HENRY FIELDING:

An Annotated Bibliography

by

H. George Hahn

Scarecrow Author Bibliographies, No. 41

The Scarecrow Press, Inc.
Metuchen, N.J., & London
1979

Library of Congress Cataloging in Publication Data

Hahn, Henry George, 1942-
    Henry Fielding : an annotated bibliography.

    (Scarecrow author bibliographies ; no. 41)
    Includes index.
    1.   Fielding, Henry, 1707-1754--Bibliography.
Z8293. 72. H33   [PR3458]   016. 823'5   79-4498
ISBN 0-8108-1212-6

To my mother and
the memory of my father

With love and gratitude

CONTENTS

PREFACE

For the better part of two centuries, Henry Fielding's critical fortunes were low.   Submerged in the wash of late eighteenth-century sentimentalism, his novels were considered vulgar and his character rakish.   And although in the nineteenth century Scott and Thackeray elevated his "lowness" to "realism" (a term that to them suggested hearty English ale, green countrysides, rollicking squires, and willing wenches), they generally continued, and even embellished, the legend of Fielding the rake.   Speaking for an age, they deemed his books improper for family reading, even if they approved his latitudinarian morality as manly and bracing.   Indeed, for well over a century after Fielding's death, Tom Jones was believed to be the perfect emblem of his author, at home in Georgian inns but unfit company in Victorian parlors.

It was Austin Dobson's biographical researches of the 1880s that began to reform the legend of the rake, and consequently the state of Fielding studies.   On new evidence, his portrayal of the humane and learned family man made Fielding sufficiently respectable for the editions of Gosse and Saintsbury to be attempted in the 1890s.   Concurrently, with the arrival of the serious study of fiction in the universities and the timely interest in realism and genre criticism, a closer examination of Fielding's novels resulted.   The new attitudes toward Fielding and fiction culminated in Henley's complete edition of 1903 and Cross' massive biography of 1918, two works that legitimatized the "life and letters" so that intensive modern scholarship could begin.

In criticism, literary history, and biography, the themes of the twentieth-century scholarly reassessment of Fielding are various.   The literary critics pay recurring attention to his craftsmanship, especially in regard to structure and characterization.   Debate on the thematic effects of Fielding's attitudes has also been keen.   Is he more the comedian or the "Christian censor"?   Does his gentle comic sense undermine his otherwise satiric temper?   Does Field-

ing view man as more benevolent or depraved? Is he more
influenced by epic or romance? By history or the picaresque? Fielding's language is also a favorite critical subject, with special interest in his narrator and ironic voice.
And his techniques of realism continue to be attractive topics
as well. As to his works in themselves, the critics are
granting the plays due notice, but most commentators regard
them merely as technical schooling for the novels. Modern
scrutiny has established the aesthetic credentials of Jonathan
Wild, Joseph Andrews, and Tom Jones, but the critics still
regard Amelia as Fielding's problem novel.

The themes of scholarship in literary history and biography likewise reveal some constants. Literary historians
attempt to define Fielding's innovations in the novel and consequently debate his status with Richardson's and, to a lesser
extent, with Smollett's. Concern with Fielding's use of literary traditions and his perception of the reading public recurs,
as does speculation about his influence on later fiction. And
in Fielding biographical scholarship, the most recent studies
are manifesting a counterreformation. With fresh data, scholars question Cross' view of Fielding's happy childhood, his
probity as a journalist, the quality of his political allegiances,
and his originality and liberalism as a legal thinker. (One
study even tarnishes the Crossian picture of Fielding the high
artist by bringing to light his operation of a puppet theatre!)
Nevertheless, the amount of critical attention devoted to the
novels alone is abundant testimony to Fielding's modern stature as the author of classics of English literature.

This bibliography therefore starts at 1900, a date
from which modern criticism of Fielding can be said to have
begun. It ends in 1978 and includes as many items from
this year as possible, up to the time the manuscript went to
press. In the main it parallels such compilations as Battestin's list of Fielding scholarship in the New Cambridge
Bibliography of English Literature, Volume II (1971); Cordasco's Henry Fielding: A List of Critical Studies Published
from 1895 to 1946 (1948); the annual bibliographies of the
Modern Humanities Research Association (since 1920) and
Philological Quarterly (since 1925); and Stoler and Fulton's
convenient list of dissertations in "Henry Fielding: A Checklist of Criticism, 1946-1975" (Bulletin of Bibliography, 33
[1976], 193-211). For older criticism, early issues of the
major journals were searched; for criticism after 1975, the
Modern Language Association catalogues and current issues
of the journals were likewise checked.

The intention of this present book is to provide a cen-
tralized, annotated docket of contemporary critical opinion
about Fielding that will aid the researcher as a quick and
convenient summary of British and American scholarship.
Annotations of the books and articles are descriptive and judgmental.   Generally, they abstract the thesis, specify it by a
pertinent example, and offer an evaluation (in word, phrase,
or tone).   Chief attention is to the criticism and biography;
annotations of editions are perfunctory.   Foreign items and
unavailable pieces are listed only, as are dissertations.   (For
most dissertations, readers are referred to Dissertation Abstracts for summaries by their authors.)   Representative
book reviews are listed after relevant entries.   No effort has
been made to cite all editions; indeed, most trade and routine
classroom editions have been purposely omitted.   Yet every
attempt has been made to provide shelter for the waifs and
strays of criticism found wandering through introductions, literary histories, and general studies of fiction.   Inevitably
there will be omissions and consequent notice of them, for
while every other author may aspire to praise, the bibliographer, like Dr. Johnson's lexicographer, can only hope to es-
cape reproach.

*   *   *

Debts are high in such an enterprise as this.   Thanks
are due to the Towson State University Library for the as-
sistance it rendered one of its faculty, to the Johns Hopkins
University Library for benefits extended an alumnus, and to
dozens of other libraries for their generosity to a stranger.
Very special thanks are due to Mr. Alan V. Poulson, whose
prompt and relentless dragooning of interlibrary loans was
invaluable; to Professor Dan L. Jones, whose encouragement
and bending of schedules kept this bibliography on a straight
course; to Professor Carl Behm III, whose good friendship,
tolerance of interruption, and Perkinsian editorial skills will
never be adequately repaid; to Professor Charles C. Mish,
bibliographer extraordinaire, whose expertise, patience, and
good humor got this book started and kept it going; and to
Cynthia C. Meyers, whose love (and typing) helped get it
finished.

H G H

Baltimore
November 1978

KEY TO ABBREVIATIONS

HF	Henry Fielding
JA	Joseph Andrews
JVL	Journal of a Voyage to Lisbon
JW	Jonathan Wild
TJ	Tom Jones

JOURNALS

AN&Q	American Notes and Queries
AUMLA	Journal of the Australasian Universities Language and Literature Association
BB	Bulletin of Bibliography
BHS	Bulletin of Hispanic Studies
BI	Books at Iowa
BNYPL	Bulletin of the New York Public Library
BSUF	Ball State University Forum
BuR	Bucknell Review
CE	College English
CEA	CEA Critic
CL	Comparative Literature
CLAJ	College Language Association Journal
CollL	College Literature
ConnR	Connecticut Review
ContempR	Contemporary Review (London)
CREL	Cahiers Roumains d'Etudes Littéraires
CritQ	Critical Quarterly
DA	Dissertation Abstracts

DAI	Dissertation Abstracts International
DR	The Dalhousie Review
DUJ	Durham University Journal
EA	Etudes Anglaises
EAL	Early American Literature
E&S	Essays and Studies by Members of the English Association
ECS	Eighteenth-Century Studies
EIC	Essays in Criticism
ELH	Journal of English Literary History
ELN	English Language Notes
EM	English Miscellany
EnlE	Enlightenment Essays
ES	English Studies
ESA	English Studies in Africa
Expl	Explicator
FMod	Filología Moderna (Madrid)
GRM	Germanisch-romanische Monatsschrift, Neue Folge
HAB	Humanities Association Bulletin (Canada)
HLQ	Huntington Library Quarterly
HSL	Hartford Studies in Literature: A Journal of Interdisciplinary Criticism
JAAC	Journal of Aesthetics and Art Criticism
JEGP	Journal of English and Germanic Philology
JGE	Journal of General Education
JNT	Journal of Narrative Technique
JUB	Journal of the University of Bombay
JWCI	Journal of the Warburg and Courtauld Institute
Lang&S	Language and Style
LJ	Library Journal
LM	London Mercury
MLJ	Modern Language Journal

MLN	Modern Language Notes
MLQ	Modern Language Quarterly
MLR	Modern Language Review
MP	Modern Philology
N&Q	Notes and Queries
NRam	New Rambler
NRF	Nouvelle Revue Française
NS	Die Neueren Sprachen
PBSA	Papers of the Bibliographical Society of America
PLL	Papers on Language and Literature
PMASAL	Papers of the Michigan Academy of Science, Arts, and Letters
PMLA	Publications of the Modern Language Association of America
PQ	Philological Quarterly
QJS	Quarterly Journal of Speech
RAA	Revue Anglo-Américaine
REL	Review of English Literature
RES	Review of English Studies
RLC	Revue de Littérature Comparée
RMS	Renaissance & Modern Studies
RS	Research Studies
SAB	South Atlantic Bulletin
SAQ	South Atlantic Quarterly
SB	Studies in Bibliography: Papers of the Bibliographical Society of the University of Virginia
SCN	Seventeenth-Century News
SE	Studies in English
SEL	Studies in English Literature, 1500-1900
SELit	Studies in English Literature (Eng. Literary Soc. of Japan)
SLI	Studies in the Literary Imagination
SNNTS	Studies in the Novel (North Texas State Univ.)

SovL	Soviet Literature
SP	Studies in Philology
SR	Sewanee Review
SSF	Studies in Short Fiction
TFSB	Tennessee Folklore Society Bulletin
TLS	[London] Times Literary Supplement
TSE	Tulane Studies in English
TSL	Tennessee Studies in Literature
TSLL	Texas Studies in Literature and Language
UTQ	University of Toronto Quarterly
UZPer	Permskii Universitet
VQR	Virginia Quarterly Review
WascanaR	Wascana Review
WF	Western Folklore
WHR	Western Humanities Review
WVUPP	West Virginia University Philological Papers
YR	Yale Review
ZAA	Zeitschrift für Anglistik und Amerikanistik (East Berlin)

I

EDITIONS AND BIBLIOGRAPHY

1 Annual Bibliography of English Language and Literature.
   Ed. for the Modern Humanities Research Association.
   London: Cambridge Univ. Press, 1921- .
   Lists current scholarship on HF.

2 Battestin, Martin C. "Fielding. " In The English Novel:
   Select Bibliographical Guides. Ed. A. E. Dyson.
   Oxford, England: Oxford Univ. Press, 1974, pp. 71-
   89.
   A selected list of texts, critical studies and commentary, biographies and letters, bibliography, and background
reading. Battestin's introduction to the list reviews the
landmarks of HF fictional criticism. Unannotated, omits all
plays, non-fiction, etc.

3 _____ . "Henry Fielding, 1707-54. " In The New Cam-
   bridge Bibliography of English Literature. Ed. George
   Watson, et al. Cambridge, England: Cambridge
   Univ. Press, 1971. Vol. II, pp. 925-948.
   A comprehensive, unannotated bibliography of primary
and secondary materials.

4 Bell, Inglis F. , and Donald Baird. "Fielding, Henry. "
   In their English Novel: A Checklist of Twentieth-
   Century Criticism. Denver: Alan Swallow, 1958,
   pp. 45-49.
   A whimsical, unannotated list of 47 critical items for
Amelia, JW, JA, Shamela, and TJ.

5 Brack, O M, Jr. , and Curt A. Zimansky. "The Charles
   B. Woods Fielding Collection. " BI, 15 (1971), 26-32.

6 Brewerton, Marti J. "Henry Fielding's The Mock Doctor:
   Or the Dumb Lady Cur'd and The Miser: A Critical
   Edition. " Diss. North Dakota. DAI, 33 (1972),
   269A.

1

7 Clark, Charles M. "The Life of Mr. Jonathan Wild The
      Great by Henry Fielding, Edited with Introduction and
      Notes. " Diss. Cornell, 1942.

8 Cordasco, Francesco. Henry Fielding: A List of Crit-
      ical Studies Published from 1895 to 1946. Eighteenth-
      Century Bibliographical Pamphlets, No. 5. Brooklyn,
      N. Y.: Long Island Univ. Press, 1948. 17 pp. Rpt.
      in Eighteenth-Century Bibliographies. Metuchen,
      N. J.: Scarecrow Press, 1970.
        An unannotated list of 224 items. Some important
   critical pieces are omitted, others misclassified.
      Review: PQ, 29 (1950), 273-275.

9 Crane, R. S. , et al. English Literature, 1660-1800: A
      Bibliography of Modern Studies. 6 vols. Princeton,
      N. J.: Princeton Univ. Press, 1952-1972.
        Reprints of the PQ annual bibliographies since 1925.
   This work is a comprehensive, largely annotated listing of
   books, articles, and reviews on 18th-century authors and
   subjects. Check "Individual Authors" throughout for scholarship on HF.

10 Cross, Wilbur L. "Bibliography. " In his History of
      Henry Fielding. New Haven, Conn. : Yale Univ.
      Press, 1918. See Vol. III, pp. 289-366.
        A primary bibliography in five parts: (1) HF's pub-
   lished works; (2) works of uncertain or doubtful authorship;
   (3) works erroneously attributed to HF; (4) dramas on HF
   and his work; and (5) letters and manuscripts.

11 _____ . "The New Fielding Collection. " Yale Alumni
      Weekly, Feb. 1913, pp. 575-576.
        Praises Frederick S. Dickson's gift of more than 1000
   volumes by and about HF to the Yale library. Dickson's aim
   was to procure everything of HF's published during the novelist's lifetime. Cross avers that the contribution makes the
   Yale collection surpass that of the Bodleian and makes it
   second only to that of the British Museum.

12 Dircks, Richard J. "Henry Fielding's A Proposal for
      Making an Effectual Provision for the Poor: An Edi-
      tion. " Diss. Fordham. DA, 23 (1962), 223.

13 Fielding, Henry. The Adventures of Joseph Andrews.
      Ed. J. Paul de Castro. London: Scholaritis Press,
      1929.

Reviews: RAA, 7 (1930), 263; TLS, 25 April 1929,
p. 343.

14 _____. An Apology for the Life of Mrs. Shamela
Andrews. Cambridge, England: St. John's College,
Gordon Fraser, 1930.

15 _____. An Apology for the Life of Mrs. Shamela
Andrews. Ed. Sheridan Baker, Jr. Berkeley: Univ.
of California Press, 1953.
"A text of questionable authority" (Charles B. Woods,
PQ, 33 [1954], 274).
Other review: TLS, 17 Sept. 1954, p. 592.

16 _____. An Apology for the Life of Mrs. Shamela
Andrews (1941). Intro. by Ian Watt. Augustan Re-
print Society, Publication No. 57. Los Angeles:
Clark Memorial Library, Univ. of California, 1956.
A reliable text. "The most valuable for scholars"
(Charles B. Woods, PQ, 36 [1957], 363).

17 _____. The Author's Farce. Ed. Charles B. Woods.
Regents Restoration Drama Series. Lincoln: Univ.
of Nebraska Press, 1966.
The original version. Includes scholarly notes and
song tunes.
Reviews: PQ, 46 (1967), 344-345; SCN, 35 (1968),
34-35.

18 _____. The Complete Works of Henry Fielding, Esq.
With an Essay on the Life, Genius and Achievement
of the Author (1902, 1903). Ed. W. E. Henley. 16
vols. Rpt. New York: Barnes & Noble, 1967.
The most comprehensive edition to date. Includes
JA (one vol.), JW (one vol.), TJ (three vols.), Amelia (two
vols.), plays and poems (five vols.), legal writings (one vol.),
and miscellaneous writings (three vols.). There are no explanatory notes, although Coleridge's notes to TJ are appended to the third volume of TJ, pp. 374-376.

19 _____. The Covent-Garden Journal. 2 vols. Ed.
Gerard E. Jensen. New Haven, Conn.: Yale Univ.
Press, 1915.
Comprises the leaders of all 72 issues of the Journal,
regardless of authorship. Slightly modernized, fully anno-
tated text with illustrations and index.

20 _____. The Criticism of Henry Fielding. Ed. Ioan
    Williams. New York: Barnes & Noble, 1970.
    An anthology of 72 extracts from HF's plays, jour-
nalism, and novels.
    Reviews: EIC, 21 (1971), 91-100; Encounter (Lon-
don), June 1970, p. 70; N&Q, Oct. 1972, p. 391; TLS, 9
July 1970, p. 746.

21 _____. The Female Husband and Other Writings.
    Ed. Claude E. Jones. English Reprint Series, No.
    17. Liverpool: Liverpool Univ. Press, 1960.
    "Shockingly inept" (Charles B. Woods, PQ, 40 [1961],
390).
    Other reviews: JEGP, 61 (1962), 189-190; MLR, 56
(1961), 631; RES, n. s. 14 (1963), 438.

22 _____. The Grub Street Opera. Ed. Leroy John
    Morrissey. Fountainwell Drama Texts. Edinburgh:
    Oliver & Boyd, 1973.

23 _____. The Grub-Street Opera. Ed. Edgar V.
    Roberts. Regents Restoration Drama Series. Lin-
    coln: Univ. of Nebraska Press, 1968.
    Good notes and appendices.
    Reviews: MLR, 66 (1971), 867-870; SCN, 29 (1971),
72-73.

24 _____. The Historical Register for the Year 1736
    and Eurydice Hissed. Ed. William W. Appleton.
    Regents Restoration Drama Series. Lincoln: Univ.
    of Nebraska Press, 1967.

25 _____. The History of the Adventures of Joseph An-
    drews and An Apology for the Life of Mrs. Shamela
    Andrews. Ed. Douglas Brooks. Oxford English
    Novels. London: Oxford Univ. Press, 1970.
    Reviews: ECS, 6 (1973), 531-533; TLS, 12 Feb.
1971, p. 178.

26 _____. The History of Tom Jones. Ed. R. P. C.
    Mutter. Harmondsworth, England: Penguin, 1966.
    Review: TLS, 17 March 1966, p. 224.

27 _____. The History of Tom Jones, a Foundling.
    Ed. Martin C. Battestin. Text ed. Fredson Bowers.
    2 vols. The Wesleyan Edition of the Works of Henry
    Fielding. Oxford, England: Clarendon Press, 1974.

The standard edition. Unmodernized text, excellent annotations.

Reviews: MLR, 71 (1976), 888-893; RES, n. s. 27 (1976), 473-475; TLS, 16 April 1976, p. 472; YR, 65 (1975), 128-133.

28 _____ . The Jacobite's Journal and Related Writings.
Ed. W. B. Coley. The Wesleyan Edition of the Works of Henry Fielding. Oxford: Clarendon Press, 1974.

The standard edition of the political writings of 1747-1748, most not reprinted since HF's lifetime. Includes (1) A Dialogue between a Gentleman from London ... and an Honest Alderman of the Country Party, (2) A Proper Answer to a Late Scurrilous Libel, and (3) the Jacobite's Journal.

Reviews: MLR, 71 (1976), 888-893; RES, n. s. (1976), 473-475; TLS, 12 Sept. 1975, p. 1029; YR, 65 (1975), 128-133.

29 _____ . Jonathan Wild. With engravings by Denis Tegetmeier. London: Golden Cockerel Press, 1932.

30 _____ . Joseph Andrews. Ed. Martin C. Battestin.
The Wesleyan Edition of the Works of Henry Fielding. Oxford, England: Clarendon Press, 1967.

The standard edition. In old spelling text with substantial notes.

Reviews: Anglia, 87 (1969), 101-103; ES, 50 (1969), 409-410; JEGP, 67 (1968), 520-522; MLR, 66 (1969), 146-147; MQR, 6 (1967), 298; PQ, 47 (1968), 379-381; RES, n. s. 19 (1968), 208-209; YR, 57 (1967), 278-282.

31 _____ . Joseph Andrews and Shamela. Ed. Martin C. Battestin. Riverside Edition. Boston: Houghton Mifflin, 1961.

Extensive notes.

Reviews: MLR, 62 (1967), 317-318; N&Q, June 1966, p. 231; TLS, 6 Jan. 1966, p. 5.

32 _____ . The Journal of a Voyage to Lisbon. Ed. Harold E. Pagliaro. New York: Nardon Press, 1963.

A good text, helpful explanatory notes (Charles B. Woods, PQ, 43 [1964], 360-361).

Other reviews: CE, 25 (1964), 640; MLR, 59 (1964), 460; N&Q, April 1964, p. 159.

33 _____ . A Journey from This World to the Next.
Ed. Claude Rawson. London: Dent, 1974.
Review: TLS, 26 July 1974, p. 811.

34 _____ . The Lover's Assistant, or New Art of Love
(1760). Ed. Claude E. Jones. Augustan Reprint
Society, Publication No. 89. Los Angeles: Clark
Memorial Library, Univ. of California, 1961.
A poor choice of text (W. B. Coley, PQ, 41 [1962],
587-588).

35 _____ . Miscellanies by Henry Fielding, Esq. Ed.
Henry Knight Miller. Vol. I. The Wesleyan Edition
of the Works of Henry Fielding. Oxford, England:
Clarendon Press, 1972.
The standard edition. Excellent notes.
Reviews: EIC, 24 (1974), 295-300; PQ, 52 (1973),
501-503; RES, n. s. 25 (1974), 212-214; TLS, 29 June 1973,
p. 740.

36 _____ . Pasquin. Ed. O M Brack, Jr. , and Curt
A. Zimansky. Iowa City: Univ. of Iowa Press, 1973.

37 _____ . Selected Essays of Henry Fielding. Ed.
Gordon Hall Gerould. The Athenaeum Press Series.
Boston: Ginn, 1905.
A representative sampling of HF's topics and tempers
as an essayist. Includes short extracts from the novels,
journals, and Miscellanies.

38 _____ . The Shakespeare Head Edition of Fielding's
Novels. 10 vols. Oxford, England: Basil Black-
well, 1926.
Includes Amelia (three vols.), JW (one vol.), JA
(two vols.), and TJ (four vols.). Good notes.

39 _____ . Tom Jones. Ed. Sheridan Baker. Norton
Critical Edition. New York: Norton, 1973.
A reliable text based on the fourth (and last) edition
of HF's lifetime. It includes helpful notes, a textual appendix, a map of Tom's route to London, and samples of early
and modern criticism on the novel.

40 _____ . Tom Thumb: and the Tragedy of Tragedies.
Ed. L. J. Morrissey. Fountainwell Drama Texts.
Edinburgh: Oliver & Boyd, 1970.

41 _____ . The True Patriot: and the History of Our

Own Times. Ed. Miriam Austin Locke. University: Univ. of Alabama Press, 1964.
A complete reprinting with lengthy annotations of the introductory essays.
Reviews: ELN, 2 (1965), 307-308; PQ, 44 (1965), 347-348; TLS, 27 Jan. 1966, p. 67.

42 _____. "The Voyages of Mr. Job Vinegar" from "The Champion" (1740). Ed. S. J. Sackett. Augustan Reprint Society, No. 67. Los Angeles: Clark Memorial Library, Univ. of California, 1958.
Comment: JNL, Dec. 1958, pp. 11-12.

43 Grundy, Isobel. "New Verse by Henry Fielding."
PMLA, 87 (1972), 213-245. See No. 799.

44 Hartog, Curt H. "The George Sherburn Collection at the University of Illinois." The Scriblerian, 2 (1970), 68-70.
Notices the "God's plenty" for HF scholars in this collection. Hartog's list is drastically selective but includes mention of originals of the plays, novels, and periodical literature in the collection.

45 Hemingson, Peter H. "Fielding and the '45: A Critical Edition of Henry Fielding's Anti-Jacobite Pamphlets." Diss. Columbia. DA, 34 (1974), 5174A.

46 Hillhouse, Theodore James. "A Critical Edition of The Tragedy of Tragedies, A Dramatic Burlesque by Henry Fielding." Diss. Yale, 1914.

47 Jobe, Alice J. "Fielding Criticism: A Twentieth-Century Selective Enumeration with Commentary." Diss. Univ. of Texas at Austin. DA, 31 (1970), 1761A.

48 _____. "Henry Fielding's Novels: Selected Criticism (1940-1969)." SNNTS, 2 (1970), 246-259.
A highly selective bibliography that lists criticism of individual novels and general novel criticism. Unannotated.

49 Kyle, Linda Davis. "Amelia by Henry Fielding: A Selective Bibliography." N&Q, May-June 1977, pp. 255-258.
An unannotated list of editions and criticism from 1751 to 1974.

50 MLA International Bibliography of Books and Articles on

the Modern Languages and Literatures.   Ed. for the
Modern Language Association.   New York: Modern
Language Association, 1922- .
Annual lists of scholarship on HF.

51   Mummendey, Richard. Language and Literature of the
Anglo-Saxon Nations as Presented in German Doctoral
Dissertations, 1885-1950: A Bibliography. Charlottes-
ville: Bibliographical Society of the Univ. of Virginia,
1954.

52   "Recent Studies in the Restoration and Eighteenth Century. " SEL, 1- (1961-).
An annual running commentary on important scholarship. Very Selective.

53   Roberts, Edgar Verne. "The Ballad Operas of Henry
Fielding, 1730-1732: A Critical Edition (The Author's
Farce, The Grub Street Opera, The Lottery, The
Mock Doctor) (Volumes One and Two). " Diss. Min-
nesota. DA, 21 (1961), 3451.

54   Stoler, John A. , with Richard Fulton. "Henry Fielding:
A Checklist of Criticism, 1946-1975. " BB, 33 (1976),
193-211.
A selected and unannotated list of 705 items (including reviews and editions) in three sections: books, articles,
and dissertations.

55   Stratman, Carl J. , ed. "Fielding, " Restoration and
18th Century Theatre Research Bibliography, 1961-
1968. Troy, N. Y. : Whitston, 1969, pp. 207-208.
A haphazard, annotated grouping of 30 recent works
on HF, not all referring to his dramatic career.

56   The Year's Work in English Studies. Ed. for the English Association. London: Oxford Univ. Press,
1921- .
A highly selective listing of current scholarship. Includes brief commentary on the scholarship.

II

FIELDING'S LIFE

57 Amory, Hugh. "Fielding's Lisbon Letters." HLQ, 35
(1971), 65-83.
An excellent analysis of HF's last days through three
letters from Lisbon and thus a main corrective to the standard view of HF as poor, cheerful, and charitable to the
last. After reprinting one and dating all of the letters from
internal evidence, Amory offers reasons for their petulant
tone--especially the quarrel over finances that stormed in
the HF household. Moreover, Amory suggests that HF's
income was much higher and his debts much greater than
other biographers have held.
This assessment of HF's financial condition should
also be read as an adjunct to the JVL.

58 _____. "Henry Fielding and the Criminal Legislation of 1751-2." PQ, 50 (1970), 175-192.
Suggests that HF's work in legal, social, and penal
theory was less influential than has been assumed. Amory
shows in great detail that though the policies of HF and of
the Committee of the House of Commons of 1751-2 followed
parallel lines, HF's were so poorly founded on investigative
facts that they were virtually useless.

59 _____. "Two Lost Fielding Manuscripts." N&Q,
May 1967, pp. 183-184.
Notices references in auction catalogues to two lost
manuscripts: a 1737 letter to bookseller John Nourse and a
1753 bond for £1892 to bookseller Andrew Millar. The
second is biographically puzzling. Was HF consolidating his
debts? Was he executing a trust?

60 Avery, Emmett L. "Fielding's Last Season with the
Haymarket Theatre." MP, 36 (1939), 283-292.
An examination of the Daily Advertiser for information about HF's career from January to May of 1737, a
somewhat hazy time for his biographers. This daily news-

paper reveals that the Haymarket was the most frequently and skillfully publicized of all the other London houses. Moreover, Avery shows that its season ran longer than was generally thought. HF's repertory there included frequent attacks on both Cibber and the government. When governmental censorship became an actuality, HF closed the theater in May.

61   Bailey, Vern D. "Fielding's Politics." Diss. California at Berkeley. DAI, 31 (1971), 6588A.

62   Battestin, Martin C. "Fielding and 'Master Punch' in Panton Street." PQ, 45 (1966), 191-208.
    Notices an episode that has escaped HF's biographers-- his ownership and management of a puppet theater in 1748. Under the name of "Madame de la Nash," HF supplied refreshments and satiric entertainments in a "large Breakfasting Room" near the Haymarket. Especially noteworthy is the theatrical war carried on between HF and Samuel Foote, a dramatic entertainer. The brief episode suggests HF's financial concerns, his exuberant energy, his sense of humor, and his catholic tastes, open even to such a humble art form as the puppet show.

63   _____, with R. R. Battestin. "Fielding, Bedford, and the Westminster Election of 1749." ECS, 11 (1977/78), 143-185.
    A major reinterpretation that shows HF to be less politically innocent and idealistic than earlier biographers have thought. The authors first establish the Duke of Bedford's generosity to HF and his family (appointments, grants, free ground rent) before revealing HF's active promotion of the interests of Trentham, Bedford's brother-in-law, in the 1749 election. They show HF using his magisterial post to advance Trentham's cause, hosting a party for his benefit, and (probably) writing parts of a campaign piece, the "first" Covent-Garden Journal for him. The Battestins include an appendix with letters of HF and his family.

64   Biron, H. C. "A Famous Magistrate." The National Review (London), 74 (1920), 669-678.
    A light account of HF's magistracy from his appointment until his death. Biron highlights the legal satire in Amelia, the Elizabeth Canning case, HF's legal pamphlets and social reform proposals. But he overstates the case for HF's legislative influence and romanticizes the cause of his death--the press of jurisprudential duties on a jaundice-, dropsy-, and asthma-ridden man.

65   Coley, W. B.   "Fielding's Two Appointments to the
     Magistracy. "   MP, 63 (1965), 144-149.
     Establishes the documents and chronology pertinent
to HF's appointments to the Middlesex and Westminster
benches.

66   _____.   "Henry Fielding and the Two Walpoles. "
     PQ, 45 (1966), 157-178.
     A close review of the relations between HF and
Robert and Horace Walpole on the grounds of HF's political
commitments.   Assessing "The Opposition, " a HF pamphlet
of 1742, and reviewing HF's papers, Coley shows that HF
departed from the Opposition but did not go into Walpole's
pay.   Cynical and disillusioned with the Opposition to Walpole, HF changed his politics in abandoning the group but
apparently refused to compromise his ethics by selling out.

67   _____.   "Henry Fielding's 'Lost' Law Book. "   MLN,
     76 (1961), 408-413.
     Speculates that HF's conduct as a lawyer may once
have been less than ethical.   He presumably advertised as
his own work two folio volumes on Crown Law, possibly to
attract briefs to himself.   Further, Coley postulates that
the folios may have been the reproduced law notes of HF's
grandfather, Sir Henry Gould, of the King's Bench.   The
book, however, was never published, and the folios have
not survived.

68   _____.   "Notes toward a 'Class Theory' of Augustan
     Literature: The Example of Fielding. "   In Literary
     Theory and Structure: Essays in Honor of William
     K. Wimsatt.   Ed. Frank Brady, et al.   New Haven,
     Conn. :   Yale Univ. Press, 1973, pp. 131-150.
     Describes the relationship between author and patron
by reference to HF.   Coley affirms that subsistence was
more important than ideology in a writer's political align-
ment.   Consequently he reasons that HF and other Augustan
authors refused to repudiate the patronage and class system,
to bemoan their dependence on it, or to withdraw cynically
from it.   Rather, recognizing their subservience, they "rest-
lessly and wittily" mocked their dependence on a patron
while continuing their employment.

69   Cross, Wilbur L.   The History of Henry Fielding.   3
     vols.   New Haven, Conn. :   Yale Univ. Press, 1918.
     The standard biography.   Its main values are three.
First, it is exhaustive.   Earlier treatments sketched an out-

line or cast an impression of HF. But Cross' 36-chapter
life is a grand sweep from 1707 to 1754 and even beyond to
chapters on HF's immediate survivors and his literary reputation through the 19th century. Within this sweep Cross
minutely details background influences such as separate chapters on the theatrical war and the riots of 1749. Exhaustive
too is the bibliography of primary works that Cross appends.

Second, it assembles much new information about HF.
Beginning with 18th-century documents, Cross establishes
the record of HF's life afresh, without the coloring of 19th-
century attitudes. From court records he fills in much
about HF's childhood, from tax records he specifies HF's
homes and movements, from church papers he provides exact information about HF's wives and children. And always,
from 18th-century letters, newspapers, and HF's own works,
Cross infers a full picture of his life, deeds, and times.

Third, Cross reveals HF's life as a unified whole:
"His development under the stress of changing circumstance
was perfectly natural and logical, like the development of a
great character in a great novel. " He shows how HF's
dramatic, legal, and journalistic career evolved into his
master calling as a novelist. And he is always at pains to
integrate HF the thorough scholar with HF the satirist quick
to respond to an immediate situation.

But an intentional problem undercuts Cross' effect.
Admitting that his massive biography grew from a "prepos-
session ... that the author of Tom Jones could not have
been the kind of man described in numerous books and essays, " Cross becomes HF's advocate more than his disin-
terested examiner. The corrective intention gets out of
hand in a desire to scotch the two favorite charges against
HF: that he led a dissipated life and that he wrote hastily
and carelessly. Cross' assertion that, e. g. , HF "never
consorted with lewd women" needs no comment, and his in-
sistence that HF used neither snuff nor tobacco assumes the
Victorian morality that Cross tries to refute. Moreover,
Cross shows HF's meticulousness in his revisions of JA and
TJ, a demonstration that itself suggests possible haste in
original composition.

For corrections of fact in Cross, one may refer to
the MLR review (by de Castro) noted below. Zirker (No.
849) is a good check against Cross' overvaluing HF's originality of thought in penal reform. And Battestin and Battestin (No. 63) are a corrective of Cross' overpraising of HF's
probity.

Reviews: Dial, 66 (1919), 407-409; JEGP, 20 (1921),
110-118; MLN, 34 (1919), 235-239; MLR, 15 (1920), 181-188;
MP, 18 (1920-21), 677-678; YR, 8 (1919), 415-424.

70 _____ . "The Legend of Henry Fielding. " YR, 8, n. s.
        (1919), 107-127.
        An undocumented attempt to show "The real Fielding
in contrast with the bibulous spendthrift and libertine of tradition. " After a compressed statement of that legend, Cross
moves to HF's defense by reviewing his charity, his con-
stancy, his long-suffering, his gallantry, and his impersonal
satire. We even learn that HF was an abstemious drinker
and smoker; indeed, he took no snuff.

71 de Castro, J. Paul. "Edmund Fielding. " N&Q, 26 Aug.
        1922, p. 178.
        Records a document certifying that HF's father
Edmund was married on 10 March 1740 for the fourth
time. He died in June of 1741.

72 _____ . "Fielding and Lyme Regis. " TLS, 4 June
        1931, p. 447.
        Suggests that when Fielding tried to run off with
Sarah Andrew of Lyme Regis, he was living in Upton Grey
in Hampshire. That was in 1725 and 1726 after he had left
Eton. Hitherto, biographers had assumed that Fielding had
gone to his grandmother at Salisbury. De Castro also notes
that Fielding may have ridden in the Vyne Hunt in North
Hampshire for these two years.

73 _____ . "Fielding and the Collier Family. " N&Q, 5
        Aug. 1916, pp. 104-105.
        Tells of HF as both lawyer and surety in an action
involving an old Wiltshire friend, Dr. Arthur Collier. When
judgment went against Collier, HF became liable for £400.

74 _____ . "Fielding as a Publicist. " N&Q, Nov. 1919,
        pp. 283-284.
        Recounts HF's participation in the prosecution of two
cases in 1750 and 1751 against justices of the peace indicted
for malfeasance in office.

75 _____ . "Fielding at Boswell Court. " N&Q, 1 April
        1916, pp. 264-265.
        Notes court records and parish rate books which
show that from 1744-1747 HF lived in Boswell Court on the
site occupied in 1916 by the Royal Courts of Justice. The
records show also that he was never in arrears of his rates.

76 _____ . "A Forgotten Salisbury Surgeon. " TLS, 13
        Jan. 1927, p. 28.

Suggests that "the famous surgeon" of the Covent-Garden Journal (11 Jan. 1752) and the surgeon who repaired Amelia's nose (Amelia, II. i) was Edward Goldwyre. The leading surgeon of Wiltshire, he lived next door to Charlotte Cradock and probably set her broken nose.

Arthur E. du Bois (TLS, 19 March 1931, p. 234) dissents to suggest that Dr. John Barker operated on Charlotte Cradock.

De Castro retorts (TLS, 26 March 1931, p. 252) that Barker did not become qualified as a medical practitioner until 1737--three years after HF's marriage to Charlotte--and thus had no hand in relieving her injury. Moreover, "Dr. Barker was an eminent physician, who would not have thanked Fielding ... for calling him a surgeon. "

77 _____. "John Ranby: Henry Fielding. " N&Q, 1 July 1916, p. 11.

Shows that HF let his country residence at Fordhook, Ealing to his friend, the distinguished surgeon John Ranby (1703-73), just before he departed for Lisbon on 26 June 1754.

78 _____. "Tom Jones. " N&Q, 10 April 1920, p. 118.

Notes that HF's grandfather John Fielding was pre-bendary successively of Yatesbury (1677), Beaminster Prima (1678), and Gillingham Major (1682). Though he had spelled his name Fielding earlier, he signed the subscription book at the last post Feilding.

79 _____. "Ursula Fielding and Tom Jones. " N&Q, 9 March 1940, pp. 164-167.

First publication of a letter by HF's second sister, 25 Oct. 1748. It notes that he and his family moved for the winter to Brownlow St. near Drury Lane, "where he intends to administer justice. " It was at that address that HF composed the final books of TJ, published 28 Feb. 1749.

79a Dobson, Austin. Fielding. English Men of Letters. London, 1883; rpt. New York: Harper, 1883; rev. 1889, 1900. 184 pp.

The first balanced biography of HF. Correcting the earlier accounts and biases, Dobson introduces many new details about HF's life. Essentially he minimizes the caricature of the rake and spendthrift by depicting "the energetic magistrate, the tender husband and father, the kindly host of his poorer friends, the practical philanthropist, the patient and magnanimous hero of the Voyage to Lisbon. " Sympathetic but sober, Dobson's investigation of the man made

possible a new assessment of HF the author by providing a
context for understanding the later works. He sounded the
theme of the reassessment by calling HF the wellspring both
of the novel of manners and of the modern novel in general.

80 _____ . "Fielding and Andrew Millar." The Library,
      3rd series, 7 (1916), 177-190.
      Details the literary relationship between HF and his
publisher Millar (1701-1768). Introduced by James Thomson
to Millar, HF earned from him nearly £ 200 for the rights
to JA. Millar published HF's other major works, as well
as Sarah Fielding's David Simple. Characteristic of Millar
was his reliance on literary advisors in determining manuscripts to publish his sound advertising techniques, and his
generosity (he gave HF £ 700 for TJ.) A poor Scotsman who
became abnormally prosperous, Millar bequeathed funds both to
David Hume and HF's two sons, William and Allen. Dr. Johnson
later praised Millar as having "raised the price of literature."

81 _____ . "A Fielding 'Find'." The National Review
      (London), 57 (1911), 983-992.
      Two newly published HF letters of 1754 to his brother
John that recount both his hopes for recovery and his pain.
Together the letters provide scene and dramatis personae for
HF's last days: a loving but homesick wife; a calculating
"friend," Margaret Collier; a thieving footman; and a "foolish" servant, Isabella Ash, who supposedly became engaged
to ex-privateer Richard Veal, captain of their Lisbon-bound
vessel, The Queen of Portugal.

82 Dudden, F. Homes. Henry Fielding: His Life, Works,
      and Times. 2 vols. Oxford, England: Clarendon
      Press, 1952. 1183 pp.
      A readable but disappointing life. Dudden promises
a "fresh" study, but delivers little more than a close para-
phrase of Cross (No. 69) in treating his three main topics:
the man, his writings, and his milieu.
      Dudden's treatment of the man is flawed in three
ways. First, it is not impartial. Concerned with defend-
ing HF's reputation, Dudden continually pictures his subject
as a paragon of dignity and integrity. Besides viewing HF
as continually high-minded in law and politics, Dudden attempts to explain away his personal peccadilloes as typical
of his times and to excuse his caustic and sometimes vulgar
writings as products of righteous indignation. Second, Dudden's account is not original. He fails to go beyond Cross
even to the point of neglecting subsequent biographical

scholarship that had thrown new light on HF's childhood,
his activities after Eton, and his personal relationships with
Cibber, Walpole, and Pope.   Moreover he errs in asserting
HF's belief in the benevolence of human nature, a conclusion
that a closer reading of the novels, if not of the recent
scholarship, disallows.   And third, in the absence of facts,
Dudden often "reconstructs" portions of HF's life from
events and characters in his works, a naive if not dangerous
practice for a biographer.
     Literary criticism in a biography is seldom acute.
And Dudden's is conventional in this respect.   His judgments
are sane, mainly of the caliber found in literary histories.
Yet he does grant detailed attention to HF's works.   His
discussion of the plays includes specification of the techniques that HF would later use in his fiction--skills of plot-
ting, humor, dramatic tricks, speedy and easy dialogue,
etc.   And his treatment of the novels provides highly useful
analytical summaries--indeed, for JA, a day-by-day account--
that graphically illustrate HF's constructional abilities.   But
here again, Dudden does not use some of the more special-
ized scholarship and criticism available to him, especially
on JW, Shamela, and Amelia.
     Dudden's treatment of HF's background is much better.
The recreation of scenes, especially of Salisbury, East
Stour, and London, is compelling and informative.   The account of the religious milieu is authoritative.   And the detail about the contexts of HF's education and dramatic and
legal careers is extensive.   Still, Cross remains the standard biography of HF.
     Reviews: PQ, 32 (1953), 268; RES n. s. 5 (1954), 302-
305; SR, 61 (1953), 316-321; TLS, 23 Jan. 1953, 56; YR, 42
(1953), 633-635.

83   Eaves, T. C. Duncan, and Ben D. Kimpel. "Henry Field-
     ing's Son by His First Wife. " N&Q, June 1968, p. 212.
     Establishes that besides two daughters by his first
wife, Charlotte, HF also had a son Henry.   The boy's
burial is recorded as 3 Aug. 1750 in the register of St.
Martin's-in-the-Fields.

84   Elwes, Winefride.   The Feilding Album.   London:
     Geoffrey Bles, 1950.
     A delightful personal account of the Roman Catholic
family of the eighth Earl of Denbigh, HF's Victorian descend-
ants.   Mrs. Elwes grants only one paragraph to the novelist who
had altered the spelling of the surname.   That paragraph contains the error of calling his father a judge and not a general (a
confusion of HF's father and maternal grandfather).

85   George, M. Dorothy. "The Sale of Fielding's Farm. "
      TLS, 26 June 1924, p. 404.
      Reprints an advertisement of the auction sale of
Fielding's farm at Ealing six months after the novelist left
for Lisbon.   This notice in the Public Advertiser of 26 Dec.
1754 lists animals (including a monkey), furniture, plate,
wines, and about forty acres.
      J. Paul de Castro (TLS, 17 July 1924, p. 449) notes
that in 1755 the farm rates were paid by John Ranby, George
II's premier sergeant-surgeon, whom Fielding mentions
honorably in TJ (VIII, 13) and in the JVL.

86   Godden, Gertrude M. Henry Fielding: A Memoir.
      London: Sampson Low, Marston, 1910.   326 pp.
      A revisionist biography that offers a sympathetic but
unbalanced view.   Godden admits nothing faintly critical of
HF.   E. g. , she glosses his conduct during the Elizabeth
Canning case, excuses his drinking as typical of his age,
and ignores any hint of his wenching.   Also she gives HF
more credit than his due for legislative reform.
      Yet Godden prints some hitherto unpublished docu-
ments, viz. , some of HF's letters of the 1750s, records of
his childhood, of his Dorset estate, of his work as a magistrate, and some old newspaper extracts.   This new material
forms the chief value of the book.

87   _____ . "Henry Fielding: Some Unpublished Letters
      and Records. " Fortnightly Review, 1 Nov. 1909, pp.
      821-832.
      Assesses newly published documents that have shed
light on some dark areas of HF's life.   (1) Chancery records tell much of the bitter Gould-Fielding contest for the
Fielding children.   (2) Sale records of the East Stour property and HF's letter to John Nourse inquiring about com-
fortable lodgings at £40 in London suggest that he was hardly poverty-stricken in 1739.   (3) Registers at St. Martin's-
in-the-Fields tell of the solemn funeral HF provided for his
wife in 1744.   (4) Oral records substantiate that HF read
TJ in manuscript to Lords Chatham and Lyttleton.   And
(5) HF's letter of 1749 to Lord Hardwick suggests his hard
work during his first years as magistrate.

88   Goldgar, Bertrand A. "Fielding's Early Plays, " "Field-
      ing, Common Sense, and Pope, " "Fielding, the
      Champion, and Cibber, " and "Fielding's Defection. "
      In his Walpole and the Wits: The Relation of Politics
      to Literature, 1722-1742.   Lincoln: Univ. of Nebras-

ka Press, 1976, pp. 98-115, 150-162, 189-196, 197-
208.
Charts HF's attitudes toward Walpole in four subsec-
tions.   In the first, Goldgar cites external evidence for HF's
support of the Lord Treasurer and finds in four plays of
1730-1731 no significant criticism of Walpole.   The second
subsection concludes that none of HF's plays until the Historical Register (1737) satirized Walpole, but that by 1737
his attitude had changed because Walpole's position--and thus
the possibility of his patronage--had weakened.   The next
subsection notices The Champion's attack on both the ministry and Cibber.   And the last suggests that HF's pamphlet,
The Opposition, critical of the Patriots, marks his defection
from the anti-Walpolian opposition.   Goldgar's important
conclusion is that HF was no ideologue; his loyalty was pri-
marily to himself because self-advancement was all-impor-
tant.

89   Harrison, Frederic.   "Bath--Somerset--Henry Field-
         ing. "   The Fortnightly Review, 106 (1919), 734-744.
         "Hometown" praise of HF in a brief review of his
life.   Stresses his learning and personal library, his associations with Somerset, and his work as a magistrate.
Spotty and unoriginal.

90   Jarvis, Rupert C.   "Fielding and the Forty-Five. "
         N&Q, Sept. 1956, pp. 391-394; Nov. 1956, pp. 479-
         482; Jan. 1957, pp. 19-34.
         An important reappraisal via HF's canon of his atti-
tudes during the Jacobite threat of the 1740s.   Jarvis
claims that because HF produced so much writing on the
subject, those years can be called a watershed in his life.
This political controversy is in the background of TJ and
may be responsible for his appointment to the Bow-Street
magistracy, a reward for his pro-government stance.

91   Jenkins, Elizabeth.   Henry Fielding.   The English
         Novelists Series.   Denver: Swallow, 1947.   102 pp.
         An occasionally graceful, occasionally eccentric,
never scholarly essay.   Jenkins's survey of HF's life is
dotted with errors: failing to mention Shamela, sending HF
to Leyden to study law (not letters), omitting notice of HF's
substantial revisions of Tom Thumb, etc.   Her remarks on
the novels are running summaries interspersed with sensitive comments but no analysis.   Jenkins replays some old
prejudices (e. g., Richardson as silly, underbred, touchy)
to heighten her portrayal of HF as a man's man.   Mainly

concerned with justifying HF's character, this slight book offers nothing new.

Reviews: New Republic, 3 Jan. 1949, p. 27; N&Q, 7 Feb. 1948, pp. 65-66; TLS, 24 Jan. 1948, p. 50.

92 Jones, B. M. Henry Fielding: Novelist and Magistrate.
      London: Allen & Unwin, 1933. 256 pp.

A highly useful view by a Middle Templar of HF as homo legis. Jones's book treats his life in three main-- but uneven--stages: the pre-law days, the Middle Temple and Western Circuit Years, and the period as magistrate. While there is a helpful chapter on legal allusions in the plays (No. 339), the rest of the first two parts is routine. But when Jones assesses HF as a magistrate, he offers a specific and balanced account.

This third section highlights HF's aims and practice on the bench, noting his theoretical severity yet his practical (if occasional) lenity. It details HF's importance in the creation of the London police force. It reveals his behavior in the celebrated Penlez and Canning cases, and not always to his credit. And it specifies--but overvalues--HF's influence on new reform legislation. Throughout the section, Jones provides important legal and social background-- especially the conditions of crime, prisons, and the courts-- to make his portrayal of HF the more accurate.

Ultimately Jones designates HF's main achievements as a magistrate as three: his contribution to penal and legislative reforms, his recommendation of salaries for magistrates, and his establishment of a detective force.

Cf. Radzinowicz (No. 99) and Zirker (No. 849), who question HF's direct influence on reform laws.

Review: TLS, 20 July 1933, p. 493.

93 Knapp, Lewis M. "Fielding's Dinners with Dodington, 1750-1752." N&Q, 20 Dec. 1952, pp. 565-566.

Reveals that George Bubb Dodington's Diary shows that HF dined with him ten times between 1750 and 1752. Knapp suggests that because little is known of their friendship, these dinners may provide a basis for reassessment.

93a McAdam, E. L., Jr. "A New Letter from Fielding."
      YR, 38 (1949), 300-10.

Quotes in full a 900-word letter from HF to Richardson in which he praises the characterization, comedy, and tragic scenes of Clarissa. This 1748 letter is important because it suggests a previous (lost) correspondence between the two novelists and because it reveals HF's warmth and friendliness to his jealous rival.

94   McKillop, Alan D.   "The Personal Relations between
         Fielding and Richardson. "   MP, 28 (1931), 423-433.
         Charts the main relations between the two novelists
between 1741 and 1754 to provide materials for an objective
survey.   For example, though HF mocks Richardson, his
praise of Clarissa is genuine.   And while Richardson--in
letter and conversation--scorns HF's "baseness, " he pur-
portedly provided for HF in Lisbon.   Cites a balanced contemporary account by Jane Collier who saw both as "ethical
writers. "   A useful corrective to seeing the authors as
pitched enemies, but there is little new information here.
Richardson emerges in his traditional role as petty and
spiteful toward HF.

95   MacLaurin, Charles.   "Henry Fielding. "   In his Mere
         Mortals: Medico-Historical Essays.   New York:
         Doran, 1925, pp. 128-135.
         Contends that HF's "sick mind" during the Elizabeth
Canning case of 1753 was a result of cancer.   "No man with
a cancer beginning to gnaw at his vitals could possibly take
the trouble to cross-examine a brazen hussy who was determined to deceive him.... "   From HF's symptoms--deep
jaundice, dropsy, wasting, and frightful appearance--Mac-
Laurin infers "a certain form of internal malignant tumour
spreading to the peritoneum. "   A speculative post-mortem
examination after 171 years may be questionable.

96   Pope, F. J.   "Fielding's Ancestors at Sharpham Park,
         Somerset. "   N&Q, Feb. 1920, p. 34.
         Verifies that the Sharpham Park estate was bought in
1657 by Richard Davidge, a London merchant.   His daughter
Sarah brought it in marriage to her husband, Henry Gould
(later Sir Henry), son and grandson of Somerset yeomen.
"Thus in Fielding the 'blue blood' he inherited from his
father was mingled with another kind of blood (yeoman and
commercial) derived from his mother. "   This is a correction of the Gould genealogy in Burke's Landed Gentry.

97   _____ .   "Henry Fielding's Boyhood. "   The British
         Archivist, 1 (Jan. 1914), 85-88.
         A discussion of the Chancery suits of 1720-1723 that
concern the trust-estate of the Fielding children.   Pope recounts the situation begun by Lady Sarah Gould's bill of
complaint that Henry's father, Col. Fielding, had misappro-
priated trust monies, neglected proper education of his children, and married an Italian Roman Catholic.

98   Pringle, Patrick.   Hue and Cry: The Story of Henry

and John Fielding and Their Bow Street Runners.
London: Wm. Morrow, 1955. 230 pp.
A popular history of the founding of the English police
system. Not original and often sensationalistic, Pringle's
book is nevertheless an accurate and entertaining depiction
of London life and crime that formed the contexts of the
Fieldings' work as magistrates. Pringle details HF's practical achievements in founding the prototype of the police:
development of crime detection techniques, of preventive
policing, of lenient but certain punishment, of police integrity, and of allaying public fear that an official police force
would threaten individual liberty. Anecdotes about the
Fielding brothers, their runners, and criminals abound.
Review: Nation, 17 March 1956, pp. 224-225.

99   Radzinowicz, Leon. "The Trend of the Proposed Re-
      forms: Henry Fielding and the Committee of 1750."
      In Vol. I of his History of English Criminal Law.
      New York: Macmillan, 1948, pp. 399-424.
A law professor's assessment of the merits and
shortcomings of HF's proposals in the inquiry on the state
of the criminal laws. Radzinowicz thus lays the groundwork
for Zirker (No. 849) by concluding that the Enquiry's penal
policy is based on two contrary inclinations: social preven-
tion of crime and harsh capital statutes. "Consequently his
tract is a mixture of bold and creative anticipation and narrow, regressive tendencies...."

100   Robbins, Alfred F. "Henry Fielding and the Civil
      Power." N&Q, 24 June 1911, p. 486.
Reprints an item from an Oct. 1751 number of The
London Morning Penny Post on HF's committing an army
colonel to prison for breach of peace and "irreverent" usage
of HF.

101   Sackett, S. J. "Fielding and Pope." N&Q, June 1959,
      pp. 200-204.
A profitable reconstruction of a literary relationship.
HF's published commentary on Pope falls into four distinct
categories. Before 1742, when the authors met, HF's reactions to Pope were ad hoc and apparently objective. Between 1744 and 1751, HF oscillated between praise and petty
carping. And from 1751 to his death, HF heaped unques-
tioned praise on Pope. It is possible that during Pope's
lifetime HF wished to please the poet to gain an ally in the
literary wars or possibly to stay out of the Dunciad. He
criticized some of Pope's works after Pope's death that he
had praised highly during his lifetime.

102   Shepperson, Archibald Bolling.   "Additions and Correc-
        tions to Facts about Fielding." MP, 51 (1954), 217-
        224.
        Five random notes.   (1) Twenty-one recognizances in
the Middlesex County records suggest that HF was an active
justice of the peace five weeks earlier than is usually thought.
(2) The one-and-a-half-year delay between his appointment in
1747 and his beginning of active duty in Middlesex results
from a leave he took to complete TJ and to write party propaganda.   (3) A number of cases before HF in 1752 were
written by him as news stories for the Whitehall Evening
Post.   (4) Publishers' advertisements make it possible to
date five of HF's later works.   And (5) HF may possibly
have written the single-issue Covent-Garden Journal of 1749,
two years before he edited the more famous periodical.

103   Stewart, Mary Margaret.   "A Correction and Further
        Note Concerning Henry Fielding as Magistrate."
        N&Q, Jan. 1973, pp. 13-15.
        Shows that although HF was duly elected chairman of
the Middlesex Sessions to succeed Thomas Lane, Lane himself had not resigned his chairmanship on becoming a Master
of Chancery.   Stewart also advances evidence from the St.
Paul's Covent Garden rate books to support HF's succession
of John Green in the Bow-Street magistracy.

104   _____.   "Henry Fielding's Letter to the Duke of
        Richmond." PQ, 50 (1971), 135-140.
        Reprints a letter of 1 April 1749 from HF to Rich-
mond.   It establishes evidence that the Bow-Street magistrate
expected a favor from the dukes of Richmond and Montagu
and that HF was connected with three notorious murder trials
of 1749, all related to incidents of smuggling in Sussex which
Richmond was determined to check.

105   _____.   "Notes on Henry Fielding as a Magistrate."
        N&Q, Sept. 1969, pp. 348-350.
        Corrections and clarifications about HF's magistracy
in 1748 and 1749.   Stewart cites contemporary newspapers
to show that (1) his immediate predecessor at Bow Street
was John Green, (2) he was chairman of the Middlesex Sessions before he was chairman of the Westminster Sessions,
and (3) he began his Middlesex magistracy by at least 17
Feb. 1749.

106   Swaen, A. E. H.   "Fielding and Goldsmith in Leyden."
        MLR, 1 (1906), 327-328.

Cites University of Leyden records to establish that
HF registered as a student of letters--not law--on 16 Feb.
1728. Further, the records disallow Goldsmith's ever having been a regular student there.

107   T---e, W.   "Fielding's First Marriage."   N&Q, 21
       July 1906, p. 47.
       Offers documentary proof that HF's first marriage
was in the church of St. Mary, Charlcombe, in Bath, 28
Nov. 1734. Also notes that his sister Sarah is buried there.

108   Taylor, Houghton W.   "Fielding upon Cibber."   MP,
       29 (1931), 73-90.
       Shows that HF's attitudes toward Cibber evolved from
the professionally cordial through the professionally satiric
to the personally satiric.   Relations were good when Cibber
sponsored Love in Several Masques.   But when Cibber rejected Don Quixote in England, HF began to ridicule Cibber's
mistreatment of others' plays, his indifference toward un-
important authors, and his poor prose style.   HF's satire became bitterly personal at the publication of Cibber's Apology
(1940), which included a hit at HF and blatant self-praise.
Using the Champion, HF attacked Cibber as unlearned and
nonsensical.   He continued the assault in 1741 in The Vernoniad, Shamela, The Opposition, and other Champion numbers.   With JA, HF's satire reached its high point.   There
he scorns Cibber for vanity, self-aggrandizement, obtuse-
ness, and hypocrisy.   Bitter and sneering, HF's assault was
more personal than anything he had written before or after.

109   Trefman, Simon.   Sam. Foote, Comedian, 1720-1777.
       New York: New York Univ. Press, 1971. See pp.
       31-35.
       Recounts the 1748 quarrel between Foote and HF.
On stage and in print Foote had mimicked HF as an ill-
kempt, begging, tobacco-chewing puppet master.   HF re-
taliated in the Jacobite's Journal by bringing Foote before
his Court of Criticism.   Trefman rightly regards HF's
scatological retaliation as gross, abusive, and less witty
than Foote's gibes.

110   Vincent, Howard P.   "The Childhood of Henry Field-
       ing."   RES, 16 (1940), 438-444.
       Suggests that recently found depositions in the case
of Fielding v. Fielding show a better picture of the novelist's
father than heretofore had existed.

111 _____. "Henry Fielding in Prison." MLR, 36
       (1941), 499-500.
       Cites a rare pamphlet of 1740 attacking HF and other
London journalists. This pamphlet alleges that before 1728
Walpole himself had sent relief to HF, then imprisoned in a
country town. Yet soon after, the pamphlet continues, HF
libelled Walpole twice and had the impudence to appear a
week later at his levée.

112 Wallace, Robert M. "Fielding's Knowledge of History
       and Biography." SP, 44 (1947), 89-107.
       A study of allusions in HF's periodicals and of the
auction list of his library. It suggests his preference for
history and biography over Latin and Greek imaginative
literature. Indeed, the number of historical and biographical
titles are second only to legal titles in his library.

113 Wells, John Edwin. "Fielding's 'Champion' and Captain
       Hercules Vinegar." MLR, 8 (1913), 165-172.
       Reveals that "Captain Hercules Vinegar" was not a
fictitious name that HF created for the pseudo-editorship of
the Champion, but instead was the name of a popular London prize fighter. HF's 1739 choice of title and editor for
his paper recalls his naming methods in the farces that he
had stopped writing by 1737.

114 _____. "Fielding's First Poem to Walpole and his
       Garret in 1730." MLN, 29 (1914), 29-30.
       Suggests that Dodsley's 1763 version of a poem by
HF on Walpole is more accurate than that of the 1743 Mis-
cellanies. Also locates HF's garret in 1730 on Picadilly
Road near Arlington Street, close by Walpole's home.

115 Wilbur, Frederick. "Henry Fielding's Life in the
       Theatre and the New Species of Writing." Diss.
       Duke. DA, 35 (1975), 6115A.

116 Willcocks, M[ary] P[atricia]. A True-Born English-
       man: Being the Life of Henry Fielding. London:
       Allen & Unwin, 1947. 288 pp.
       A popular biography attempting to show that all of
HF's actions and thought grew out of his humanity and zest
for life.
       Generally Willcocks has digested her sources well,
even to the point of feeling obliged to defend HF. She keeps
close to the important facts as set down by Cross, but occasionally admits a legend (e.g., HF's writing plays on tobacco

wrappers) and misrepresents a name or title (e. g. , the
Political Register for the Historical Register and Herbert
Walter for Peter Walter).   Willcocks' criticism is weaker
than her scholarship, for she allows lively plot summaries
with biographical asides to stand for analysis.
Nevertheless this life is enjoyable, for its energetic
and dramatic presentation takes hold, and HF--man and
legend--comes alive.   Fifteen illustrations.
Reviews: Queen's Quarterly, 55 (1949), 517-518;
N. Y. Times Book Review, 7 March 1948, p. 6; Sat. Rev.,
3 April 1948, 29-30; TLS, 1 Nov. 1947, p. 567 and 24 Jan.
1948, p. 50.

117   Willy, Margaret.   "Portrait of a Man: Henry Field-
        ing. "   In her Life Was Their Cry.   London: Evans,
        1950, pp. 98-152.
        An uncritical sketch of HF's life.   Drawn wholly
from secondary sources, it is accurate in its broad outline
but is impaired by factual errors and omissions and blunted
by commonplaces.   For example, Willy claims that HF
studied law (not letters) at Leyden and omits mention of
both his authorship of Shamela and his premarital relationship with Mary Daniel.   Likewise she continues the legend
that "reckless good living killed him" and finds TJ's main
merit to be "its rollicking gusto and its zest for adventure."

118   Wright, Kenneth D.   "Henry Fielding and the Theatre
        Act of 1737. "   QJS, 50 (1964), 252-258.
        Specifies contemporary sources that hold HF largely
responsible for the Licensing Act.   Colley Cibber, Benjamin
Victor, Arthur Murphy, and the newspaper Common Sense
all allow that his dramatic satire on Walpole was the proxi-
mate cause of the act.   Oddly enough, there was little
printed opposition to the act, even by HF and other theater
people, probably for fear of governmental retaliation.   The
act became law in 1737; its chief provisions included the
closing of non-Westminster theaters, the censoring of plays
by the Lord Chamberlain, and the licensing of theaters.
Penalties for violation were £ 50 per offense or the revoca-
tion of license of an approved theater.

119   Zirker, Malvin R. , Jr.   "Fielding and Reform in the
        1750s. "   SEL, 7 (1967), 433-465.
        Discounts HF's importance in the official reform
movement of the 1750s.   Zirker sees him as no more than
a witness to and supporter of the seminal Committee of Reform of 1750.   With members such as Pitt and Oglethorpe,

the Committee would have had little need for a Bow Street magistrate's theories. Moreover, HF's views were more superficial than those of the Committee.   E. g. , he saw punishment as crucial; they stressed the revision of capital laws.   Indeed, HF's pamphlets on reform were only two of 18 that appeared between 1750 and 1760.   With reform a favorite issue with all from the King to the projectors, HF's was a typical, not a significant, voice.   See Zirker's book (No. 849) for an extended account.

III

GENERAL CRITICISM

120   Allen, Walter.   "Henry Fielding. "   In his Six Great
      Novelists. "   London: Hamish Hamilton,   1955, pp.
      38-63.
      A review and appreciation of HF as man and author.
Allen offers nothing new or distinctive.

121   Alter, Robert.   Fielding and the Nature of the Novel.
      Cambridge, Mass.:   Harvard Univ. Press 1968.   211
      pp.
      A corrective of the dismissal of HF as a novelist
weak in characterization and artificial in design.   Alter contends that the basic principles of HF's novels are antithesis
and balance, both of which create a conscious artifice to
distance the reader to allow a properly moral perspective
of the novels' actions.
      In the derivative but useful chapter, "The Uses of
Style, " Alter shows that HF cultivates his reader by prefaces, asides, stage speeches, scenes, and similes.   But
mainly it is by an irony that implies both complicity with
the narrator and superiority to the characters that HF establishes a judgmental attitude in his readers.   This artifice
of language conditions the reader for the artifice both in
character and design of JA and TJ.
      In the closely analyzed "The Design of Character, "
Alter explains HF's "integration of character, " the strate-
gies he uses to relate his people to one another and to the
novel's larger moral vision.   While HF refuses to treat
their inner lives, he assesses their motives morally--and
with the right touch of psychological nuance.   Moreover, he
renders the characters complex by a subtle irony that reveals their natures.   (By an analysis of HF's language, e. g.,
Alter shows Aunt Western to be both a satiric butt and a
pathetic old woman.)   Further, Alter shows that HF groups
his characters in various paradigms to reveal their moral
relationships.
      Likewise, in "The Architectonic Novel, " Alter illus-
trates HF's purposeful artifice in the general structures of

JA and TJ.   In close detail he specifies five structures that
allow the novels' unity, viz.   literary parallels, repeated incidents creating a moral continuity, repeated incidents that
aid a coherent plot, thematic parallels, and larger balances
(trains of circumstances, etc.).

A strong advocate of HF's sophistication and complex
craftsmanship, Alter throughout insists that HF has been
misjudged because critics assess him by the standards of
the modern empathetic novel and not by those of the evalu-
ative novel which he invented.   And herein is the chief value
of Alter's study.   It teaches us that the nature of the HF
novel is a purposeful artifice that delights in itself.   Moreover, we may agree when Alter suggests that HF offers
useful guidance for the novel's future: Awareness of the
necessity of art as contrivance will liberate the novelist to
view confused contemporary experience from a distance and
to fix it clearly in a pattern.

For Alter's chapters on Amelia and HF criticism,
see Nos. 718 and 122.

Reviews: Criticism, 12 (1970), 76-78; DR, 49 (1969),
268-270; Genre, 3 (1970), 289-291; JEGP, 68 (1969), 529-
535; RES, n. s. 22 (1971), 89-93; SNNTS, 2 (1970), 239-245.

122   _____.   "On the Critical Dismissal of Fielding:
        Post-Puritanism in Literary Criticism. "   Salmagundi,
        1 (1966), 11-28.

Attacks those critics (e. g. , Leavis and Kermode)
who allege HF's inferiority in matters of technique and
morality.   Alter believes such allegations based on a puritanical view of morality and on a correspondent aesthetic
view that judges all fiction by a tragic standard.   Such criticism attacks Tom Jones's sexual escapades, e. g. , because
HF refuses to weight them with moral significance.   Thus,
to these critics HF's characters are superficial because
they lack mythopoeic resonance, a conclusion based on the
assumption that good fiction must be morally problematic.
These assumptions disallow a competent view of HF's comic
novel.

123   Amory, Hugh.   "Law and the Structure of Fielding's
        Novels. "   Diss. Columbia.   DA, 27 (1966), 451A.

124   Ashmore, Charles D.   "Henry Fielding's 'Art of Life':
        A Study in the Ethics of the Novel. "   Diss. Emory.
        DA, 19 (1959), 2610.

125   Auty, Susan G.   "The New Species of Writing Founded

by Mr. Fielding. " In her Comic Spirit of Eighteenth-
Century Novels.   Port Washington, N. Y.:   Kennikat,
1975, pp. 34-54.
    Overstates the benevolent comic effect at the expense
of the satiric effect in HF.   Auty claims that by keeping
fear, pain, and death out of his novels, HF opens them to
mirthful treatment and in fact sees the ridiculous as matter
more for mirth than for censure.   Auty concludes that HF
treats even his "unpleasant" characters tolerantly.   This
seems a narrow reading, for it cannot account for JW and
Amelia and, by implication, cancels the moral and satiric
effects of the novels.

126   Baker, Ernest A.   Intellectual Realism: From Richard-
      son to Sterne.   Vol. IV of A History of the English
      Novel.   London: H. F. and G. Witherby, 1930.
      See pp. 77-196.
    From the most ample history of the English novel
(10 volumes).   Baker's thesis in this volume is that "the
cardinal achievement of the period was the establishment of ...
intellectual realism, which is synonymous with the novels of
Fielding. "   Through five biographical-cum-critical chapters,
Baker illustrates HF's mastery of this technique.   Indeed,
he judges HF's ultimate importance to be in his shaping the
external realism of Defoe and the psychological realism of
Richardson into a coherent, stable presentation of life by
means of an intelligent, uninvolved narrator.   In JA and TJ
this central intelligence allows a comic but certain presentation of reality.   And though in Amelia the central intelligence breaks down, HF's achievement in realism in the
earlier two novels makes him "the Shakespeare of English
fiction. "

127   Baker, Myra M.   "Satiric Characterizations in the
      Novels of Henry Fielding. " Diss. Alabama. DA,
      27 (1967), 3033A.

128   Baker, Sheridan W. , Jr.   "Fielding and the Irony of
      Form. "   ECS, 2 (1968), 138-154.
    Argues that the reader's perception of the difference
between the neat structures and the chaotic events of JA and
TJ allows a detachment from the events and makes possible
a participation in the ironic amusement prompted by the
narrator.

129   _____.   "Henry Fielding and the Cliché. " Criti-
      cism, 1 (1959), 354-361.

Notes six clichés that HF repeats in his works.   Yet, Baker claims, HF uses them deliberately as a base for variations of phrase and meaning.   His use of them suggests a reliance on durable and permanent ideas that can represent the verities of human nature.   (The six clichés are "voracious pike, " "Nature and Fortune, " literature as a "Bill of Fare, " "je ne sais quoi, " "solid comfort, " and courtship as hunting hares, deer, or foxes.)

130 _____. "Setting, Character, and Situation in the Plays and Novels of Henry Fielding. " Diss. California at Berkeley, 1950.

131 Banerji, H. K. Henry Fielding, Playwright, Journalist and Master of the Art of Fiction: His Life and Works (1929). Rpt. New York: Russell & Russell, 1962, 342 pp.
Purports that because little attention has been paid to HF's plays, pamphlets, and journalism, a true estimate of him has not emerged.   Banerji's chief idea is that HF's realism developed because of his "attention to the living world around him"; indeed, his acute observation of actual people, manners, and events are at the heart of his neglected writings.   Yet in ten chapters, including three superficial ones on the novels, Banerji does little to show how the realism of these writings allows a true estimate of HF.   He notes their topicality and integrates his review of them with facts about HF's life, but all this produces is a highlighting of contents and a summary of previously existing factual data, neither one a basis for the "true estimate" of HF. Still, Banerji's chapters on the plays, the Champion, and the political pamphlets are useful as reviews and checklists, however uncritical.
Reviews: LM, 21 (1930), 373-375; PQ, 10 (1931), 200-201; RAA, 7 (1930), 62; TLS, 3 April 1930, p. 293.

132 Bassein, Beth Ann C. "Crime and Punishment in the Novels of Defoe, Fielding, and Godwin. " Diss. Missouri at Columbia. DA, 22 (1962), 2783.

133 Battestin, Martin C. "Introduction. " In his edition, Twentieth-Century Interpretations of Tom Jones. Englewood Cliffs, N. J.: Prentice-Hall, 1968, pp. 1-15.
Highlights the current "revival" of HF, his life, and the religious, moral, and aesthetic content of TJ.   Seeing Providence and Prudence as the novel's great themes,

Battestin suggests that its benign and orderly universe, its
Palladian structure, and its omniscient, witty narrator make
TJ the consummate work of Augustan literature.
   Other essays in the collection are from Leavis (No.
219), Watt (No. 708), Empson (No. 590), Wright (No. 304),
Crane (No. 575), Booth (No. 557), and Alter (No. 121).

134   Beach, Joseph Warren. "Psychology: Fielding." In
      his Twentieth-Century Novel: Studies in Technique.
      New York: Appleton, 1932, pp. 25-30.
   Cites HF as the most philosophical of the 18th-century
novelists by virtue of his regard of the novel as a philosophical essay.   In his psychological analysis of characters, HF
makes no attempt either to identify with or to dramatize
feelings or mentality.   Rather, he generalizes a character's
psychology so that the reader may see the relationship between mental reactions and general moral make-up.

135   Beasley, Jerry C.   "Romance and the 'New' Novels of
      Richardson, Fielding, and Smollett." SEL, 16 (1976),
      437-450.
   Gauges the anti-romantic climate of the 1740s, dominated by didactic allegories and propagandistic satires loose-
ly disguised as romance.   This climate of reaction to the
romance encouraged the new "realistic" fiction of Richardson, Fielding, and Smollett.   Yet though their anti-romantic
traits are seen in their rejection both of the marvelous and
of extravagances in plot and character, their work still re-
tains traces of the old romances, especially sentimental
love and reversals of fortune.

136   Beatty, Richmond Croom.   "Criticism in Fielding's
      Narratives and His Estimate of Critics." PMLA, 49
      (1934), 1087-1100.
   An unsystematic listing of literary-critical passages
from the narratives.   Beatty concludes that HF's views are
sane and practical and that his theories on character, subject matter, and digressions are pioneer in the novel.
Beatty also illustrates HF's scorn for contemporary critics--
"worms" and "common slanderers" as he styled them.   This
contempt, Beatty suggests, arises from two influences:
HF's unfavorable personal treatment by the critics and the
low and rigid state of 18th-century criticism as dominated
by Rymer, Bysshe, and Dennis.

137   Berger, Tjard W.   "Don Quixote" in Deutschland.
      Heidelberg: J. Hörning, 1908.   See pp. 38-47.

138   Billi, Mirella Mancioli. <u>Strutture narrative nel ro-
       manzo di Henry Fielding.</u> Milan: Bompiani, 1974.
       116 pp.

139   Bissell, Frederick Olds, Jr. <u>Fielding's Theory of the
       Novel</u> (1933). Rpt. New York: Cooper Square, 1969.
       86 pp.
       An uncritical summary of HF's explicit critical theory.
Bissell's purpose is to describe the sources of that theory,
to present and interpret it, and to show its application in
JA and TJ.   His book delivers little of that promise.
       Chapter I, "The Sources of Fielding's Theory, " is a
helpful review of the general traditions (chivalric romance,
picaresque novel, and burlesque romance) and the specific
authors (Scarron, Marivaux, Cervantes, etc.) influencing
his theory.   These sources are presented but not interpreted
in light of their impact on HF's theory.
       Likewise, the second and third chapters on JA and TJ
are superficial.   Each chapter simply extracts HF's direct
statements about fiction from the prefatory chapters of the
two novels.   These are convenient summaries in check-list
form, but Bissell's occasional comments on them never
accrue to a general interpretation.   The last chapter, "Fielding's Application of His Theory, " is still more disappointing
because it summarizes the preceding chapters of summary.
       Never does Bissell infer HF's theory from the narra-
tives themselves nor does he notice the theory as HF expounds it in his journalism.   Still, the book is useful as a
quick reference for a compact reproduction of HF's explicit
poetics in JA and TJ.

140   Blanchard, Frederic T. <u>Fielding the Novelist: A
       Study in Historical Criticism.</u> New Haven, Conn. :
       Yale Univ. Press, 1926.   655 pp.   Incorporates his
       "Coleridge's Estimate of Fielding, " <u>C. M. Gayley
       Anniversary Papers.</u> Berkeley: Univ. of California
       Press, 1922, pp. 155-163.
       A thoroughly detailed record of HF's critical fortunes
from 1742 to 1925.   Blanchard shows that from the beginning of his career, the recurring critical problem of HF
was biographical.   Irrelevancies and inaccuracies colored
his literary reputation to produce misunderstanding, disdain,
and neglect of his works.   In his survey, Blanchard reviews even the most minute commentary, often merely illustrative dicta in letters and speeches, but he devotes his
closest attention to the most influential of HF's observers.
       Oddly enough, as Blanchard shows, though HF was a

popular success in his own time, his 18th-century critical reception was characterized by political animosity, personal malice, or mere neglect of his "low" works. Authors such as Richardson, Smollett, Johnson, and Walpole reacted violently to him, while Arthur Murphy's careless essay of 1762, culled from newspaper attacks, rumors, and dubious anecdotes, established HF for over a century as a rake and hasty artist. And though Sir Walter Scott praised HF's literary craftsmanship, he claimed that HF's personal moral and ethical faults led to the creation of the rake-like Tom Jones and Booth. Thackeray's 1851 portrayal of HF as penitent rake and supreme artist, like Scott's assessment, accepted Murphy's scandalous account as a premise, the effect of which was to ban HF from Victorian parlors and reading rooms. Believing him a roysterer, most vocal critics of the 19th century implied to genteel readers that his novels had no serious purpose, were hastily thrown together, and included "low" characters and scenes derived from his own depraved character.

The reaction began in 1883 when Austin Dobson's sane biography scotched Murphy's and Thackeray's slurs by providing new details about HF's later life that showed him a tender, moral, and learned man. Dobson's reassessment coincided with an awakened interest in realism, genre study, and textual scholarship. Editions by Leslie Stephen (1882), George Saintsbury (1893), Edmund Gosse (1899), and W. H. Henley (1903) attested to the reassessment of HF. And professional university critics such as Wilbur Cross and Walter Raleigh turned detailed attention to HF's achievement. It remained only for Cross' great biography of 1918 to establish accurately HF's life from a wholesale and meticulous investigation.

Blanchard's ample bibliography of sources and detailed analytical index complement his 18-chapter survey to make this book a formidable history of applied criticism. Reviews: MLR, 22 (1927), 225-228; RAA, 5 (1927), 57-59; RES, o. s. 3 (1927), 227-232.

141 Booth, Wayne. "The Self-Conscious Narrator in Comic Fiction before Tristram Shandy." PMLA, 67 (1952), 163-185.
A history of the narrator who intrudes into his novel. Booth specifies Sterne's debt to HF, whose intrusive, self-conscious narrator represents the true order and form of his novels. Booth shows also why HF's intrusions are functional and not ornamental. Generally the intrusions (1) characterize the reader morally, (2) generate an intimacy

between narrator and reader, (3) insure a comic purpose,
and (4) comment on the narrator's procedures.

141a Borinski, Ludwig. "Fieldings Früwerk" and "Fieldings grosse Romane. " In his Der englische Roman
des 18. Jahrhunderts. Frankfurt am Main: Athenaum
Verlag, 1968, pp. 149-82, 183-232.

142 Bradbury, Malcolm. "The Comic Novel in Sterne and
Fielding. " In The Winged Skull: Papers from the
Laurence Sterne Bicentenary Conference. Ed. Arthur
H. Cash and John M. Stedmond. Kent, Ohio: Kent
State Univ. Press, 1971, pp. 124-131.
A reflective but undetailed commentary. Bradbury
suggests that HF's comedy is a "self-conscious fictive styli-
zation, " an attitude toward a real world balanced and re-
fined by art. But Sterne's comedy is a condition of life in
which his hero is frustrated in a world without balance and
neat endings. HF's comedy is attitudinal, Sterne's repre-
sentational. HF's works by commentary, Sterne's by identification.

143 Braudy, Leo. "Fielding: Public History and Individual
Perception. " In his Narrative Form in History and
Fiction: Hume, Fielding, and Gibbon. Princeton,
N. J.: Princeton Univ. Press, 1970, pp. 91-212.
Argues for the development of HF's narrative form
from a "spontaneity" in JA, to a pure pattern in JW, to a
synthesis of both in TJ, to a technique that fuses public life
and private morality in Amelia. Braudy attempts to check
the moralistic and "static" readings of the novels by suggesting that HF's approach is "dynamic" (for it concerns
characters in a movement of time) and epistemological (for
it also concerns the apprehension--by HF and his characters--
of complex facts of existence).
Braudy's otherwise insightful commentary is impaired
by his disregard of weighty scholarly opinion that believes
JW to have been substantially completed before the publication of JA.

144 Bredvold, Louis L "The Novel: Fielding, Smollett,
Sterne. " In his Literature of the Restoration and the
18th Century, 1660-1798. Vol. III in A History of
English Literature. Ed. Hardin Craig. 1950; rpt.
London: Collier-Macmillan, 1969, pp. 148-156.
Another restatement of the usual facts found in literary
histories.

145   Bronson, Bertrand H.   "Strange Relations: The Author
      and His Audience. "   In his Facets of The Enlighten-
      ment: Studies in English Literature and Its Contexts.
      Berkeley: Univ. of California Press, 1968, pp. 298-
      325.
      Notices the common "oral" narrative technique of
Chaucer and HF.   But Bronson concludes that HF's is retro-
grade from the psychological realism achieved by Richardson's epistolary method, for what HF's technique gains in
relating reader and author it loses by distancing the characters from the author.

146   Bruce, Donald.   Radical Doctor Smollett (1964).   Rpt.
      Boston: Houghton Mifflin, 1965.   See pp. 154-156.
      Indicts HF as "an exponent of conformity" in his style
(Addisonian), his use of the classics (often "pseudo-Virgil-
ian"), his philosophy (unoriginal), and his view of society
(reactionary).

147   Burke, John J. , Jr.   "History without History: Field-
      ing's Theory of Fiction. "   In A Provision of Human
      Nature: Essays on Fielding and Others.   Ed. Donald
      Kay.   University: Univ. of Alabama Press, 1977, pp.
      45-63.
      Argues that HF's theory of fiction emerges from his
displeasure with the distortions of historiography.   Burke
suggests that in JW a cynical HF presents a negative example
attacking historiographical abuses.   In JA he presents a
positive alternative as he shows the writer's service to the
public to be in his bringing them happiness by "new species"
of comic writing.   And in TJ he moves in an autobiographi-
cal direction to establish that the writer's own experience
and humanity produce good fiction.   Thus Burke interprets
HF's theory as socially motivated: the imperative of fiction
is to offer the reader some happiness in an otherwise difficult world.   He does not attempt to fit Amelia into his argument.

148   Burton, Richard.   "Eighteenth-Century Beginnings:
      Fielding. "   In his Masters of the English Novel: A
      Study of Principles and Personalities.   New York:
      Holt, 1909, pp. 48-71.
      Perpetuates the legend of HF's checkered career, ir-
regular living, and spendthrift ways and views him as a
man's man at Richardson's expense.   Further, Burton rejects HF's novels in unexpurgated form as unfit for household reading.   He highlights TJ, granting high praise to its

"realism" and varied characters. But because he thinks the book reverts to picaresque type, Burton regards it as insignificant in the history of the English novel.

149   Butt, John. Fielding. Writers and Their Work, No. 57. London: Longmans, Green, 1954; rev., 1959. 35 pp.
A compact appreciation of HF's literary development. This pamphlet shows his progress from stage wit to lampooner to didactic novelist. Within Butt's main focus on these general phases is an account of the technical problems HF faced, such as persuading the reader of Tom's and Booth's reforms, adapting the "road" novel to the domesticity of Amelia, balancing concerns of character with social concerns, and modifying traditional forms such as the epic and travel literature. Generally sensible with no erratic judgments.

150   Caliumi, Grazia. Il romanzo di Henry Fielding. Milan: Istituto Editoriale Cisalpino, 1959.

151   Capers, Connie. "From Drama to Novel: A Study of Fielding's Development." DAI, 31 (1971), 5353A (New Mexico).

152   Castillo Cofiño, Rosa. "Los conceptos del amor en la novelística de Henry Fielding." Diss. Univ. of Madrid 1973.

153   Child, Harold. "Fielding and Smollett." In Vol. X of The Cambridge History of English Literature. Ed. A. W. Ward and A. R. Waller. Cambridge, England: Cambridge Univ. Press, 1913, pp. 20-45.
A conventional outline of HF's and Smollett's lives and works aimed at measuring their influence on the British novel. Child counterpoints HF's polished style, structure, and character analysis with Smollett's raw wit, episodic ability, and typical characters. He regards HF's main legacy to fiction to be the foundation of the novel of character. A dubious conclusion in light of more modern scholarship.

153a Cleary, Thomas R. "Fielding: Style for an Age of Sensibility." In Transactions of the Samuel Johnson Society of the Northwest. Vol. VI. Calgary, Alberta: Samuel Johnson Society of the Northwest, 1973, pp. 91-96.
Contests the bromide of seeing HF as a novelist inter-

ested mainly in his story or the product of his narration.
Instead, Cleary calls him a novelist whose concern is more
with the process of telling his story. Especially in TJ HF
appears a novelist of sensibility, imposing his mind and feelings on the action.

154   Coley, William B.   "The Background of Fielding's
      Laughter. "   ELH, 26 (1959), 229-252.
      States the claim of HF as satirist to redress emphasis
on HF as moralist. By reference to the intellectual milieu,
Coley specifies three main influences on HF's comic view.
First, Robert South's sermonic use of "witty seriousness"
and impatience with "dull gravity" afforded example and
sanction for HF. Second, Shaftesbury's approval of burlesque
and the dialogue structure were as influential on HF as were
his philosophical pronouncements. A third influence was
Swift, whose Scriblerian satire showing how the "high" is
really "low, " the sublime really ridiculous, the ideal really
base, can be found throughout HF's work.

155   _____. "Fielding's Comic: A Study of the Relation
      Between Wit and Seriousness in a Comic Augustan. "
      Diss. Yale.   DAI, 30 (1970), 4403A.

156   _____. "Gide and Fielding. "   CL, 11 (1959), 1-15.
      Recalls that Gide's journal contains high praise of HF.
Especially, Gide sees him as an anti-religionist whose mis-
trust of perfection and whose refusal to relate piety to good
nature and religion to honor make him anything but an "Augustan Gospel singer" or, as others have called him, an
earnest and orthodox "Christian censor. "

157   Combs, William W. , Jr.   "Man and Society in Field-
      ing's Works. "   Diss. Harvard, 1962.

158   Conti, Paola C.   "Natura e civiltà in Henry Fielding. "
      EM, 19 (1968), 105-132.

159   Cooke, Arthur L.   "Fielding and the Writers of Heroic
      Romance. "   PMLA, 62 (1947), 984-994.
      Shows that HF's theory of prose fiction is similar to
that of the romance writers (especially Scudery and La Cal-
prenède) whose work he disparaged. Both theories used the
principles of the epic. Both insisted on an identification
with history. Both insisted on probability over the marvelous.
Both stressed the moral purpose of fiction. Both demanded
unity. And both agreed on genius, learning, social knowledge,
and feeling as requisites of the author.

160   Cooper, Frank B.   "The Structure of the Novels of
       Henry Fielding. "   Diss. Claremont.   DAI, 30 (1970),
       5404A.

161   Daiches, David.   A Critical History of English Litera-
       ture.   New York: Ronald, 1950.   Vol. II.   See pp.
       713-727.
       A good general review of HF's novelistic development
with sensible critical comments on the individual works.
Daiches' approach is often social besides; e. g. , he regards
HF's good-natured man as "a revolt against the idealization
of sophistication found ... in Lord Chesterfield's letters to
his son. "

162   Davis, Charles G.   "Satire on the Reader in the Novels
       of Henry Fielding. "   Diss. North Carolina at Chapel
       Hill.   DAI, 31 (1971), 6006A.

163   Deppe, Wolfgang G.   History versus Romance.   Ein
       Beitrag zur Entwicklungsgeschichte und zum Verständnis
       der Literaturtheorie Henry Fieldings.   Münster: Neue
       Beiträge zur Englischen Philologie, 1965.   Band 4, 178 pp.

164   Derstine, Virginia.   "Fielding's Shift in Instructional
       Method as Reflected in His Early Prose Fiction. "
       Diss. Washington.   DA, 21 (1961), 3780.

165   Devine, Mary E.   "Fielding on Walpole: A Study of
       Henry Fielding's Major Political Satires. "   Diss.
       Loyola of Chicago, 1964.

166   Dibelius, W.   "Henry Fielding. "   In his Englische
       Romankunst.   Berlin: Mayer & Müller, 1910, pp. 85-
       155.

167   Digeon, Aurélien.   The Novels of Fielding.   London:
       Routledge, 1925.   255 pp.   Originally pub. in French.
       Paris, 1923.
       The first major appreciation of HF that does not admit
discussion of his virtues and vices as grounds for analysis.
Although in the first chapter, which is biographical, Digeon
does often carp at Richardson and Smollett, his book is
finally a careful and sensitive examination of HF's development as a novelist.
       Essentially Digeon traces that development from the
plays (impersonal and governed both by literary tradition
and the taste of the paying public) through JW ("an intellec-

tual criticism" in irony) through JA and TJ (which merge
irony and comic sentimentality) to Amelia (which strains between sentimental and didactic tension).

The chief merits of this examination are Digeon's continual reference to the structure of the novels (especially to
their dramatic architecture) and to the tradition of "psychological realism" that HF established (his ability to show motive through action).   Yet Digeon's predilection for the comic
structure flaws his appreciation of Amelia, which he judges
by the terms of JA and TJ and not as an experiment in
fiction; thus he unfavorably contrasts the many plots of
Amelia with the unity of action of TJ.

Besides structure and psychological realism, Digeon
regards HF's tone, narrative mastery, and philosophical
comedy as his main legacy to the English novel: Through
Dickens and Thackeray to Meredith, "the English novel has
followed Fielding's law: it is a domestic novel interrupted ...
by the humorous comments of the author. "

168   Doland, Virginia M.   "Versions of Pastoral in Henry
        Fielding's Prose Fiction. "   Diss. U. S. C.   DAI, 31
        (1970), 1222A.

169   Dooley, D. J.   "Some Uses and Mutations of the Pica-
        resque. "   DR, 37 (1958), 363-377.

A useful review of the picaresque from the 16th into
the 20th century.   At first an anti-romance, it was changed
by HF.   His hero is honest, not roguish, and his subject
is folly, not knavery.   Further, he departed from the picaresque tradition in his imposition of form--especially plot-
ting and unified action--and he continued the irony of the
picaresque but without its cynicism.   Thus in HF's novels
the romance and anti-romance (picaresque) coexist.

170   Duber, Rudolph.   "Beitrage zu Fieldings Romantech-
        nik. "   Diss. Halle, 1910.

171   Dyson, A. E.   "Satiric and Comic Theory in Relation
        to Fielding. "   MLQ, 18 (1957), 225-237.

An important essay that places HF in the Augustan
climate that nurtured satire and comedy.   Dyson shows that
if in spirit HF was a satiric idealist, in practice he was a
comic humorist.   In his work good humor ultimately breaks
in to undermine his satire, for he is not misanthropic enough
to sustain the disgust he pretends to feel.   HF's comparative
failure as a satirist accounts largely for his success as a
comic writer.   His progression from Shamela and JW to JA

and TJ manifests his shift from the satiric ideal to the comic norm.

172   Elistratova, Anna.   "Henry Fielding (1707-1754), " SovL
      October 1954, pp. 161-166.
      A Marxist review for the HF bicentennial.   Jargon-
ridden, the article offers more praise than analysis of the
novels, regarding them as part of "the fight for a democratic national culture. "   Specifically it praises HF for his
attack on the hypocrisy and greed of the "upper classes, "
his protest against adventurist wars, his "contempt for the
selfish moneyed interests masquerading as bourgeois vir-
ture, " and his championing of the common man.   Aesthe-
tically, it cites HF's typical characters and principles of
realism as important to the establishment of Socialist realism.

173   England, Denzil.   "Henry Fielding. "   Contemp R, 186
      (1954), 218-223.
      A popular sketch of HF's life and works for the bi-
centennial of his death.

174   Ernle, Lord.   "Founders of the Modern Novel: Field-
      ing. "   Edinburgh Review, 243 (1926).   Rpt. in his
      The Light Reading of Our Ancestors: Chapters in the
      Growth of the English Novel.   London: Hutchinson,
      n. d. , pp. 205-244.
      Typical of many other historical/appreciative accounts.
This essay reviews HF's life and fiction with great delight
and little originality.   There is high praise for HF's putting
himself into his books by his nature, humor, and tolerance.
An engaging note is that Amelia's noselessness may well
have been the text for Sterne's chapter on noses in Tristram
Shandy.

175   Evans, William E.   "Poetic Justice and the Endings of
      Henry Fielding's Novels. "   Diss. Ohio State.   DAI,
      34 (1973), 2555A.

176   Farrell, William J.   "Fielding's Familiar Style. "
      ELH, 34 (1967), 65-77.
      Modifies the criticism defending HF's narrative dis-
tance as a means of gaining objectivity.   Farrell suggests
that HF's familiar style (especially in the aside and full
conversation) reduces the distance between the story and the
storyteller to produce greater credibility.

177   Fischer, Hildegard. <u>Das subjektive Element in den Ro-
      manen Fieldings.</u> Ohlau: Eschenhagen, 1933. 84 pp.

178   Fox, Ralph. "The Novel as Epic." In his <u>Novel and
      the People.</u> 1937; rpt London: Cobbett, 1944, pp.
      53-63.
         A Marxist commentary with allusions to HF. Fox
      sees HF using the novel to examine the new English society,
      "a brutal world ... of conquering capitalism." He praises
      HF both for his belief in man's ability to master the world
      and for his realism and objectivity which bespeak a ma-
      terialist aesthetic.

179   Frolich, Armin. "Fieldings Humor in seinen Romanen."
      Diss. Leipzig, 1918.

180   Gerould, Gordon Hall. "The Dominance of the Novel."
      In his <u>Patterns of English and American Fiction: A
      History</u> (1942). Rpt. New York: Russell & Russell,
      1966, pp. 74-101.
         The same brief outline of HF's work common to all
      short histories of the British novel. Nothing distinctive.

181   Golden, Morris. <u>Fielding's Moral Psychology.</u> Am-
      herst: Univ. of Massachusetts Press, 1966. 171 pp.
         A disappointment. While Golden's intention is "to
      describe Fielding's theory of psychology and its connection
      with his view of morality," his means are the restatement
      of clichés, the reworking of thoughts of other scholars, and
      the repetition of both in a bland prose. Ultimately this
      study is an extensive restatement of the idea that HF's
      works evidence tension between the selfish and generous
      passions. Or as Golden's jargon refashions this bromide:
      HF's crucial problem is "how to establish an outgoing sym-
      pathy in an enclosed mind."
         In "The Enclosed Self" Golden presents the customary
      review of the main philosophical thought of the day--Mande-
      ville, Shaftesbury, et al.--and recalls the usual thoughts
      about good nature, happiness as a human goal, and hypocrisy
      as a great sin. "Fielding's System of Psychology" strains
      to establish a system where only random pronouncements
      exist. That HF wavers between Mandeville and Shaftesbury
      is clear; but because Golden can never really show a system
      for HF, he must resort to pointing to illustrations of both
      philosophies in the novels and essays in his chapter on "The
      Psychology of the Novels." "Environment" makes some in-
      teresting points to suggest how social position can affect

character before, as one reviewer notes, the last chapter,
"Fantasy and Reality, " confuses Golden's fantasy with HF's
reality.
Reviews: JEGP, 66 (1967), 591-594; Novel, 1 (1968),
286-288.

182 Green, Emanuel. Henry Fielding: His Works: An
     Independent Criticism. London: Harrison & Sons,
     1909. 33 pp.
A vituperative tract that labels HF a "most despicable
character" and summarily dismisses his major works as
"low. " For Green, the plays are "obstetric, unhealthy, and
nauseous, " JA is weak in style, plot interest, and delicacy,
TJ is "naughty" and indelicate, and Amelia is "an offense
against every standard rule of decency. " This ludicrously
abusive account concludes that "the world has hardly derived
either profit or benefit" from HF's works.

183 Hammond, Geraldine E. "Evidences of the Dramatist's
     Technique in Henry Fielding's Novels. " Bulletin of
     the University of Wichita, 16 (1941), 3-27.
A review of influences on HF's novels--the epic, Cervantes, the picaresque, and Richardson--and a detailed illustration of HF's own dramatic craft in JA, TJ, and Amelia.
Essentially, Hammond points to HF's many direct references
to the stage, comedy of manners and burlesque elements,
reliance on dialogue, speed of scenes, internal climaxes,
revelation of character, character quirks, malapropisms
and dialect, "humor" names, suggestion of scenery, and
stage directions.

184 Harmen, Mary M. Campbell. "Exposition in the
     Novels of Henry Fielding. " Diss. Catholic. DAI, 34
     (1973), 1911A.

185 Harrison, Bernard. "The Philosophical Context" and
     "Fielding and the Philosophers. " Chapters in his
     Henry Fielding's Tom Jones: The Novelist as Moral
     Philosopher, 1975.
     See No. 602.

186 Hartelius, Kirsten. "Satire i Henry Fieldings romaner."
     Extracta, 1 (1968), 104-111.

187 Hassall, Anthony J. "Fielding's Puppet Image. " PQ,
     53 (1974), 71-83.
     Examines HF's use of the puppet image in four plays,

JW, and TJ.   Not only a vehicle for political and moral
satire, the puppet image defines the nature and structure of
HF's best work: the author as master controlling and sometimes talking through his character-puppets and mediating between them and the audience.

188   Hatfield, Glenn W.   Henry Fielding and the Language
      of Irony.   Chicago: Univ. of Chicago Press, 1968.
      224 pp.   Incorporates "Puffs and Pollitricks: Jonathan
      Wild and the Political Corruption of Language," PQ,
      46 (1967), 248-267; "Quacks, Pettifoggers, and Par-
      sons: Fielding's Case against the Learned Profes-
      sions," TSLL, 9 (1967), 69-83; and "'The Serpent and
      the Dove':   'Prudence' in Tom Jones," MP, 65 (1967),
      17-32.
A study of HF's attitude toward the corruption and cor-
ruptibility of the language.   Hatfield shows how HF uses
irony both to expose the popular decay of English words and
to restore to them their exact, though not original, meanings.
      Chapter I, "The Corruption of Language," first estab-
lishes HF's general concern with the contemporary prostitution of language.   His explicit attacks on corrupt language
extend from the Champion of 1740, which put Colley Cibber
on trial for the murder of the English language, to the Covent-
Garden Journal of 1752, whose "Modern Glossary" ironically
defines honor as duelling, worth as power, rank, and wealth,
gallantry as fornication and adultery, etc.   The chapter then
suggests HF's reliance on the linguistic theory of Locke,
and especially his thoughts about "confused ideas in words."
The second chapter, "Words and Ideas," extends discussion
of Locke's influence on HF, particularly regarding the imperfect connection between words and ideas in the human
mind.
      The third chapter, "Language and Society," if thin in
analysis is rich in illustration.   In it Hatfield combs HF's
works to produce a catalogue of linguistic abuses perpetrated
by four classes of offenders: writers and critics, politi-
cians, polite society, and the professions.   These last HF
attacked in the belief that their jargon often masks an in-
sincerity that results in a debasing of humanistic values.
      Hatfield's final three chapters show how HF devises
methods to immunize his own meanings from the corruption
of the words in which he must express them.   "Irony and
Action" argues that HF articulates his meanings by playing
off corrupt (ironic) words against true (dramatic) renderings
of them.   Thus JA, JW, and TJ harbor both the exact and

the popular meanings of charity, greatness, and prudence.
HF applies the debased meaning of, say, charity to Trulliber
verbally and then positively defines it in the actions of
Adams.   Ironic, negative meanings receive their true signifi-
cations in dramatic, positive acts.   Chapter V, "The Serpent
and the Dove," explains how this blending of irony and dramatic action defines prudence, the main ethical term of TJ.
And the last chapter, "'A Mirrour for the Understanding,'"
asserts that HF's "dramatized authorship" in his narrator
is a final means of overcoming the corrupt medium of a debased language.
    Ultimately Hatfield's book reconstitutes HF as a stylist
by showing how his attitude toward language embodies his
social and moral attitudes.   And though the book does not
substantially offer what could be a useful contrast with the
ironic voice of Swift, it does place HF squarely among
Swift, Pope, and Johnson, who all recognized the relationship between a declining civilization and a decaying language.
    Reviews: JEGP, 68 (1969), 529-535; MLQ, 30 (1969),
149-151; PQ, 48 (1969), 356; QJS, 55 (1969), 86; RES, n. s.
20 (1969), 507-508; SNNTS, 2 (1970), 230-238; TLS, 2 Jan.
1969, p. 8.

189 _____. "Quacks, Pettifoggers, and Parsons: Field-
        ing's Case Against the Learned Professions." TSLL,
        9 (1967), 69-83.
        See No. 188.

190 Henley, William Ernest. "Essay on the Life, Genius,
        and Achievement of the Author." In his edition, The
        Complete Works of Henry Fielding, Esq.   16 vols.
        London: Heinemann, 1903. Vol. XVI, pp. v-xlvi.
    An important Edwardian statement and a blistering
attack on the Victorian myth of HF, perpetrated largely by
Thackeray.   Henley concedes HF's healthy sexuality--"Young
ravens must have food"--as irrelevant to a judgment of him.
And though brushing aside his plays as "burrowing ground"
for the historian, Henley stresses HF as a serious artist
in all that he wrote and as a magnanimous man in all that
he did.   While Henley's essay is a clear call for a re-
appraisal of HF, its exuberant advocacy frequently swamps
its critical sensibility.

191 "Henry Fielding." TLS, 8 Oct. 1954, p. 641.
    A bicentennial appreciation exhuming all the common-
places: the hearty, rakish HF, his brilliantly earthy English
masterpieces, his sense of humor, etc.

192   Hill, Rowland M. "Setting in the Novels of Henry
        Fielding. " Bulletin of the Citadel, 7 (1943), 26-52.
        Avers that the sparsity of setting in HF's novels de-
rives from (1) his dramatic habit of using few stage proper-
ties, (2) his suspicion that colorful background would retard
the narrative, and (3) the picaresque tradition that subordin-
ated setting to caricature and story. Nevertheless, Hill
contends that HF's experiments in setting are notable, for
his mock-heroic settings promote realism and satire by contrast. And while HF hesitates to depict interiors, he excels
at mob- and sea-scenes, buildings and countrysides. Often
brief, such scenes provide both realistic atmosphere and a
unity of impression among incidents.

193   Holly, Grant I. "Fielding's Enchanted Glass: A Study
        of the World as Language in Selected Comic Prose. "
        Diss. Rochester. DA, 35 (1974), 2226A.

194   Homann, Wilhelm. "Fielding as Humorist. " Diss.
        Marburg, 1900.

195   Horn, András. "Social Morality: Fielding. " In his
        Byron's "Don Juan" and the Eighteenth-Century English
        Novel (1962). Rpt. Norwood, 1976, pp. 9-27.
        Discusses the influences on Don Juan of HF (social
morality), Sterne (subjectivism), and Smollett (picaresque
elements). Horn explains that HF's novels and Byron's
poem share a consistent moral attitude characterized by
tolerance and active humanitarianism; ultimately they fuse
their "eroticism and social conscience into a positive whole."
Includes a useful sketch of the determining currents in the
authors' cultural milieu.

196   Hughes, Leo. "The Influence of Fielding's Milieu upon
        his Humor. " SE (1944), 269-297.
        Lists some of the obvious social influences on HF's
comic practice. Hughes notes that the Horatian dictum to
teach and entertain, the popular encouragement to write at
a low level, and the literary and political factionalism all
retarded his success as a playwright. Hughes sees JA as
the zenith of HF's humor, for it was influenced by the most
favorable conditions of his life--recent admission to the bar,
the countryside of the western circuit, and happy family life.
TJ (with less warmth, gaiety, and humor) and Amelia (with
the virtual absence of humor) reflect the unhappy years--the
deaths of his first wife and his daughter in 1743 and 1744,
the rigors of city and professional life, and his own declining health.

197   Humphreys, A. R.   "Fielding's Irony: Its Methods and
      Effects. "   RES, o. s. 18 (1942), 183-196.
      Suggests that HF's irony, unlike Swift's, is corrective
and orthodox, an irony of integration rather than of disintegra-
tion.   By asking the reader to join him as an observer--and
not to join his characters as a participant--HF establishes a
kinship and oneness of view pointed by common sense.   He
shows "normal" people what is "abnormal" in society, unlike
Swift who often satirizes his reader for being "abnormal. "
Specific methods of HF's irony include the rhythmical assur-
ance, cogency and symmetry of the sentence, reduction of
complex behavior to formalization, formal-antithetical style,
and mock-heroic characterization.

198   Hunter, J. Paul.   Occasional Form: Henry Fielding
      and the Chains of Circumstance.   Baltimore: Johns
      Hopkins Univ. Press, 1975.   263 pp.   Incorporates
      "Fielding's Reflexive Plays and the Rhetoric of Dis-
      covery. "   SLI, 5 (1972), 65-100.
      Sets HF's major works (JW curiously excepted) in
their cultural contexts to show how contemporary forces
("chains of circumstance") moved him to use ad-hoc rhetorical tactics ("occasional forms").   The importance of Hunter's study is dual.   First, it shows that HF's literary
stimulus ultimately is more to be found in modern political,
religious, and literary events than in older literary forms
(e. g. , the epic).   And consequently, Hunter's book maintains that HF's literary identity is defined in the tension
between his allegiance to "timeless" old values and the
"timely" imperatives that he could not avoid.   Roughly
stated, Hunter's HF has a classical heart and a contemporary head.
      The first chapter, "The Many Masquerades of Henry
Fielding, " is a general but accurate discussion of how HF
reflects the basic cultural shift from medieval to modern
that was in progress in the 18th century.   The liberating
but rootless and urban sensibility of the Whigs was dis-
placing the Tory authoritarian, rural, and ordered consciousness.   And HF, aristocratic but non-affluent, of the
country but in the city, classically educated but involved in
"hackney" writing, felt the pressures of the alternatives.
His solution, Hunter suggests, is to use the demands of the
new age to adapt the old values.
      There are two chapters on the plays.   "Fielding Among
the Giants" explains how the Tragedy of Tragedies is a
primer to HF's basic ideas and techniques.   The play illustrates his dilemma between conflicting past and present

values.   "Fielding's Reflexive Plays and the Rhetoric of
Discovery" shows how his rehearsal plays illustrate his concern with autonomy of action, the dynamics of authorial interpretation, the technique of multiple satire, and the displacement of the word in the 1720s and 1730s.
    "Historical Registers for the Year 1740" is a largely
unoriginal chapter that reminds us of HF's use of Shamela
to criticize some contemporary attitudes and people (theological, political, and literary).
    Hunter provides five chapters on the major novels.
"Some Contexts for Joseph Andrews" examines some contemporary controversies (e. g. , deistic disputes and the
"holiness movement") that HF uses to produce the reader's
expectations in the novel. Likewise, "Some Models for
Tom Jones" establishes HF's rhetorical uses of the originals
of Thwackum and Square, Fénelon's Télémaque, Virgil, the
biblical expulsion myth, and Methodism. "The Conquest of
Space: Motion and Pause in Joseph Andrews and Tom
Jones" is a brilliant explanation of HF's use of the contemporary journey motif. It also views the interpolated tales
in these novels as parodies of popular fiction. "Occasions
Large and Small: Symmetry and the Limits of Symmetry in
Tom Jones" is most instructive when it argues that "the
cultural consciousness of Tom Jones is that of 1745, when
constitutional government was threatened by nostalgia for
the old ways and universal absolutes. " Thus Hunter sees
Tom as a Hanoverian model, the new man of English society, and Paradise Hall ultimately as a paradigm of the
new order. It is on the basis of its cultural consciousness
that Hunter terms TJ an epic. Finally, "Flight into the Interior" is a sensitive reading of what went wrong in Amelia.
It accounts for the main critical indictments against HF's
last novel, relates it to JA and TJ, and speculates on the
influences HF and Richardson exerted on each other.
    Reviews: Criticism, 19 (1977), 99-102; PQ, 55 (1976),
468; RES, n. s. 28 (1977), 475; SAQ, 75 (1976), 525-526; SR,
85 (1977), 652-653.

199 Irwin, Michael. Henry Fielding: The Tentative Realist.
    Oxford, England: Clarendon Press, 1967. 147 pp.
    An explanation of why HF failed to write a truly real-
istic novel. Principally, Irwin sees HF wavering between
a basic intention to moralize and a lesser intention to tell
an entertaining story. It is that wavering that makes his
realism tentative.
    Irwin suggests that in the plays HF subordinates form
to his moral intentions. But because his artificial, Restora-

tion-derived plots would not square with an imperative Augustan didacticism, the plays become almost formless "revues," as HF is forced by that imperative to satirize social abuses. This problem continues in the novels, according to Irwin. JW is retarded by the inconsistency between its romantic plot (in which society's values are upheld) and its ironic plot (in which society's values are attacked). JA's "loose-leaf" structure pits the narrative interest (Joseph's story) against the moral interest (Adams's story) to produce a spasmodic quality. TJ's moral "predestination" of its characters impedes their presentation. And Amelia fails to achieve a consistent realism for four reasons: its didacticism strains the story, the Booth and Amelia plots compete for primacy, Booth's beliefs are never dramatized, and the sentimental touches are often obtrusive.

Irwin concludes that HF was essentially committed to a didactically moral intention and that that commitment was of greater interest to his contemporary readers than was realism.

This argument is generally plausible. But it too often assumes HF's moral intentions without presenting cogent biographical (or social) reasons for them. And its reduction of HF's "failure" to a system of intentional inconsistency implies a failure in his development as a novelist that the facts of his literary biography do not allow.

Reviews: N&Q, Dec. 1968, pp. 474-477; Novel, 2 (1968), 79-80; RES, n.s. 20 (1969), 249-250; TLS, 19 Oct. 1967, p. 985; YR, 57 (1967), 278-282.

200   Irwin, W. R. "Satire and Comedy in the Works of Henry Fielding." ELH, 13 (1946), 168-188.
Documents HF's comments that the basis of his comedy and satire is affectation, his chief method, exposure. From his early dramatic satire on literary affectation--in actors, editors, playwrights, critics, booksellers, and readers--he developed a sense of narrative comedy that could include greater ethical and technical refinements.

201   Iser, Wolfgang, ed. Henry Fielding und der englische Roman des 18. Jahrhunderts. Darmstadt: Wissenschaftliche Buchgesellschaft, 1972. 505 pp.
Reprints critical essays by Sherburn (Nos. 268 and 755), Humphreys (No. 197), M. Mack (No. 471), Kettle (No. 624), Crane (No. 572), Spilka (Nos. 279 and 490), Van Ghent (No. 703), Erzgräber (No. 730), Empson (No. 590), Coley (No. 156), Coolidge (No. 727), Ehrenpreis (No. 441), Baker

(No. 719), Cazenave (No. 566), Iser (No. 456), E. C. Mack
(No. 225), Watt (No. 296), Sherwood (No. 269), Kermode
(No. 212), Booth (No. 141), and Stanzel (No. 692).

202 _____. Die Weltanschauung Henry Fieldings.
Tübingen: Max Niemeyer, 1952. 320 pp.
Reviews: MLR, 49 (1954), 114; RES, n. s. 5 (1954),
302-305.

203 Jackson, Holbrook. "Henry Fielding." In his Great
English Novelists (1908). Rpt. Freeport, N. Y.: Books
for Libraries Press, 1967, pp. 64-86.
Claims, in pertinent part, that in HF's novels "virtue
and instinct may be identical." Such oversimplification also
informs Jackson's belief that HF has no finesse, for he
evokes only emotional extremes from his readers.

204 Jensen, Gerard E. "Fashionable Society in Fielding's
Time." PMLA, 31 (1916), 79-89.
Sketches "Vanity Fair" in HF's life and works. Jensen
notes that the fictional Boobies, Didappers, Bellastons, and
Fellamars symbolize HF's dislike of the immorality of
fashionable society and its effect on the lower classes which
aped it. Jensen suggests that HF's pictures of an insolent,
imitative public that gamed, brawled, drank, etc. derived
from his daily contact as a magistrate with the lower classes.

205 Joesten, Maria. Die philosophie Fieldings. Kölner
anglistische Arbeiten, vol. XV. Leipzig: Bernard
Tauchnitz, 1932. 107 pp.

206 Johnson, Maurice. Fielding's Art of Fiction: Eleven
Essays on Shamela, Joseph Andrews, Tom Jones, and
Amelia. Philadelphia: Univ. of Pennsylvania Press,
1961. 182 pp.
Diverse, largely unrelated essays on HF's fictional
techniques. Johnson's aim is worthy, to establish the artistic integrity of HF's fiction, and his method is usually
intense, a close analysis of structures and specific passages.
But the book's quality is uneven; some chapters are derivative, some incisive, and some obvious. Moreover, while a
thesis flickers occasionally--the relationship in the novels
between literature and life or art and reality--it never glows.
See Nos. 407, 459-461, 617, 619-621, 736-738 for
annotations of the separate chapters.
Reviews: MLR, 58 (1963), 464; PQ, 41 (1962), 588-
590; SAQ, 61 (1962), 422-423; TLS, 3 Aug. 1962, p. 555.

207   Jordan, Burt A.   "The Moral Code in Fielding's
      Novels: Jonathan Wild, Joseph Andrews, Tom Jones,
      and Amelia."   Diss. South Carolina.   DAI, 31 (1970),
      360A.

208   Kalpakgian, Mitchell A.   "The Idea of the Marvelous
      or Wonderful in Fielding's Novels."   Diss. Iowa.   DA,
      35 (1974), 2227A.

209   Karl, Frederick R.   "Henry Fielding: The Novel, the
      Epic, and the Comic Sense of life,"   A Reader's Guide
      to the Eighteenth-Century English Novel.   New York:
      Noonday, 1974, pp. 146-182.
      Notes that HF's only development is from the burlesque
to the mainstream of novel writing.   By "reshaping narrative, character, plot, theme, and language, Fielding turned
prose fiction away from romance and epic" to social comedy.
Karl's theory, however, cannot account for Amelia.

210   Kaul, A. N.   "The Adjudication of Fielding's Comedy."
      In his Action of English Comedy: Studies in the En-
      counter of Abstraction from Shakespeare to Shaw.   New
      Haven, Conn.:   Yale Univ. Press, 1970, pp. 150-192.
      Discusses JA, TJ, and Amelia in terms of their use
of sentimental and sensual love.   Kaul sees HF as an advocate of neither type.   Rather, he believes HF to be a judge
whose deliberations lead him to regard each as partial and
misleading.   Indeed, Kaul suggests that by contrasting these
types of love, HF dramatizes "the dilemma of a whole culture polarized between the claims of body and soul, passion
and virtue, pleasure and happiness."

211   Kay, Donald, ed.   A Provision of Human Nature: Es-
      says on Fielding and Others in Honor of Miriam Austin
      Locke.   University: Univ. of Alabama Press, 1977.
      207 pp.
      Includes seven essays on HF.   See Williamson (No.
302), Durant (No. 322), Hutchens (No. 608), Burke (No.
147), Wolfe (No. 847), Miller (No. 650), and Eaves (No.
729).

212   Kermode, Frank.   "Richardson and Fielding."   Cam-
      bridge Journal, 4 (1950), 106-114.
      Compares the two authors in matters of texture and
structure, finally ruling Richardson the better novelist.
After citing HF's superiority in the verbal suggestiveness
of texture (e. g., his style) and Richardson's in the unity of

structure (e. g. , the simple, mythic plot), he faults HF's superficial vision, theatrical use of chance, and simplification of moral issues.   Kermode's estimation is clear in his final association of Richardson with Shakespeare and HF with Ben Jonson.

213   Knowles, A. S.   "Defoe, Swift, and Fielding: Notes on the Retirement Theme. "   In Quick Springs of Sense: Studies in the 18th Century.   Ed.   Larry Champion. Athens: Univ. of Georgia, 1974, pp. 121-136.
Notices the retirement theme in Robinson Crusoe and Gulliver's Travels before showing HF's use of it.   In JA Wilson's retirement is idyllic and in JW Heartfree expresses the desirability of retreat.   Both novels take the conventional Horatian-Augustan view of the theme.   But in TJ, HF reverses his technique.   The Man of the Hill's retirement is characterized by relief, not joy, by oddity, not simplicity, and by misanthropy, not benevolence.   Knowles concludes that the Man of the Hill is a prototype of Manfred or Melmoth the Wanderer and that by a negative technique HF pays tribute to the conventional Horatian theme.

214   Krause, Lothar P.   "The Conflict Between Social Communities and Individuals in the Novels of Henry Fielding. "   Diss. Pittsburgh.   DAI, 30 (1970), 4991A.

215   Kropf, Carl R.   "Educational Theory and Human Nature in Fielding's Works. "   PMLA, 89 (1974), 113-120.
Notices inconsistency in HF's thought about the relationship between human nature and education.   In The Fathers he sees education as crucial in determining character.   In JA HF leaves the relationship moot and ambivalent.   In TJ he regards education as irrelevant to character.   And in Amelia he suggests that while character is predetermined and cannot be transformed, it can be mended or repaired by education.

216   Kurtz, Eric W.   "Fielding's Thoughtful Laughter. " Diss. Yale.   DA, 28 (1967), 234A.

217   LaFrance, Marston.   "Fielding's Use of the 'Humor' Tradition. "   BuR, 17 (1969), 53-63.
Suggests that HF's mode of characterization is that of the "humors" tradition of Ben Jonson and Congreve.   The humors of HF's central characters derive from the excess of their innocent humanity.   But those of the impeding characters--e. g. , Wild, Lady Booby, Blifil, Col. James, etc. --

emerge from self-interest, a human monstrosity. LaFrance
suggests that the scenes of the novels can generally be conceived as a dramatic opposition among the humors of various
characters and that this opposition becomes an ethical as
well as an artistic device.

218   Lane, William G. "Relationships between Some of
       Fielding's Major and Minor Works." Boston Univ.
       Studies in English, 5 (1961), 219-231.
       A random and superficial notice of traits in the True
Patriot, the Covent-Garden Journal, A Journey from This
World to the Next, and the JVL (e. g. , HF's love of virtue
and goodness, satiric attitude, and character depiction).
Lane tenuously links them to the major fiction.

219   Leavis, F. R. The Great Tradition (1948). Rpt. New
       York: New York Univ. Press, 1963. See pp. 2-4.
       A reputable dissent. Leavis holds that "life isn't long
enough to permit one's giving much time to Fielding" because he lacks rich matter and subtle organization, especially in TJ. Yet Leavis allows that HF opens the central tradition of the novel and is important because he thereby leads
to Jane Austen. More a charge than a case.

220   Lepage, Peter V. "Fielding's Immanent Symbology."
       Diss. Bowling Green. DA, 25 (1964/65), 5282.

221   Levine, George R. Henry Fielding and the Dry Mock:
       A Study of the Techniques of Irony in His Early Works.
       The Hague: Mouton, 1967. 160 pp.
       A slight but able classification of HF's ironic tech-
niques in selected plays, the Champion, JW, and JA, i. e. ,
between 1728 and 1742. After a chapter on ironic usage in
the 18th century that distinguishes among conventional forms,
Levine focuses chapters on HF's persona, his mode of verbal irony, and his use of dramatic irony. Moreover, in a
separate chapter on JA, Levine attempts to show that the
irony itself becomes a mode of characterization.
       Though the classification is useful as a checklist of
HF's early ironic practices, there are curious lapses. E. g. ,
Levine neglects Shamela and treats the plays, the Champion,
and the Miscellanies in an arbitrarily selective way. Further, Levine's conclusion that HF's ironic techniques are
only conventional is weakened by his failure to contrast them
with those of other 18th-century authors besides Swift.
       Reviews: PQ, 47 (1968), 382-383.

222 Loftis, John E., III. "The Moral Art of Henry Fielding." Diss. Emory. DAI, 32 (1972), 6382A.

223 Macallister, Hamilton. Fielding. New York: Arco,
1971. 140 pp.
A passable introduction for the undergraduate. The
biographical sections are at times inaccurate and at other
times overly imaginative in linking HF's life to his literature. And though there are some invalid judgments on
Richardson and Dr. Johnson, the larger approach to the
novels is both conventional and readable, its judgments prudent and derivative. JA and TJ get two chapters each--
their themes and structures emphasized--but the plays and
periodical writings are critically ignored.

224 McCutcheon, Roger P. "Richardson, Fielding, Smollett, Sterne." In his Eighteenth-Century English Literature. Home University Library, No. 212. Oxford,
England: Oxford Univ. Press, 1950, pp. 49-65.
A cursory review of the standard facts.

225 Mack, Edward C. "Pamela's Stepdaughters: The
Heroines of Smollett and Fielding." CE, 8 (1947),
293-301.
Explains that HF's heroines--deriving from the 18th-
century concept of the ideal woman--represent three phases
of his art. Fanny (like a Smollett heroine) is a sweet,
youthful, and passive object of sentiment and desire. Sophia
is the boldest, a sentimental and moral, yet gay, sensible,
and courageous woman who leads to Austen's Elizabeth. And
Amelia, tenderhearted, but prudish and passive, is the consummate wife. Mack concludes that in HF's novels the 18th-
century ideal of woman becomes a reality.

226 McKillop, Alan Dugald. "Henry Fielding." In his
Early Masters of English Fiction. Lawrence: Univ.
Press of Kansas, 1956, pp. 98-146.
The most intelligent short survey of HF's novels. The
basic historical facts are here, and McKillop deepens his
account by a lucid criticism of humor in HF as aesthetic experience rather than as didactic tool. Also instructive are
the explanations of HF's intrusive narrator as a force of
unity and his use of antithesis for moralistic purposes.

227 Maresca, Thomas E. "Fielding." In his Epic to
Novel. Columbus: Ohio State Univ. Press, 1974, pp.
181-234.

A densely exegetical chapter suggesting that HF's novels must be criticized in the same terms by which he conceived them--as epics. Thus, Maresca notices the epic structure and allusion in the novels. JA has close affinities with Books III and IV of The Faerie Queen; TJ recreates the classical epic in a boldly original way; and Amelia becomes a modern reenactment of the Aeneid with touches of Paradise Lost. Maresca's stress is on the symmetry of the novels, and this chapter includes valuable charts specifying that symmetry. Still, though he argues fervently, he tends to stint other structural influences.

228   Milward, Peter. "Shakespeare and Fielding. " SELit
        (Eng. No.), 48 (1972), 33-42.
        Only a glance at the Shakesperian influence in the plays, JA, and TJ. Milward especially suggests that TJ is largely indebted to Shakespeare's four "great" tragedies in plot, character, and phrase (e. g. , the Romeo and Juliet main story and the Lear-like juxtaposition of Tom and Blifil suggesting the Edgar-Edmund pairing).

229   Moore, Robert Etheridge. "Hogarth's Role in Field-
        ing's Novels. " In his Hogarth's Literary Relationships
        (1948). Rpt. New York: Octagon, 1969, pp. 107-162.
        Outlines Hogarth's influence on HF. Not only did HF copy scenes and characters from Hogarth, but more importantly he used the artist's techniques of depicting exuberant activity, drawing plot and character, promoting humor, and fostering sound moral teaching.

230   Moulton, Charles W. , ed. "Henry Fielding, 1707-
        1754, " The Library of Literary Criticism. Buffalo,
        N. Y. : Moulton, 1902, III, 338-365.
        A useful guide, via brief excerpts, to 18th- and 19th-century commentaries on HF.

231   Neuendorf, Mary M. "The Great Man in the Works of
        Henry Fielding. " Diss. Rice. DA, 25 (1964/65),
        2498.

232   New, Melvyn. "'The Grease of God': The Form of
        18th-Century English Fiction. " PMLA, 91 (1976),
        235-243.
        A dissent from the providential world-view interpretation of the 18th-century English novel. In a few paragraphs on HF, New suggests that, because of contemporary intellectual doubt, the role of God is problematic for HF. Thus his

attitude toward providence in his fiction is at times serious and hopeful and at other times ironic. New claims that HF's central irony is that he could exercise more real power over his novels than God could over the world.

233 Newhouse, Edward B. "Poetic Theory and Practice in the Novels of Henry Fielding. " Diss. Ball State. DAI, 32 (1972), 5194A.

234 "Numéro special pour le 200e anniversaire de la mort d'Henry Fielding. " Les Lettres françaises. No. 536 (30 Sept. -7 oct. 1954). Review: PQ, 34 (1955), 288.

235 "Our Immortal Fielding. " TLS, 24 Jan. 1948, p. 50. A review article resuscitating the old complaints against Richardson's "namby-pamby sentimentality" and "sermonizing. " Sees HF questioning the middle-class "puritanical virtues" and "prudential insurance" embodied in Pamela. Similarly, the article offers the conventional caricature of HF as massive, masculine, and common-sensical.

236 Park, William. "Fielding and Richardson. " PMLA, 1966 (81), 381-388. An important survey of the common ground of HF, Richardson, and other novelists of the 1740s and 1750s. First, Park notices their similar theory of the novel. All see fiction to be a positive moral example, history focused on general nature, and all use the same stock characters and plots. Second, he specifies their common assumptions about man, society, and the world. Their heroes, e. g., become social conformists, though they are still radical individualists in their solitariness. In the novels the notion of happiness is usually the family in the country. And the novels posit a static society and a view of history as static. Though a tendency to generalization may weaken his essay at points, Park establishes the intellectual milieu that makes it possible to talk of a mid-century novel and to avoid seeing HF and Richardson as continually at odds.

237 _____ . "What Was New about the 'New Species of Writing' ? " SNNTS, 2 (1970), 112-130. Holds that the main innovation of Richardson and HF in their invention of the novel is their assembling and refashioning of earlier fictional patterns, techniques, and ideas. Park offers a useful model of the mid-18th-century novel that illustrates the workings of these elements.

238   Pastalosky, Rosa. Henry Fielding y la tradición
       picaresca. Buenos Aires: Solar/Hachette, 1970.

239   Paulson, Ronald, ed. Fielding: A Collection of Criti-
       cal Essays. Twentieth Century Views Series. Engle-
       wood Cliffs, N. J.: Prentice-Hall, 1962. 186 pp.
       Paulson's introduction discusses the critical implica-
tions of the 13 essays included in this anthology. They are
by Humphreys (No. 197), Rogers (No. 377), Watt (Nos. 412
and 708), Mack (No. 471), Spilka (No. 490), Digeon (No.
502), Gide (No. 596a), Kettle (No. 624), Murry (No. 654),
Empson (No. 590), Sherburn (No. 755), and Coolidge (No.
727).

240   _____. "Fielding the Satirist," "Fielding the Anti-
       Romanticist," "Fielding the Novelist." In his Satire
       and the Novel in Eighteenth-Century England. New
       Haven, Conn.: Yale Univ. Press, 1967, pp. 52-164.
       A brilliant assessment of HF's development showing
his merging of satire with the new fictional form of the
novel. The plays reveal HF as a child of both the Whig and
Tory satirists with their different conceptions of human nature. Paulson examines the main thematic and formal features of the plays to demonstrate HF's satiric habits: use
of the villain, the farcical construction, the judicial metaphor, and the commentator.
       But in JA it is the innocent and not the villain who is
central to the fiction. Yet, though HF stresses the positive,
he depicts reality by satiric means. The juxtapositions between a character's professions and performance and the
use of the innocents as touchstones to expose the ridiculous
in their predators are two main satiric devices. Moreover,
Paulson shows that HF's objection to Pamela was based on
the heroine's subjective viewpoint which blurs the reader's
moral perspective by disallowing a view of the whole. HF's
satiric methods thus render a more objective reality because they are viewed from an omniscient distance in which
motives can be most clearly seen.
       In JA, HF becomes interested in motive; he drama-
tizes it by action and "his progression toward Tom Jones
can be said to be from law and a study of action (satire) to
justice and an interest in being (novel)." Thus he is at
pains to approximate a continuous and cumulative experience
for his characters to let them be judged not on one action--
a legal view--but on a series of actions--a more just view.
Only in a flow of experience can motive truly emerge, and
with it a true judgment of reality by reader and commentator.
Short sections on Shamela and Amelia as well.

241 _____, and Thomas Lockwood, eds. Henry Fielding: The Critical Heritage. The Critical Heritage
Series. London: Routledge, 1969. 454 pp.
    An anthology of 180 opinions about HF's works. Re-
produced in unmodernized text, these opinions date from
1730 to 1787. Represented are the famous (e. g. , Chesterfield), the not-so-famous (e. g. , Thomas Birch), the infa-
mous (e. g. , Eliza Haywood), and the pseudonymous (e. g. ,
"Cynic") in their letters, leaders, speeches, and squibs.
Yet they are more historically than critically important, for
they most often represent reaction than analysis.
    In the introduction to the volume, Paulson and Lock-
wood offer a distillation of 18th-century reactions to HF's
plays and novels. Identifying the basic conflict running
through this mass of early commentary as the distrust of
HF's "lowness" versus the praise of his realism, they also
note the recurring biographical fallacy in it.
    Of special note is the treatment that Paulson and Lock-
wood afford Arthur Murphy, HF's first editor and biographer
(the bulk of whose influential 1762 essay on HF is included
in the volume). Long disdained by HF apologists for his
portrayal of the novelist as the rake, he was also, the editors remind us, responsible for articulating a most modern
view of HF as a writer divided between a tendency to political satire and an equally strong one to realism, a dilemma
that must be faced in any final judgment on the novels.
    In all, this is a useful collection of rare and "fresh"
opinion about HF that no serious student should neglect.
    Reviews: EIC, 21 (1971), 91-100; TLS, 29 Jan. 1970,
p. 103.

242 Persky, Charles. "The Comic Alternative: A Study
of Henry Fielding and His Novels from Shamela to
Tom Jones. " Diss. Harvard 1968.

243 Phelps, William Lyon. "Fielding, Smollett, Sterne. "
In his Advance of the English Novel. New York:
Dodd, Mead, 1916, pp. 53-78.
    Claims that HF's use of the personal essay in JA and
TJ breaks the continuity of the narrative, destroys its illusion, and disconcerts the reader. Phelps believes that
these "insincere" essays also established a bad tradition in
English fiction. Besides this personal style, there is Fielding's humor, which gives his novels a richness, variety,
and complexity not found in Richardson. And Fielding's
male characters are superior to Richardson's because he is
a humorist: "Say what you will about the equality of the

sexes, man is essentially a comic character; and woman, tragic. " Concludes by calling Richardson an analyst, HF a realist, and Smollett a naturalist.

244 Plumb, J. H. "Henry Fielding: The Journey through Gin Lane. " Horizon, 6 (Winter 1964), 74-83.
A popular appreciation written from the viewpoint that the English scene shaped HF's works and made him the first novelist of social criticism.

245 Pracht, Erwin. "Bittere Enttäuschung und erschütteter Optimismus in Fieldings Spätwerk?" ZAA, 7 (1959), 288-293.

246 _____. "Henry Fielding zu Fragen der Roman- theorie. " ZAA, 3 (1955), 152-174.

247 Price, Martin. "Fielding: The Comedy of Forms. " In his To the Palace of Wisdom: Studies in Order and Energy from Dryden to Blake. Garden City, N. Y.: Doubleday, 1964, pp. 286-312.
Designates HF's central theme as "the opposition be- tween the flow of soul--of selfless generosity--and the struc- tures--screens, defenses, moats of indifference people build around themselves. " This generosity is an energy that tests "respectable" social forms and is manifest in the symmetrical arrangements in the novels, e. g. Blifil's selfishness versus Tom's good will. Yet, Price suggests, HF is under no illu- sion that generosity will win out, so he subverts the logical expectation of the hero's doom with a comic resolution, a reward for his facing moral consequences. HF is not out to reorder society but to re-establish the basis of its conduct by exposing it through its conduct to low characters or people reduced in fortune.

248 Pritchett, V. S. "The Ancestor. " In his Living Novel. New York: Reynal & Hitchcock, 1947, pp. 17-23.
A light appreciation claiming that the English novel grew from JW, JA, and TJ in character creation, humor, didacticism, horseplay, gregarious viewpoint, sociability, and satire. And in Amelia, HF points in the direction of Dickens in domestic realism and sentimentalism.

249 Proper, Coenraad B. E. "Henry Fielding. " In his Social Elements in English Prose Fiction between 1700 and 1832. Amsterdam: H. J. Paris, 1929, pp. 49- 62.

Calls TJ HF's most political novel, for in it he emerges
as a Whig and anti-Jacobite. Curiously, Proper fails to
mention the political ingredients of JW, but his essay highlights the social matter in HF's fiction. By HF's day the
social atmosphere was such that his audience accepted--and
expected--moralism in art. And thus HF's social matter is
always colored by a corrective, though he himself does not
strive for a social millennium. All the novels are socially
oriented in their roving from class to class, their concern
with the daily business of life, and their localization of
scene. But it is Amelia that is HF's most "social" work.
In an unsystematic and tripping account, Proper notes gin
shops, usurers, prisons, pawn shops, and sponging houses--
all governed by greed--among Fielding's social concerns.

250   Rader, Ralph W. "Idea and Structure in Fielding's
      Novels. " Diss. Indiana. DA, 19 (1958), 1367.

251   Radtke, Bruno. Henry Fielding als Kritiker. Leipzig:
      Mayer & Müller, 1926.
      Review: PQ, 7 (1927), 180.

252   Rawson, Claude J. "Cannibalism and Fiction. Part
      II: Love and Eating in Fielding, Mailer, Genet, and
      Wittig. " Genre, 11 (1978), 227-313.
      Recalls that HF uses the lust/hunger metaphor to
attack love that is crudely gluttonous. HF's "point is not
that sexual activity is as bad or as crude as gourmandizing,
but that gourmandizing is not capable of higher manifesta-
tions whereas sexual activity is. " Yet from HF's recurring
use of the metaphor Rawson infers HF's sense of guilt about
violating Christian tenets of chastity. [Part I of Rawson's
article concerns Swift, Flaubert, et al.]

253   _____ . "Gentlemen and Dancing Masters: Thoughts
      on Fielding, Chesterfield, and the Genteel. " ECS, 1
      (1967), 127-158.
      See No. 255.

254   _____ . Henry Fielding. Profiles in Literature
      Series. London: Routledge & Kegan Paul, 1968.
      162 pp.
      An introduction to HF through 42 extracts with direct
commentary. Arranged in 14 sections both by subject (e. g. ,
"Professions and Codes, " "Benevolence and Love, " etc.)
and by technique (e. g. , "Irony, " "Dialogue, " etc.), Rawson's
book provides practical insights on recurring features of HF's

non-dramatic prose. Though its ad hoc nature precludes a
general thesis, Henry Fielding should be an early port of
call for a reader new to HF.

255 _____ . Henry Fielding and the Augustan Ideal Under
Stress: "Nature's Dance of Death" and Other Studies.
London: Routledge & Kegan Paul, 1972. 266 pp. In-
corporates "Gentleman and Dancing Masters, " ECS, 1
(1967), 127-158; "Nature's Dance of Death, " ECS, 3
(1970), 307-338, 491-522; "Fielding's Good Merchant:
The Problem of Heartfree in Jonathan Wild, " MP, 69
(1972), 292-313; and "The Hero as Clown: Jonathan
Wild, Felix Krull and Others, " Studies in the Eighteenth Century, Vol. II. Toronto: Univ. of Toronto
Press, 1973, pp. 17-52.
An attempt to reveal the change wrought in HF's style
by his loss of confidence in the Augustan notion of Nature,
"that animating ideal or live fiction of order and coherence. "
But Rawson bases his study on cultural contexts that, however real, he only asserts and does not describe: that by
HF's time the moral, social, and aesthetic harmonies of
the Augustan Age were under threat. Nevertheless, the
first part of his book, "Nature's Dance of Death" examines
the stylistic effects of HF's supposed perception of a culture
under stress. The second part, "Heroes, Clowns and School-
boys, " studies the crisis in the Augustan genre of mock-
heroic, with specific reference to JW.
Because all seven chapters have appeared earlier as
articles or papers, Rawson's book has a patched quality.
Moreover, his method is to ruminate at length on passages
from HF to produce commentary about HF's artistry. The
book's disjunct thesis and corollary static methodology virtually precludes abstraction of its specific content. Yet
Rawson's insights are often brilliant (and always bright),
however unfortunately shaded by his own opaque prose.
Chapter I, "Gentleman and Dancing Masters: Thoughts
on Fielding, Chesterfield and the Genteel, " aims to establish
HF's--and the general Augustan--belief that good breeding
proceeds from morality. The second chapter, "Nature and
the Masteries of Style in Fielding, Swift and Pope, " reveals HF's early use of antithesis (reflecting his perception
of a balanced world). And "Nature, Cruel Circumstance
and the Rage for Order: Amelia with Reflections on Defoe,
Smollett and Orwell, " the third chapter, argues that HF's
earlier ironic appeals to Nature's ordering role, become,
in Amelia, grim and sarcastic recriminations of Fortune.
Sarcasm becomes the stylistic signal of the breaking of a

world or Nature that could, by 1751, only be acknowledged but never explained, as in JA and TJ.

Part II of Rawson's book regards JW as a case study of HF's redaction of the favorite Augustan type of mock-heroic. In Chapter IV, "The Hero as Clown: Jonathan Wild, Felix Krull and Others," Rawson contends (radically) that HF's story is more comic than satiric, that HF consciously links his hero-villain to the amiable tradition of the rogue as clown. By this reading, JW becomes a "stylized farce." "Epic vs. History: Jonathan Wild and Augustan Mock-Heroic" further calls JW "mock-historical" (rather than "mock-epic"), not only because HF alludes to parallel historical facts, but also because he was growing uncomfortable with epic morality.

The next chapter, "The World of Wild and Ubu," uses Jarry's Ubu as an analogy to what may be in JW "black-clownish reversals of moral form." The last chapter is "Fielding's Good Merchant: an Appendix on the Problem of Heartfree and Other 'Good' Characters in Fielding." It includes disparate reflections on the ambiguity of goodness and greatness, on the failure of HF to take Heartfree's moral dignity seriously, and on Heartfree and Parson Adams as admirable characters.

Reviews: CritQ, 15 (1973), 187; JEGP, 74 (1975), 131-134; MLQ, 34 (1973), 470-473; MP, 74 (1977), 102-107; PQ, 52 (1973), 504-505; RES, n. s. 25 (1974), 212-214; SAQ, 73 (1974), 411-412.

256 _____ . "Nature's Dance of Death: Part I. Urbanity and Strain in Fielding, Swift and Pope." ECS, 3 (1970), 307-338.
See No. 255.

257 _____ . "Some Considerations on Authorial Intrusion in Fielding's Novels and Plays." DUJ, 33 (1971), 32-44.
An important, deeply analytical essay that specifies HF's controlling presence in his characters' dialogue. Throughout Rawson shows HF's fictional dialogue to be superior to his dramatic dialogue of usually stylized epigrammatic routine. To demonstrate how HF shapes the fictional narrative to the service of his tone and theme, Rawson analyzes the vitality of the verbal exchanges, HF's framing and linking the parts of dialogue by direct intrusion, stylized context, or third-character presence, and his mastery of dialect and modulation.

258 _____ , ed. Henry Fielding: A Critical Anthology.

Penguin Critical Anthology Series. Harmondsworth,
England: Penguin, 1973. 619 pp.

259 Rogers, Katharine M. "Sensitive Feminism vs. Conventional Sympathy: Richardson and Fielding on Wom-
en." Novel, 9 (1976), 256-270.
An accurate yet unbalanced contrast. By an analysis
of selections from his fiction, Rogers shows Richardson to
be sympathetic to sexual equality, personal autonomy, and
feminine intellectualism. Yet her conclusions about HF on
women do not issue from so thorough an analysis. While
she conclusively establishes Richardson as a radical femi-
nist, she only repeats the truism with sparse examples that
HF "accepted the male chauvinism of his culture."

260 Rogers, Pat. "Fielding." In his Augustan Vision.
New York: Harper & Row, 1974, pp. 275-285.
Recreates the 18th-century setting to reveal HF as an
author in the high Augustan tradition whose "career spans
the transition from the literature of perception to the literature of experience." This restatement of a critical commonplace locates HF's main effect on the history of the novel in
his blending--through his narrator--of judgments of and feeling for his characters.

261 Rojahn-Deyk, Barbara. Henry Fielding: Untersuchungen zu Wesen und Funktion der Ironie in seiner frühen
Prosa. Nuremberg: Verlag Hans Carl, 1973. 217 pp.

262 Romein, Tunis. "Omnisciences, Uncertainty, and the
Reader's Role in the Novels of Fielding." Diss. Texas
at Austin. DAI, 38 (1978), 7349A.

263 Sacks, Sheldon. Fiction and the Shape of Belief: A
Study of Henry Fielding with Glances at Swift, Johnson,
and Richardson. Berkeley: Univ. of California Press,
1964. 278 pp.
An example of rhetorical criticism that attempts to
show how HF embodies his beliefs in his novels. Sacks regards the novels largely as persuasive works that body forth
their beliefs in "formal signals which control our response
to characters, acts, and thoughts."
The first and last of the book's six chapters are theoretical and polemical. In them Sacks distinguishes the fictional types of satire, apologue, and novel. He suggests
reasons for the difficulty in approaching ideas embodied in
novels, the chief of which is that past criticism has muddled

the important distinctions among these fictional types.
Sacks's "glances" at works of Swift, Johnson, and Richardson serve thus to distinguish HF's novels from variant fictional genres.

His central chapters explain the seven classes of signals in HF's novels by which he conveys his ideas: (1) the "split commentator" who both narrates and criticizes; (2) the "fallible paragons" who represent a positive ethical norm but who err in judgment (Adams, Allworthy, Harrison); (3) the "nondiscursive female paragons" who are often objects of value judgments (Fanny, Sophia, Amelia); (4) species characters and "walking concepts" who are labeled for our evaluation (Tittle, Tattle, Col. Bath); (5) male heroes testing and being tested by modes of belief and behavior; (6) narrators of digressive tales who expound formulated ideas (Wilson, the Man of the Hill, Mrs. Bennet); and (7) characters who have important value judgments made about them but who do not evaluate others (Jenny Jones, Maj. James).

Besides its graceless presentation, the book's chief faults are two. First, it virtually obliterates HF as a comic novelist. And second, its complex theoretical and analytical apparatus brings us arduously to a rather obvious conclusion: that an author conveys his ideas through his characters, their actions, speeches, and the reactions they provoke from other characters. Moreover, Sacks's discovery of HF's beliefs is hardly original: Christianity, a desire for judgment by motive, a general charity, and a negative attitude toward Stoicism, moral turpitude, and hypocrisy.

Reviews: CE, 27 (1966), 654; JEGP, 65 (1966), 602-604; JGE, 17 (1966), 332-335; SAQ, 64 (1965), 568-569; YR, 55 (1965), 129-130.

264   Saintsbury, George. "The Four Wheels of the Novel Wain." In his English Novel. London: Dent, 1913, pp. 77-132.

Flatly asserts that Richardson's greatest creation was his successor and superior, HF. Saintsbury continues the legend of HF as rakish and improvident, yet shows him outdistancing Richardson on three counts: his characters are more "personal," his scenes more visual, and his dialogue more vivid.

Saintsbury finally regards HF's launching a new form in TJ as his legacy to the novel: range, diversity of character, and humor. Curiously, he fails to mention HF's originality in sweeping aside the delusion of actual fact and of abandoning the first-person point of view.

265   Sells, Larry F. "Fielding's Central Triad: Repetition

and Variation in the Novels." Diss. Pennsylvania
State. DAI, 32 (1971), 932A.

266 Seltman, Kent D.   "Henry Fielding, the Preacher: A
Study of the Layman's Sermons in Historical and Rhetorical Context." Diss. Nebraska. DA, 35 (1975),
5425A.

267 Sherbo, Arthur.   Studies in the Eighteenth-Century
English Novel. East Lansing: Michigan State Univ.
Press, 1969, pp. 1-127.
   Six (of ten) disparate chapters on HF's novels.   Sherbo stridently attacks much criticism of the novels and terms
it invalid for failure to advance adequate textual evidence in
support of its contentions.   Consequently, this book "corrects" what has come to be regarded as doctrine in six
areas.   (1) "The Narrator in Fielding's Novels" holds that
little difference exists between HF the real author and the
narrator he creates.   Sherbo is painstaking in setting forth
traits of the narrator's external and internal character by a
close textual reading.   He rejects most criticism on HF's
narrator as pettifogging.   (2) "'Inside' and 'Outside' Readers
in Fielding's Novels" defines the presence of the postulated
or "inside" audience which the narrator, for comic purposes, calls to the attention of the real or "outside" readers.   (3) "Some Aspects of Fielding's Style" is a tedious
catalogue-essay of HF's favorite phrases and mannerisms
to suggest that his prose style was more constant than de-
velopmental.   (4) "Fielding's Amelia: A Reinterpretation"
argues against the critical grain to conclude that HF's last
novel contains all the same playful usages of language as
do JA and TJ.   Sherbo's assessment is based largely on
passages concerning Mr. Trent.   By showing these few
episodes as comic, he "reinterprets" only these few episodes
and certainly not the whole novel.   (5) "The 'Moral Basis'
of Joseph Andrews" is a heated attack on Battestin's reading
of the novel as latitudinarian in its philosophy and sophisticated in construction (No. 422).   Sherbo questions Battestin's sources and parallel passages and accuses him of a
preconceived conclusion.   Sherbo himself concludes only
that JA is delightful reading but not good fiction in the
modern sense.   (6) Finally, "Naked Innocence in Joseph
Andrews" disputes Spilka's equation of Adams' nakedness
with innocence (No. 490) by showing from textual details
that Adams is never stark naked.
       Sherbo has a keen eye for the literal.   Sometimes
tedious, often caustic, he nevertheless repays the reader

with his close scrutiny of the text by revealing clay toes on some critical idols.
Reviews: PQ, 50 (1971), 398; TLS, 14 Aug. 1970, p. 896.

268   Sherburn, George.   "Fielding's Social Outlook. "   PQ, 35 (1956), 1-23.   Rpt. in Eighteenth-Century English Literature.   Ed. James L. Clifford.   New York: Oxford Univ. Press, 1959.
Views HF as fundamentally a moralist.   This important essay highlights his ideas about society and the individual. HF posits the divine plan and a stratified society made workable by the individual sense of duty to the whole.   And always he asserts human moral responsibility.   Though Fielding is no systematic thinker, these ideas undergird his works.

269   Sherwood, Irma Z.   "The Novelists as Commentators. " In The Age of Johnson: Essays Presented to Chauncey Brewster Tinker.   Ed. Frederick W. Hilles and Wilmarth S. Lewis.   New Haven, Conn. :   Yale Univ. Press, 1949, pp. 113-126.
Observes that the frequent authorial commentary in the 18th-century novel was due largely to the spirit of criticism and morality then current.   But because the novel was a new form, authors liberally used techniques from familiar genres, especially the sermon, conduct book, polite letter, and essay.   Each employs formal diction, illustration, and usually a moral.   Like other 18th-century novelists, HF often speaks in his own voice or lets "mentor character, " heroes, or villains comment for him.   Sherwood states that if direct moral commentary led to the weakening of a character's or a story's plausibility, in the best of the novels (e. g. , TJ) it never smothers the narrative.   Indeed, familiar with such commentary, the readers probably expected it.

270   Shesgreen, Sean.   Literary Portraits in the Novels of Henry Fielding.   DeKalb: Northern Illinois Univ. Press, 1972.   206 pp.
A workmanlike study that corrects the scholarship that sees HF's characterization achieved by dialogue and action only.   Shesgreen focuses on the literary portrait as a main device of HF's craft.   He shows that in formally depicting character, HF uses four types: the biographical character sketch (e. g. , Jonathan Wild), the psychological or moral sketch (e. g. , Aunt Western), the idealized portrait (e. g. , Fanny), and the portrait caricature (e. g. , Didapper).

Examining the emblematic content of the portraits, Shesgreen shows how the formulaic sketches of JW evolve through the physionomical and Hogarthian renderings of JA to the sophisticated "cumulative" characterization of TJ and the psychological studies in Amelia. Always Shesgreen connects the portraits to HF's fundamental moralism to reveal the literary portrait as ultimately an ethical medium.
Reviews: MP, 72 (1975), 321-324.

271   Simon, Irène. "Early Theories of Prose Fiction: Congreve and Fielding. " In Imagined Worlds Essays on Some English Novels and Novelists in Honour of John Butt. Ed. Maynard Mack and Ian Gregor.   London: Methuen, 1968, pp. 19-36.
Claims Congreve's main theoretical contribution in the Preface to Incognita to be the demand for form in fiction. But HF's was to show how form could be achieved. Essentially, by applying epic theory (with its unity of design) to the roman comique (with its comic picaresque, authorial asides, etc.), he developed a theory on which a new fiction could be based and judged.

272   Slagle, Kenneth. The English Country Squire as Depicted in English Prose Fiction from 1740 to 1800. 1938; rpt. New York: Octagon, 1970.   149 pp.
Reviews the manners, thought, customs, and social position of the country squire in selected 18th-century novels. References to HF and Shamela, JA, TJ, and Amelia throughout.

273   Smith, J. Oates. "Masquerade and Marriage: Fielding's Comedies of Identity. " BSUF, 6(1965), 10-21.
Sees the antipodal symbols of masquerade and marriage as the "central myth" of nearly all of HF's work. That myth involves the world's hypocrisy militating against a good marriage.

274   Smith, Leroy W. "Fielding and Mandeville: The 'War Against Virtue. '" Criticism, 3 (1961), 7-15.
An important caution against seeing only the benevolist influence in HF, for his thought was inclined to the skeptic and self-love philosophies as well, especially those of Mandeville.   With Mandeville, e. g. , he recognizes the drive for dominance by the selfish passions and views the world as hypocritical and corrupt.   HF's pamphlets and programs aimed at curing society's ills suggest his belief that evil passions guide the human will.

275   Sokolyanski, M. G. "Istorizm Fildinga: na Materiale
       'Komicheskikh Epopei'" ["Fielding's Historicism: The
       Evidence of the 'Comic Epics'"]. NDFN, 1 (1974),
       34-42.

276 _____. "Literaturnaya Parodiya v Romanakh H.
       Fildinga" ["Literary Parody in the Novels of H. Field-
       ing"]. UZPer, 270 (1973), 35-46.

277 _____. Tvorčestvo Genri Fildinga: Kniga Očerkov
       [The Works of Henry Fielding: A Book of Essays].
       Kiev: Izd. Kievskogo Univ., 1975. 174 pp.

278   Spector, Robert Donald, ed. Essays on the Eighteenth-
       Century Novel. Bloomington: Indiana Univ. Press,
       1965.
       Includes essays by Crane (No. 572), Kermode (No.
212), and Spilka (No. 490).

279   Spilka, Mark. "Fielding and the Epic Impulse." Criti-
       cism, 11 (1969), 68-77.
       An important essay showing HF's "epic impulse" to be
his awareness of the vast changes in 18th-century life and
not a sense of cool classical imitation of heroic poems.
Ridiculing the closed society changing around him, his
novels are at once mock epics and documentaries of the social, personal, and domestic life of the individual. The
cultural change from the epic's unified world picture to a
culture in which individual perspectives become dominant
impelled HF to depict an individual quest for self-fulfill-
ment. And that, Spilka asserts, is HF's chief legacy to
the novel: More so than Defoe and Richardson, it is HF
"who gives the novel social breadth and abundance, who provides for the fullest exploration of public life, or for those
relations with others by which self-realization is achieved."

280   Steeves, Harrison R. "A Manly Man (Henry Field-
       ing)." In his Before Jane Austen: The Shaping of
       the English Novel in the 18th-Century. New York:
       Holt, 1965, pp. 103-130.
       An unbalanced and superficial review of the novels.
This chapter leans heavily on a plot summary and conventional judgments of TJ. JA and Amelia are only acknowledged.

281   Stevenson, Lionel. "The First Masterpieces (1740-
       1755)." In his English Novel: A Panorama. Boston:
       Houghton Mifflin, 1960, pp. 79-119.

After Baker (No. 126), the most intelligent literary-historical review of the English novel. Stevenson offers sensible critical judgments as well, but he occasionally subscribes to a dubious commonplace (e. g. , HF's sudden, unplanned change of direction from satire to the novel in JA).

282   Stevick, Philip. "Fielding and the Meaning of History."
       PMLA, 79 (1964), 561-568.
       A difficult argument that labors to explain that HF's comic form is an image of man in time. Because he could not accept the primitivist notion that history was in a decline, HF resolves his novels socially, with the hero in comic harmony with his world. This resolution "is an affirmation of the values implicit in one's time" and is thus virtually an affirmation of the progressive view of history.

283   _____. "Fielding: The Novelist as Philosopher of History." Diss. Ohio State. DA, 24 (1963/64), 2912.

284   Stitzel, Judith G. "Comedy and the Serious Moralist:
       The Concept of Good-Nature in the Novels of Henry
       Fielding. " Diss. Minnesota. DA, 29 (1969), 2686A.

285   Stuart, Walter H. "The Role of Narrator in the Novels
       of Fielding. " Diss. Wisconsin. DA, 24 (1963/64),
       2489.

286   Studt, Annelise. "Fieldings Charakterromane. " Britannica, 13 (1936), 101-118.

287   Swann, George Rogers. "Fielding and Empirical Realism. " In his Philosophical Parallelisms in Six English
       Novelists: The Conception of Good, Evil and Human
       Nature. Philadelphia: Univ. of Pennsylvania, 1929,
       pp. 46-64.
       Specifies the essential similarities between HF and
       Hume. E. g. , both agree on and develop the Shaftesburian ethic; both reject moral causality (HF's heroes are saved not by their good virtue but by their good fortune); both see human nature motivated by the passions (HF's characters can be interpreted by a stimulus-response pattern); and both make sympathy the basis of valid ethical standards but make public utility the standard for moral conduct.

288   Thomsen, Enjar. Studier i Fieldings romaner. Copenhagen: Jesperson og Pio, 1930. 88 pp.

289   Thornbury, E. Margaret. Henry Fielding's Theory of

the Comic Prose Epic. 1931; rpt. New York: Russell
& Russell, 1966. 202 pp.
An attempt to explain both HF's use of epic theory and
his innovations in writing JA and TJ.
"Fielding's Library, " Chapter I, aims to show the subjects that influenced HF. Thornbury notes that his library
was replete with the books of the ancients and with English
history. In it, Renaissance critical theory was also well
represented.
In "The General Problem of the Modern Epic, " Thornbury reviews Renaissance critical theory to isolate its crucial issues. Should art instruct or entertain? Should the
epic follow Homerian or Virgilian form? Should the Aristotelian rules be followed? In sum, she shows that most of
the theorists concluded that the modern epic should be national, realistic, and probable. With these conclusions HF
would agree in practice.
Thornbury's next two chapters notice the 17th-century
French influences on HF. "French Epics and Epic Theories"
highlights the thought of Georges de Scudery, Desmarets,
and Chapelain who, in prefaces to their own epics, argued
for the appropriateness of a modern Christian epic. "Fénélon,
Boileau, Le Bossu, and Madame Dacier" is especially useful in implying Le Bossu's influence on HF. Thornbury particularly notes the importance to HF of Le Bossu's dicta on
the epic as didactic, the importance of the good but imperfect hero, and the uses of plot and character motivation.
Likewise, "Epic Theory in England, Dryden to Fielding" glances at native thought represented in HF's library.
This chapter is a useful review of the relevance of the Ancients versus Moderns issue and of the speculations of such
authors as Davenant, Hobbes, Dryden, Blackmore, Dennis,
Addison, and Pope.
In the following two chapters, Thornbury looks directly
at HF. Unfortunately, however, she does little more than
notice HF's specific comments on the epic in JA and TJ
and offer some examples of his epic practice. "The Definition of the Comic Prose Epic: Joseph Andrews, " e. g. , is
disappointing. Thornbury merely summarizes sections of
HF's Preface, notes the epic rules he lists in Book I, 1,
and lists five epic principles that he follows (causative central plot, epic battle, "irrelevant" interpolated tales, the
formula of discovery, and use of native matter). In the
next chapter, "Development of Principle of Epic Structure:
Tom Jones, " she argues for the influence of Le Bossu in
the novel. Thornbury cites his comments on the unities of
time and action, on the fortunate outcome, on the good but

imperfect hero, and on the moral purpose.   In each case
she provides an example from TJ.
    Chapter VIII, "The Verisimilar and the Marvellous, "
attempts to account for HF's realism.   His mimetic inclinations lead him to call his novels history, biography, and
epic and prompt him to achieve verisimilitude of character
by creating typical characters marked by individual eccen-
tricities.   As to the marvellous, HF simply defines it as
the surprising but probable and thus defends his use of coincidence.   "Fielding's Theory of Comedy" asserts how he
bases his comic thought on traditional theories and complements them with his own theory of the ridiculous.
    Thornbury provides a list of the 653 titles in HF's
library.
    Reviews: JEGP, 32 (1933), 417-418; MLR, 28 (1933),
110-111.

290   Tichý, A.   "Remarks on the Flow of Time in the Novels
       of Fielding. "   Brno Studies in English, 2 (1960).

291   Van der Voorde, Frans P.   Henry Fielding: Critic and
       Satirist (1931).   Rpt. New York: Haskell House, 1966.
       232 pp.
       A stunted attempt to examine HF as a satirist.   While
Van der Voorde exhaustively musters examples of HF's
satire, he never develops a synthesis of them in terms of
HF's rationale and tone.
       The first chapter is a random review of the social/po-
litical contexts of HF's times.   As such, however, it merely
distills standard scholarship, especially of Dorothy George,
J. R. Green, and W. E. H. Lecky, to conclude oversimply
that the wealthy were corrupt and the poor savage.   The
next chapter, "Fielding's Life and Principal Works, " is still
more superficial.   It repeats the standard biographical facts,
but neither updates them with the recent findings of Vincent
and Wells nor reinterprets them after the insights of Digeon.
In terms of the book's thesis, the first two chapters are
gratuitous, for Van der Voorde leaves them unrelated to HF
as a satirist.
       His next three chapters assemble, respectively, in-
stances of HF's literary, political, and social satire.   Again,
there is nothing new in these sections, their main character
being the parading of HF's favorite satiric butts.   Occasionally, Van der Voorde will allow his own errors to mis-
construe HF's thought, as when his equation of country
Tories with Jacobites leads him to mistake HF's attitude
toward Squire Western.

Besides its catalogue quality, there is a greater problem with Van der Voorde's book. It makes no careful attempt to assess the reasons for HF's satire. Van der Voorde's claim that "Love of country is the ground of Fielding's satire" evolves from his naive acceptance of HF's pronouncement against personal satire, a stock public utterance of most 18th-century satirists. Thus Van der Voorde forces himself to identify patriotic abstractions rather than to consider personal spleen as evidence of HF's motives. Moreover, Van der Voorde skirts the nagging problems of how HF's satire coexists with his comedy and of what the blend does to his general tone. Ultimately, this book is a harvest of HF's satiric ideas that leaves the milling of them to its reader.

292 Van Doren, Carl. "The Greatest English Man of Letters." Nation (New York), 6 June 1923, pp. 659-660.
A relaxed personal essay recounting a game the author played with himself--determining the greatest English author. Deciding that the man as much as the artist must influence his decision, Van Doren cites Aristotelian magnanimity as his criterion. On that standard he rejects many authors from Chaucer to Shaw before settling on HF for his abundance, wisdom, vitality, courage, eloquence, scholarship, and high-mindedness.

293 Van Loon, Nelles Hart. "The Comic and the Sentimental in the Novels of Henry Fielding." Diss. Toronto. DAI, 38 (1977), 3461A.

294 Wagenknecht, Edward. "Fielding and the Prose Epic." In his Cavalcade of the English Novel, 2nd ed. New York: Holt, 1954, pp. 58-68.
A repetition of scholarship on structure, characterization, and philosophy in HF's novels. A bit extreme is Wagenknecht's comment on TJ that, "Reacting against Richardsonian formalism, [HF] falls in danger of Rousseauism."

295 Wallace, Robert M. "Henry Fielding's Narrative Method: Its Historical and Biographical Origins." Diss. North Carolina at Chapel Hill, 1945.

296 Watt, L. P. "The Naming of Characters in Defoe, Richardson, and Fielding." RES, 25 (1949), 322-338.
A thoughtful look at naming in the novels. All three use realistic names for their main characters. But Defoe often uses aliases, and his failure to name secondary

characters tells us much about unstable social roles and
Defoe's view of social relationships. Richardson's heroines'
names reflect the influence of the romance, but the addition
of a realistic surname suggests the essence of his works:
love versus duty to family. These names specify the individuality of his characters. HF's names come by way of
the classics, comedy, and satire. More interested in manners than men, he avoids suggesting that his characters are
unique, for he insists that they are representative of all
mankind.

297 Watt, Ian. "Fielding and the Epic Theory of the Novel."
     In his Rise of the Novel: Studies in Defoe, Richard-
     son, and Fielding. Berkeley: Univ. of Calif. Press,
     1957, pp. 239-259.
     Disputes that the epic influence on HF is great, for,
though he approximates the epic in some practical effects
(depiction of a social panorama, verisimilitude, surprise,
and mock-epic touches), he uses it only to enlist its prestige for the novel, a form in great disrepute in 1742.

298 Wess, Robert V. "Modes of Fictional Structure in
     Henry Fielding and Jane Austen." Diss. Chicago,
     1970.

299 Whiteford, Robert Naylor. "Samuel Richardson, Henry
     Fielding, Sarah Fielding, and Tobias Smollett." In
     his Motives in English Fiction. New York and London:
     Putnam's, 1918, pp. 86-118.
     A generalized approach that attempts to isolate the
leading "formative motives" of English fiction. Pamela gets
the back of the hand as a "beautiful feminine mongoose"
forever "scribbling, blubbering, and kissing." Whiteford
offers conventional praise of the humor of Adams, the
causality of the plot of TJ, and the pathos of scenes in
Amelia. "In final summary then we can say that Fielding
successfully moulded for the English novel a correct form
of atmosphere, motivation, and characterization, and manu-
factured a dialogue that characterizes by avoiding the method
of letting things get cold on the pages of a report as was
the custom of Richardson."

300 Williams, Aubrey. "Interpositions of Providence and
     the Design of Fielding's Novels." SAQ, 70 (1971),
     265-286.
     An essential article asserting providence as the grand
design of HF's four novels and thus rejecting criticism that

sees HF's use of providence variously as comic, careless,
or ironic.   Williams first offers external evidence for HF's
conventionally Christian attitude toward providence by reviewing his 1752 tract, Examples of the Interposition of
Providence in the Detection and Punishment of Murder.
Then Williams advances internal evidence, HF's linking
most of the "improbabilities" and "coincidences" in the novels
to a direct comment on their relationship to divine providence.   Williams also sees HF's use of providence as working in or through human choices or natural events so that
characters can be tested and rewarded or punished.

301   Williams, Murial Brittain.   Marriage: Fielding's Mir-
      ror of Morality.   University: Univ. of Alabama Press,
      1973.   168 pp.
      A lucid study suggesting that HF's attitude toward mar-
riage is an index to his moral vision.   His thoughts on marriage evolve from a pagan ethic in the plays to a morally
Christian one in Amelia.   This evolution parallels HF's
shift from a burlesque view of imperfect humanity (in JA
and JW) to an anxiety for harmony effected by regenerate
mankind (in TJ and Amelia).   Though details on the social
background of marriage are neglected, the book's assessment of individual works is to the mark.
      Reviews: LJ, 15 Feb. 1974, p. 489; PQ, 53 (1974),
708-709.

302   Williamson, Eugene.   "Guiding Principles in Fielding's
      Criticism of the Critics."   In A Provision of Human
      Nature: Essays on Fielding and Others in Honor of
      Miriam Austin Locke.   Ed. Donald Kay.   University:
      Univ. of Alabama Press, 1977, pp. 1-24.
      A useful review of HF's contemporary critical for-
tunes, his attitudes toward critics, and his principles for a
just criticism.   Williamson suggests that the attacks on HF's
work, e. g. , those with a narrow moral and political bias,
led to his general disdain of critics.   Throughout his career
he faults their irresponsibility by depicting them as ignorant,
pedantic, or unscrupulous.   Consequently, Williamson suggests, HF's own criticism extols impartiality, experimenta-
tion, sensitivity, and knowledge of critical theory and culture.

303   Work, James A.   "Henry Fielding, Christian Censor."
      In The Age of Johnson: Essays Presented to Chauncey
      Brewster Tinker.   Ed. Frederick W. Hilles and Wil-
      marth S. Lewis.   New Haven, Conn.:   Yale Univ.
      Press, 1949, pp. 139-148.

A major essay that holds HF to be the most important moralist of his time, whose driving force was the propagation of Christian doctrine and conduct. Essentially, Work sees HF as an orthodox, low-church, conservative Christian and anything but a Stoic, deist, or enthusiast. And though he offers sparse reference to the works other than the Champion, Work enumerates HF's basic beliefs in revealed religion, spiritual reward and punishment, the Trinity, free will and good works. Seeing the cause of England's evils as a general neglect of religion, HF preached Christianity in his works.

304   Wright, Andrew.   Henry Fielding: Mask and Feast. Berkeley: Univ. of California Press, 1965.   214 pp.
     Argues that HF's interest is to provide cultivated delight for a cultivated audience and that the comic mode preempts the moral and the satiric in JA and TJ.   Wright sees HF as a masked master of revels who serves up an aesthetic feast.   Conscious of an imperfect real world, HF offers his readers a festive and artificial world, the contemplation of which produces a civilizing effect.   Through five chapters, then, Wright stresses the rhetorical power of HF's novels.
     "The Festive Stance" establishes the celebratory mode by tuning in on the narrator's comic voice and by outlining the form of the novels.   Wright's formal distinctions, however, are more announced than analyzed.   "The Comic Structures" explains the elaborate designs of the novels and insists that HF's is a conscious arrangement to control reality.   "Tableau" suggests that the novels are a set of speaking pictures focused and refocused by the narrator's comic epic voice that distances the reader to allow him enjoyment of the scenes.   "Character as Bas Relief" locates the essence of HF's characterization in the use of sparse but vivid details, the "economical number of strokes serving to bring the characters not to life but to liveliness. Verisimilitude is scamped and indeed scorned." This chapter includes good outlines of the main characters.   The last chapter, "Language and Style," designates HF's versatility of styles and usages--the metaphor, cliché, class language, professional jargon, and the panegyric and plain styles.
     Wright allows JA, TJ, and Amelia subsections in each of these chapters, an arrangement that causes disconcerting repetition and bothersome cross-referencing.   More disturbing, however, is his inclusion of Amelia, a novel anything but festive and celebratory.   Wright argues that by the time of its writing HF had become disgusted with society and that his sourness and dropping of the festive viewpoint flaw the

book. Perhaps. But then the inclusion of Amelia may con-
stitute the flaw in Wright's book. His comments on it are
some of the most perceptive in the study, but they are
islands far off the coast of his thesis. To include Amelia
begs inclusion of JW if only for completeness and range.
More valuable would have been the ignoring of Amelia and
the deepening of analysis of the clearly festive novels, JA
and TJ.

Reviews: CE, 27 (1966), 515; ELN, 4 (1966), 142-144;
JEGP, 65 (1966), 196-198; MLR, 61 (1966), 499-501; MP,
64 (1966), 81-82; RES, n. s. 17 (1966), 326-327; TLS, 11 Feb.
1965, p. 108.

IV

THE PLAYS

305 Appleton, William W. "Introduction." In his edition,
     "The Historical Register for the Year 1736" and "Eury-
     dice Hiss'd." Regent's Restoration Drama Series.
     Lincoln: Univ. of Nebraska Press, 1967, pp. lx-xviii.
     Specifies the social, theatrical, and political satire of
The Historical Register. While many commentators regard
the play as the main cause of Walpole's closing the theater,
Appleton exonerates HF of primary responsibility. He notes
that by 1737 three causes had intensified to threaten the
theater: (1) parliamentary movements to control actors,
audiences, and profanity; (2) growing displeasure with the
low artistic state of the stage; and (3) the desire of the
patent theaters to check the popularity of the non-patent
houses. The Golden Rump (an anonymous and libellous
farce) and HF's play merely provided the occasion for passage of the Licensing Act. Appleton offers no introductory
comment on Eurydice Hiss'd.

306 Avery, Emmett L. "An Early Performance of Field-
     ing's Historical Register." MLN, 49 (1934), 407.
     Refers to an entry in Viscount Percival's diary to offer
the earliest date postulated for the performance: 22 March
1737.

307 _____. "Fielding's Universal Gallant." Research
     Studies, State College of Washington, 6 (1938), 46.
     Suggests that though the Universal Gallant had been
ready for production for over a year, HF delayed its appearance until 1735. Perhaps because he recognized the comedy's
weaknesses, he left it unproduced and brought it forth only
when he had no stronger play to offer.

308 _____. "Some Notes on Fielding's Plays." Re-
     search Studies, State College of Washington, 3 (1935),
     48-50.
     Offers the dates of first and early performances of

The Historical Register, Don Quixote in England, the Covent-
Garden Tragedy, and Eurydice Hiss'd from a search of the
Daily Advertiser.

309   Baker, Sheridan. "Political Allusion in Fielding's
      Author's Farce, Mock Doctor, and Tumble-Down Dick."
      PMLA, 77 (1962), 221-231.
      A close detailing of the anti-Walpoliana in these plays
of the 1730s. Baker emphasizes HF's association of Colley
Cibber, Dr. John Misaubin, and John Rich with Walpole.

310   Banerji, H. K. "Beginnings of Literary Career" and
      "Triumphs and Reverses as a Playwright." In his
      Henry Fielding: Playwright, Journalist, and Master of
      the Art of Fiction (1929). Rpt. New York: Russell &
      Russell, 1962, pp. 14-33, 34-77.
      See No. 131.

311   Bateson, F. W. "Henry Fielding." In his English
      Comic Drama, 1700-1750. 1929; rpt. New York:
      Russell & Russell, 1963, pp. 115-143.
      Reviews highlights of HF's comedies, farces, and bur-
lesques to conclude that it is in the last--especially in The
Author's Farce, Tom Thumb, Pasquin, and the Historical
Register--that HF is most successful. That success resides
in his tendency to concreteness. Comedy demands a generalizing, universalizing power that HF, at home in a world
of particulars, lacked. But in the specific, timely characters and situations of the burlesques, he cogently dramatizes
the ridiculous. Moreover, each play includes a character
as commentator, a device that allows HF to moralize specifically as would the personae in the novels.

312   Boas, Frederic S. "Henry Fielding." In his Intro-
      duction to Eighteenth-Century Drama, 1700-1780. Ox-
      ford, England: Clarendon Press, 1953, pp. 220-238.
      Sketchy summaries of some of the plays that conclude
with the commonplace that HF's long apprenticeship to the
stage sharpened his techniques later in the novels.

313   Brown, Jack Robert. "Four Plays by Henry Fielding."
      Diss. Northwestern, 1937.

314   _____. "From Aaron Hill to Henry Fielding?" PQ,
      18 (1939), 85-88.
      Postulates that if Hill's letter is to HF, then HF may
be the playwright of A Rehearsal of Kings.

315 _____. "Henry Fielding's Grub-Street Opera."
MLQ, 16 (1955), 32-41.
Shows this first attempt at direct political satire to be
both largely non-partisan and light-hearted. HF's targets
are corruption in general, whether of the ministry or the
Opposition. The main plot line of the mismanagement of a
household by its servants allows the political allegory to
mock the efforts at dominance by Walpole, Pulteney, and
others.

316 Burnette, Patricia Lou Bauer. "The Polemical Structure of Fielding's Plays." Diss. Indiana. DAI, 32
(1972), 6921A.

317 Carrière, Martine. "Fileding: dramaturge se veut-il
moraliste?" Caliban, 3, no. 2 (1967), 21-28.

318 Colmer, Dorothy. "Fielding's Debt to John Lacy in
The Mock Doctor." ELN, 9 (1971), 35-39.
Specifies HF's use of some details in two of John
Lacy's plays. From Lacy's Dumb Lady (1669) he borrowed
four scenes centering on the revenge of Gregory, the mock
doctor, on his wife Dorcas. And from Lacy's Old Troop
(1664) he borrowed Gregory's mock French accent. Colmer
thus shows that HF's debt in The Mock Doctor was not only
to Molière's Le Médecin malgré lui.

319 Craik, T. W. "Fielding's 'Tom Thumb' Plays." In
Augustan Worlds: Essays in Honour of A. R. Humphreys. Ed. J. C. Hilson et al. Leicester: Leicester
Univ. Press, 1977, pp. 165-174.
A spotty comparison of passages from the three versions of Tom Thumb for the purpose of illustrating HF's
stylistic progress.

320 de Castro, J. Paul. "Revivals of Fielding's Plays."
N&Q, 11 Jan. 1941, p. 35.
Recalls a 1932 revival of Tom Thumb at the Malvern
festival.

321 Ducrocq, Jean. Le Théâtre de Fielding: 1728-1737 et
ses prolongements dans l'oeuvre romanesque. Etudes
Anglaises 55. Paris: Didier, 1975. 664 pp.

322 Durant, Jack D. "The 'Art of Thriving' in Fielding's
Comedies." In A Provision of Human Nature: Essays
on Fielding and Others in Honor of Miriam Austin

<u>Locke.</u>   Ed. Donald Kay.   University: Univ. of Ala-
bama Press, 1977, pp. 25-35.
Shows how "thriving"--HF's term for self-interest--is
thematic in his eight comedies.   In each, hard thrivers
abuse others to upset familial or social order.   Yet the
thriving theme presents a structural problem for the comic
resolution of these plays, because the good-natured characters who oppose it often are above the conflict or are without resources to avert it.   Durant suggests that the plays
allow the self-serving thrivers to prevail so that only arbi-
trary or fortuitous occurrences can resolve the conflict for
the good-natured.   He calls the plays "comedies of warn-
ing" which put the audience on guard against the powerful
thrivers who dominate the world.

323   Folkenflik, Robert.   "'The Author's Farce' and 'Othello.'"   <u>N&Q</u>, April 1976, pp. 163-164.
Notes some echoes of <u>Othello</u> in Act III of <u>The Author's
Farce.</u>   Folkenflik suggests that HF travesties Shakespeare's
play as a means of ridiculing the pretensions of the Italian
opera and thus offers an early example of his allusive art.

324   Goggin, Leo P.   "The Development of Fielding's Technique as a Writer of Comedies."   Diss. Chicago, 1950.

325   _____.   "Development of Techniques in Fielding's
Comedies."   <u>PMLA</u>, 67 (1952), 769-781.
An instructive essay suggesting that HF's eight comedies from 1727 to 1743 reveal an improvement in technique
that may well have been crucial to the novels.   Goggin measures this development on three standards: indirect repre-
sentation (reportage on stage of off-stage action), characterization, and dialogue.   In every case, Goggin shows an improvement in HF's verisimilitude, integration of elements,
and vividness.

326   _____.   "Fielding and the Select Comedies of Mr.
de Molière."   <u>PQ</u>, 31 (1952), 344-350.
Shows that HF wrote the <u>Mock Doctor</u> with only the
French text of Molière's <u>Le Médecin malgré lui</u> before him.
However, Goggin compares passages to reveal that HF wrote
<u>The Miser</u> with both Molière's <u>L'Avare</u> and the translation,
the <u>Select Comedies,</u> before him.

327   _____.   "Fielding's <u>The Masquerade.</u>"   <u>PQ</u>, 36
(1957), 475-487.
Discusses this poem, HF's first printed work (1728),

as an attack on immorality through the vehicle of the masquerade.   Goggin shows that, besides its lampoon of "Count
Ugly" Heidegger, the poem stresses three evils of the masquerade: the moral irresponsibility of disguise, the positive
encouragement of vice, and the deception that traps the un-
wary.   The poem's dual importance is that it establishes
the masquerade as a satiric target for HF and supports his
being in London between 1725 and 1728.

328   Goldgar, Bertrand A.   "The Politics of Fielding's
        Coffee-House Politician. "   PQ, 49 (1970), 424-429.
        Shows that this play (originally titled Rape upon Rape)
has as its background the conviction and subsequent pardon
for rape of Francis Charteris, an associate of Walpole.   Because Walpole was widely thought responsible for the pardon,
Fielding merges an attack on the administration with a
general social satire.   Justice Squeezum in the play may
represent Walpole himself.   This is a unique essay, for
around 1730, the play's production date, Fielding is generally
held to be politically uncommitted.

329   Hassall, Anthony J.   "The Authorial Dimension in the
        Plays of Henry Fielding. "   Komos, 1 (1967), 4-18.
        Shows that HF first experiments with the authorial di-
mension in ten of his 25 plays.   Hassall explains that the
two main uses of the device are the authorial commentary
(e. g. , in the "rehearsal" plays) and the juxtaposition of the
author's life and character with his work (e. g. , Luckless
in The Author's Farce).   The essay is important in that
Hassall specifies the groundwork for this ironic technique
that HF would perfect in the novels.

330   Horn, Robert D.   "The Farce Technique in the Dramatic
        Work of Henry Fielding and Samuel Foote and Its Influ-
        ence on the Märchensatiren of Ludwig Tieck. "   Diss.
        Michigan, 1930.

331   Hughes, Helen Sard.   "Fielding's Indebtedness to James
        Ralph. "   MP, 20 (1922), 19-34.
        Notes that Ralph, HF's co-editor on the Champion,
published The Touch-Stone in 1728, a half-serious, half-
jesting book of essays ridiculing contemporary folly.   Its
subjects include music, opera, plays, poetry, audiences,
masquerades, etc.   Hughes shows that borrowings and ana-
logues from this book are evident in HF's Author's Farce
and Tom Thumb.

332   Hughes, Leo.   "Some Representative Farces. "   In his

Century of English Farce. Princeton, N. J.: Princeton Univ. Press, 1956, pp. 259-263.
A brief demonstration of how HF adapted Molière's Le Médecin malgré lui to The Mock Doctor (1732) and Regnard's Retour Imprevu to the Intriguing Chambermaid (1734). He prepared both for the talents of Kitty Clive.

333 Hume, Robert D. "Marital Discord in English Comedy from Dryden to Fielding." MP, 74 (1977), 248-272.
Shows in part how The Modern Husband (1732) attacks the "criminal conversation" law which allowed a husband to gain heavy damages from anyone who had cuckolded him. Consequently it depicts the bad results of an economic view of marriage that looks forward to Amelia.

334 Hunter, J. Paul. "Historical Registers for the Year 1740." In his Occasional Form: Henry Fielding and the Chains of Circumstance. Baltimore: Johns Hopkins Univ. Press, 1975, pp. 76-93.
See No. 198.

335 _____. "The Many Masquerades of Henry Fielding, " "Fielding among the Giants, " and "Fielding's Reflexive Plays and the Rhetoric of Discovery. " In his Occasional Form: Henry Fielding and the Chains of Circumstance. Baltimore: Johns Hopkins Univ. Press, 1975, pp. 2-21, 22-47, 48-75.
See No. 198.

336 Irwin, Michael. "Didacticism in Fielding's Plays. " In his Henry Fielding: The Tentative Realist. Oxford, England: Clarendon Press, 1967, pp. 24-40.
See No. 199.

337 Jaggard, William. "Revivals of Fielding's Plays. " N&Q, 4 Jan. 1941, p. 15.
Notes that TJ was converted into a comic opera and acted at Covent-Garden in 1769 and was revived at the Apollo Theatre in 1907. Asserts also that Tom Thumb was rewritten as a burletta and acted at Covent Garden in 1780.

338 Johnson, Jeffrey L. L. "The Good-natured Young Man and Virtuous Young Woman in the Comedies of Henry Fielding. " Diss. Florida State. DAI, 30 (1970), 5411A.

339 Jones, B. M. "Legal Allusions in the Plays. " In his

Henry Fielding: Novelist and Magistrate. London:
Allen & Unwin, 1933, pp. 30-50.
See No. 92.
A useful thematic overview. Jones suggests that HF's
plays include nearly 500 legal allusions. Noticing them
selectively, he isolates two traits of lawyers that HF attacked in the plays, viz. "their proneness to stirring up
litigation and their pretentious employment of legal jargon
in their speech." Moreover, HF's criticism of the dishonesty, greed, and ignorance of the justices of the peace
and the state of law as it regarded marriage and divorce
are recurrent subjects.

340   Kaiser, John L. "A Study of the Plays by Henry Field-
       ing As a Commentary on the Early 18th Century
       Theater." Diss. St. John's University, 1962.

341   Kern, Jean B. "Fielding's Dramatic Satire." PQ, 54
       (1975), 239-257.
       Analyzes the devices of HF's dramatic satire. Essen-
tially, Kern shows HF to be an experimenter, for in the
absence of critical theory about non-poetic satire, he was
forced to try or adapt a variety of satiric structures of
techniques. His adaptations were diverse: Molière's in-
secure, ironic character; Buckingham's rehearsal format;
Gay's mixture of song and short scene; Pope's veiled names
and rhetorical tricks; and The Craftsman's invective and
direct attacks on Walpole. Indeed, most of HF's dramatic
satires and rehearsals, ballad operas, or burlesque comedies feature ironic rhetoric and a masked persona (the vir
bonus, the bad playwright, the stupid critic, the overzealous
editor) to focus the satire. Kern concludes that all eight
of HF's dramatic satires have more vitality than intensity,
a quality that reveals his basic comic interest and desire
to entertain an audience.

342   Kinder, Marsha. "Henry Fielding's Dramatic Experi-
       mentation: A Preface to His Fiction." Diss. U. C. L. A.
       DA, 28 (1967), 633A.

343   _____. "The Improved Author's Farce: An Analy-
       sis of the 1734 Revisions." Costerus, 6 (1972), 35-43.
       Compares passages from the 1730 original with the
1734 revision to suggest three technical improvements: an
increase in the narrator's (Luckless's) reliability, a wider
satiric range (including dishonesty in business, law, and
government), and a more controlled use of verbal irony.
These developments continue in HF's prose fiction.

344 Krentz, Irving W. "A Study of Henry Fielding's
Plays." Diss. Wisconsin. <u>DA</u>, 16 (1956), 2165.

345 Lewis, P. E. "Three Notes on Fielding's Plays."
N&Q, July 1974, pp. 253-255.
(1) HF drew upon The British Stage (1724), the first
burlesque of English pantomime, for elements in three of
his dramatic satires. (2) "Merlin's cave" in Pasquin is a
satiric allusion to a contemporary theatrical spectacle. And
(3) the original of Apollo in The Historical Register is
Charles Fleetwood, the patentee of Drury Lane.

346 Lewis, Peter. "Fielding's The Covent-Garden Tragedy
and Philips' The Distrest Mother." DUJ, 37 (1976),
33-46.
A detailed commentary on HF's burlesque of Ambrose
Philips' 1712 play, probably the most popular pseudo-classical tragedy. Setting the action in a brothel, HF leveled
Philips' tragedy by a thorough burlesque of plot, character,
speech, and Philipian tendencies (e.g., the over use of the
question and exclamation). Moreover, Lewis outlines the
Grub-Street Journal's counter-attack on HF's burlesque for
its mockery of Pope's periodical.

347 _____. "A Note on Chrononhotonthologus." N&Q,
Feb. 1978, pp. 43-44.
Notes that generally Henry Carey's 1734 play has
fewer specific parodies than does The Tragedy of Tragedies
(1731) on which it was modeled.

348 Loftis, John. "The Displacement of the Restoration
Tradition, 1728-1737." In his Comedy and Society
from Congreve to Fielding. Stanford, Cal.: Stanford
Univ. Press, 1959, pp. 101-132.
Notes HF's role in the departure from the stylized
Restoration comedy. Especially in The Modern Husband
(1732), he breaks abruptly from the Restoration pattern by
his analysis of character and motive, his use of natural
dialogue, and his humorless presentation of fashionable de-
bauchery. The Universal Gallant (1735) continues this departure. In it, HF becomes "the embittered analyst of the
personality and of society" and so nears the mood of the
novel.

349 _____. "Fielding and the Stage Licensing Act of
1737." In his Politics of Drama in Augustan England.
Oxford, England: Clarendon Press, 1963, pp. 128-153.

Charts HF's attacks on Walpole's government from
1734 to 1737, which helped passage of the Licensing Act.
Loftis suggests that of its two main provisions, the one
limiting the number of theaters was more damaging than the
one calling for licensing of plays. Its effects were the reduction of a market for plays, a more mediocre drama, and
a transfer of creative energy to the novel.

350   Macey, Samuel L. "Fielding's Tom Thumb as the
       Heir to Buckingham's Rehearsal." TSLL, 10 (1969),
       405-414.
       Notes points of theatrical satire in Tom Thumb (other
than its well-known parodies) that relate it to The Rehearsal.
The drama of heroics, blood, and bombast was still popular
in HF's day, long after Buckingham's 1672 satire on it, so
HF's play hits again at the absurdity of the great man, the
massacres, and the inflated speeches as an aristocratic objection to popular taste.

351   Masengill, Jeanne Addison. "Variant Forms of Field-
       ing's Coffee-House Politician." SB, 5 (1953), 178-182.
       Concludes that HF's 1730 play exists in only one edi-
tion.   That edition has three issues, and the third issue
exists in two states.

352   Metcalf, John Calvin. "Henry Fielding, Critic." SR,
       19 (1911), 138-154.
       Recalls that in his plays HF attacks the heroic drama,
current adaptations of Shakespeare, and Italian and French
importations.   At the heart of his attack is a hatred of
"rules," bombast, pedantry, and pretension.   Metcalf suggests that these antipathies allow HF to bring "English criticism back to nature and common-sense, after its captivity
in the box-tree walks of the pseudo-classical garden."

353   Michon, Jacques. "Du Beggar's Opera au Grub Street
       Opera." EA, 24 (1971), 166-170.

354   Moore, Robert E. "Hogarth and Fielding Invade the
       Theater." In his Hogarth's Literary Relationships
       (1948). Rpt. New York: Octagon, 1969, pp. 77-106.
       Suggests that though HF's debt to the artist Hogarth
is not remarkably great in the plays, the same temperament
spurred both to inveigh against current dramatic fare.   Both
ridicule pantomime, opera, heroic tragedy, and Shakesperian
"improvement."   Moreover, their literary relationship was
close, Hogarth illustrating some of HF's work (e. g., Tom

Thumb), and HF borrowing characters and scenes from Hogarth (e. g. , Col. Charteris, Mother Needham, Dr. Misaubin
of The Harlot's Progress).   Moore notes also specific allusions to Hogarth's work in HF's plays.

355   Morrissey, LeRoy J.   "Critical Introduction. "   In his
      edition, "Tom Thumb" and "The Tragedy of Tragedies."
      Berkeley: Univ. of California Press, 1970, pp. 1-9.
      Presents the background and stage history of Tom
Thumb and its redaction, The Tragedy of Tragedies.   Morrissey stresses the innovativeness of the plays as stage versions of classical satura (potpourri) with a contemporary
debt to the Scriblerian parodies of Swift and Pope.   The influence of the Scriblerians is clear, but Morrissey's reference to satura is puzzling, for in these plays HF is far
closer to straight parody than to the plotless "revue" form
that he perfected in the Historical Register.

356   _____ .   "Fielding's First Political Satire. "   Anglia,
      90 (1972), 325-348.
      A noteworthy detailing of the political background to
specify the directness of HF's attack on Walpole and the
government in The Tragedy of Tragedies (1731).   Besides
ad-hominem attacks on Walpole's ancestry, economic policy,
and corruption figured in Tom Thumb, HF alludes to many
others in the court.   Grizzle is the burly Lord Townshend
who fell out with Walpole.   The appetitive and buxom Hun-
camunca is Anne, Princess Royal.   The virago Dollalolla
is Queen Caroline to the blustering weakling King Arthur,
butt of George II.   And Glumdalca is Elizabeth Farnese,
the lusty Gubernadora del Reno, out-negotiated by Walpole
in the Treaty of Seville.   Morrissey's article is important
in its demonstration that the theatrical satire in the play is
not primary and by its suggestion that the political satire
was the main cause for its contemporary popularity.

357   _____ .   "Henry Fielding and the Ballad Opera. "
      ECS, 4 (1971), 386-402.
      A look at HF's choice of music in his nine ballad
operas.   Morrissey suggests that his choice was determined
both by the tastes of the town and theater managers and by
the availability of printed music.   John Watts, e. g. , the
leading publisher of ballad operas with music, had a treasury
of wood blocks with popular scores.   A playwright aspiring
to see his ballad opera in print, then, would do well to use
scores already printed by Watts and collected in his six-
volume Musical Miscellany.

358   Moss, Harold Gene. "A Note on Fielding's Selection
      of Handel's 'Si Cari' for 'The Lottery.'" N&Q, June
      1972, pp. 225-226.
      Suggests that HF's use of this song in the first ver-
sion of The Lottery (1732) was intended to satirize the monarchy and the Walpole government by allusion to the promis-
cuity of the Prince of Wales. He borrowed the song from
Handel's Admetus, which the government was backing.

359   _____. "Satire and Travesty in Fielding's The
      Grub-Street Opera." Theatre Survey, 15 (1974), 38-
      50.
      Suggests that HF extensively used borrowed music and
lyrics in the play to mask his satire on Walpole and the
Royal family. On the basis of the practice of Gay and the
authors of The Craftsman, Moss believes that in the event
of a libel charge by the government, HF could claim that
his satire was merely a travesty of other plays.

360   Nichols, Charles W. "The Date of Tumble-Down Dick."
      MLN, 36 (1921), 312-313.
      Shows that on the basis of contemporary advertise-
ments, the play's date can be established as 29 April 1736.
It had been variously dated 1737 and 1744.

361   Nichols, Charles W. "Fielding and the Cibbers." PQ,
      1 (1922), 278-289.
      Suggests that HF's treatment of Colley Cibber and Mr.
and Mrs. Theophilus Cibber in Pasquin and The Historical
Register for the Year 1736 was not original with him and
was based on humorous events involving the Cibbers. HF's
satire is directed only against their professional activities
not against their personalities or characters.

362   _____. "Fielding Notes." MLN, 34 (1919), 220-
      224.
      Three bibliographical notes suggesting that Pasquin
was a careful composition, that The Historical Register was
on the boards as early as 24 March 1737, and that a newly
discovered 1737 letter by HF to Common Sense argues for
the propriety of politics on the stage.

363   _____. "Fielding's Satire on Pantomime." PMLA,
      46 (1931), 1107-1112.
      Shows that in mocking pantomime in his plays HF ran
counter to popular taste. In attacking it he was trying to
influence the better part of his audience to take a higher

view of the stage. HF thought that pantomimes--such as those of John Rich--increased prices and lowered tastes at the theater.

364 _____. "Fielding's Satirical Plays of 1736 and 1737: Pasquin, Tumble-Down Dick, The Historical Register for the Year 1736, and Eurydice Hiss'd. Edited with a Historical Introduction and Explanatory Notes." Diss. Yale. DAI, 33 (1972), 731A.

365 _____. "Fielding's Tumble-Down Dick." MLN, 38 (1923), 410-416.
Shows Tumble-Down Dick to be structurally compatible both with Pasquin, to which it was appended, and with Pritchard's Fall of Phaeton, which it burlesqued. A study of parallel sections from Pritchard's play and HF's parody of it further illustrates the satire.

366 _____. "A New Note on Fielding's Historical Register." MLN, 38 (1923), 507-508.
A discovery of a 1737 news item heralding the appearance of the play "thought to contain the finest Humour and the genteelest Satire, of any thing published a long Time."

367 _____. "Social Satire in Fielding's Pasquin and The Historical Register." PQ, 3 (1924), 309-317.
A useful reminder that these plays are more than just political satire. HF's satire is social as well in its blasts at the Italian opera--and Farinelli--public auctions, adulation, polite conversation, and general social vices such as gaming, running into debt, and intriguing.

368 Nicoll, Allardyce. "Forms of Drama." In his History of Early Eighteenth-Century Drama, 1700-1750. Cambridge, England: Cambridge Univ. Press, 1925, pp. 262-265.
Cites HF as the most important dramatist of the rehearsal type of satiric play. Includes random examples from some of them to illustrate his satiric touches.

369 Oden, Richard L. "Fielding's Drama in Relation to Restoration Comedy and to Tom Jones." Diss. Tulane. DA, 29 (1969), 3106A.

370 Ohnsorg, Richard. "John Lacys Dumb Lady, Mrs. Centlivres Love's Contrivance, und Fieldings Mock Doctor in ihrem Verhältnis zu einander und zu ihrer gemeinschaftlichen Quellen." Diss. Hamburg, 1900.

371   Raynard, Martine. "Fielding et l'unité dramatique de
       The Historical Register for the Year 1736." Caliban,
       8 (1972), 41-53.

372   Rence, Robert J. "The Burlesque Techniques Em-
       ployed by James Robinson Planché in His Dramatic
       Works and Their Relationship to the English Burlesque
       Tradition Between Henry Fielding and W. S. Gilbert."
       Diss. Minnesota. DA, 29 (1967), 2367A.

373   Roberts, Edgar V. "Eighteenth-Century Ballad Opera:
       The Contribution of Henry Fielding." Drama Survey,
       1 (1961-1962), 71-85.
       Recognizes HF as the most important London playwright
of the 1730s and one of the most significant of the century.
Roberts reviews his contributions in nearly a dozen ballad
operas. Though the essay lacks specificity, it touches on
the genre's main traits and HF's mastery of them. He
shows HF excelling in literary skills that allow him to perfect this popular stage type, especially by his satirical outlook centering on human self-delusion, his use of the many-
faceted rogue, and his artistry in dialect, argument, and
general word-play.

374   _____. "Fielding's Ballad Opera The Lottery (1732)
       and the English State Lottery of 1731." HLQ, 27
       (1963), 39-52.
       A detailed and clear account of the official workings,
dishonest practices, and popular vocabulary associated with
the 1731 lottery, subject of HF's play.

375   _____. "Henry Fielding and Richard Leveridge:
       Authorship of 'The Roast Beef of Old England.'" HLQ,
       27 (1963), 175-181.
       Ascribes original authorship largely to HF but credits
Leveridge with the music and certain verses. HF used ver-
sions in his ballad operas The Grub-Street Opera (1731) and
Don Quixote in England (1734).

376   _____. "Possible Additions to Airs 6 and 7 of
       Henry Fielding's Ballad Opera The Lottery (1732)."
       N&Q, Dec. 1962, pp. 455-456.
       Reprints two additions to airs that were probably in-
cluded in The Lottery but not in any printed edition of it.
They were first printed in some song books and miscellanies
of the 1730s and 1740s.

377   Rogers, Winfield H.   "Fielding's Early Aesthetic and
       Technique. " SP, 50 (1943), 529-551.
       An important essay that shows HF's plays developing
the aesthetic on which the later, great works rest. First,
he uses farce as a criticism of life. Second, the "hu-
mours" theory becomes the basis of his analysis of human
motivation. Third, his use of words as symbols ("great
man, " "good nature, " etc.) approaches allegory. And
fourth, he develops a comprehensive allegorical method of
interpreting life.

378 _____ . "The Significance of Fielding's Temple
       Beau. " PMLA, 55 (1940), 440-444.
       A noteworthy explanation of HF's early use of a domi-
nant symbol to express an attitude. Deriving from Spectator
No. 105's discussion of a pedant, The Temple Beau extends it as a symbol to satirize a family gripped by a ruling
passion of pedantry. This use of a unifying symbol pre-
figures his mature satiric technique, e. g. , the "great-man"
symbol of JW and the mob in TJ.

379   Rudolph, Valerie C.   "People and Puppets: Fielding's
       Burlesque of the 'Recognition Scene' in The Author's
       Farce. "   PLL, 11 (1975), 31-38.
       Contends that HF burlesques the popular dramatic use
of the "recognition scene. " By blurring its realistic presentation (in which the fiction is believed) with the fantastic
(in which it is not believed), he thereby presents the confusion of popular ethical and aesthetic values. Thus in Act
III the Court of the Goddess of Nonsense appears not only
as a mythic figure from a fantastic underworld, but also as
the reality of theatrical commercialism.

380 _____ .   "Theatrical Verisimilitude and Political Be-
       lief in the Plays of Henry Fielding. " Diss. Iowa.
       DAI, 32 (1971), 1485A.

381   Scouten, Arthur H.   The London Stage, 1660-1800.
       Part III: 1729-1747. 2 vols. Carbondale: Southern
       Illinois Univ. Press, 1961. References to HF passim.
       An indispensable tool for information on dates and
theaters of performances, players, box office receipts, etc.
Scouten records much information for 27 of HF's plays between 1729 and 1747. Moreover, in a substantial introduction (pp. xix-clxxxviii) he provides material on the loca-
tion and descriptions of the playhouses, theater accommoda-
tions and practices, financing, the Licensing Act, the audi-

ence, advertising, the demands of action, costumes, and
scenery. References to HF reveal him in various roles,
e.g., training actors, advertising, and accusing the door-
keepers of theft.

382   Sellery, J'nan. "Language and Moral Intelligence in
       the Enlightenment: Fielding's Plays and Pope's Dun-
       ciad, Part I. " EnlE, 1 (1970), 17-26.
       Shows that HF and Pope share the same concern for
the morally responsible purpose of art. Thus, both satirize
the audience whose only desire is to be diverted. Its noisy
and uncontrolled behavior is attacked by HF in The Author's
Farce (1730), Pasquin (1736), and The Historical Register
(1736). As the physical audience embodies the degeneration
of taste, the plays depict the problems of the authors in
such a society. It is to this audience, e.g., that Medley,
the stage playwright of The Historical Register, must appeal,
yet by his irony he keys his moral meaning to more perceptive members of the audience.
       Part II of this article, on pages 108-119, centers on
Pope's Dunciad, not on HF's plays.

383   Shaw, George Bernard. "Preface" to the First Volume
       of Plays: Pleasant and Unpleasant (1906). Rpt. in
       Vol. III of Complete Plays with Prefaces. New York:
       Dodd, Mead, 1963, p. xvi.
       Refers to HF as "the greatest practising dramatist,
with the single exception of Shakespeare, produced by England between the Middle Ages and the nineteenth century. "
Shaw further praises HF for devoting his genius to exposing
parliamentary corruption.

384   Smith, Dane F. "The Rise and Fall of Henry Field-
       ing, Grand Mogul of Satirical Farce. " In his Plays
       about the Theatre in England from "The Rehearsal" in
       1671 to the Licensing Act of 1737. London: Oxford
       Univ. Press, 1936, pp. 205-237.
       Specifies HF's satire on the contemporary theater in
Pasquin, Tumble-Down Dick, and Eurydice. Smith also recalls how HF's satire on Walpole as Quidam in the Historical Register of 1736 and as Pillage in Eurydice Hiss'd
helped precipitate the Licensing Act.

385   Stonehill, Charles. "Fielding's The Miser. " TLS, 22
       Oct. 1925, p. 698.
       Claims possession of a folio edition of The Miser that
was probably printed before the play was acted and was

suppressed by HF for its unsightly format. Stonehill suggests that HF corrected the text and reset the type for the edition of 1733.
    Cf. Stanley E. Read, "Fielding's Miser." HLQ, 1 (1931), 211-213. Suggests that Stonehill's folio version is not the true first edition because an octavo copy pre-dates it. Seeing the folio as a careless reprint of the octavo, Read suggests that the folio was intended to go with a collection of translations from Molière, and was thought to be literary rather than theatrical in appeal. Thus the absence of a dramatis personae in the folio.

386 Sullivan, William A. "Fielding's Dramatic Comedies: The Influence of Congreve and Molière." Diss. Louisiana State. DAI, 32 (1972), 3966A.

387 Swaen, A. E. H. "Fielding's The Intriguing Chambermaid." Neophilologus, 29 (1944), 117-120.
    Shows that though this play of 1733/1734 is directly adapted from Le Retour imprevu of Regnard, its remote source is Plautus' Mostellaria. When HF Englished the French play, he restored the Plautine spirits, or devils, that Regnard had deleted.

388 Swanson, Gayle Ruff. "Henry Fielding and the Psychology of Womanhood." Diss. South Carolina. DAI, 38 (1977), 7761A.

389 Thomas, Jerrald P. "Henry Fielding's Comedies of Manners: A Study in the Eighteenth Century Problem Play." Diss. Kansas State. DA, 35 (1975), 5369A.

390 Weide, Erwin. Henry Fieldings Komödien und die Restaurationskomödie. Dichtung, Wort, und Sprache, Vol. 10. Hamburg: Hansischer Gildenverlag, 1947. 140 pp.

391 Wells, John Edwin. "Some New Facts Concerning Fielding's Tumble-Down Dick and Pasquin." MLN, 28 (1913), 137-142.
    Offers the idea that HF redacted Pasquin to satirize John Rich both for Rich's refusal to produce the play and for Rich's own satire on it, Marforio. Also, Tumble-Down Dick; or Phaeton in the Suds is a satire on Rich's Fall of Phaeton.

392 Williams, Murial Brittain. "Marriage in the Plays."

In her Marriage: Fielding's Mirror of Morality. University: Univ. of Alabama Press, 1973, pp. 23-42. See No. 301.

393   Wood, David C. "The Dramatic Tradition of Henry Fielding's Regular Comedies. " Diss. Bowling Green. DAI, 30 (1970), 4428A.

394   Woods, Charles B. "Cibber in Fielding's Author's Farce: Three Notes." PQ, 44 (1965), 145-151. Identifies three references to Cibber in the play.   In Act I (iv) Jack accuses Cibber directly of ignoring authors' plays; in Act II, Marplay is Cibber as a cobbler of others' plots; and in Act III, Sir Farcical Comick is Cibber ridiculed for his notorious misuse of language.

395   _____. "The 'Miss Lucy' Plays of Fielding and Garrick." PQ, 41 (1962), 294-310. Suggests a collaboration between HF and Garrick. HF's popular Virgin Unmask'd (1735) spurred Garrick's production of a sequel, Lethe (1740).   In both plays, Kitty Clive played Miss Lucy, as she was to again in Miss Lucy in Town (1742), a play in which textual evidence suggests the joint authorship of HF and Garrick.

396   _____. "Notes on Three of Fielding's Plays. " PMLA, 52 (1937), 369-373. Establishes the topical backgrounds for three plays. (1) The Letter-Writers (1731) derives from a wave of gangster terrorism that swept England and was characterized by letters of threat and extortion.   (2) The Modern Husband (1732) draws its theme from the contemporary practice which enabled a man to make money legally from his wife's adultery.   And (3) Eurydice Hiss'd (1737) is a double allegory based on current literary and political events--the rejection of HF afterpiece and the Excise Bill of Walpole.

397   _____. "Studies in the Dramatic Works of Henry Fielding. " Diss. Harvard, 1935.

398   _____. "Theobald and Fielding's Don Tragedio. " ELN, 2 (1965), 266-271 Claims that allusions to thunder, repetition, and failed tragedies in The Pleasures of the Town suggest the identity of Don Tragedio to be Lewis Theobald, a playwright and scholar famous for those traits.

399   Wright, Kenneth Daulton.   "Henry Fielding and the
      London Stage, 1730-1737. "   Diss. Ohio State.   <u>DA</u>,
      21 (1960), 1293-94.

V

SHAMELA

400 Amory, Hugh. "Shamela as Aesopic Satire." ELH,
  38 (1971), 239-253.
  Claims that for satiric purposes HF associates Shamela's
authorship with a corporation of Colley Cibber, Conyers Middleton, and Richardson. Their respective books--Cibber's
Apology, Middleton's Life of Cicero, and Richardson's Pam-
ela--are ultimately no more than romances that "explain the
success of [naive and candid] parvenus by their superior
moral merit" and that therefore they bear close resemblance
to Shamela.

401 Baker, Sheridan W., Jr. "Introduction." In his edition, An Apology for the Life of Mrs. Shamela Andrews. Berkeley: Univ. of California Press, 1953,
  pp. xi-xxxiv.
  A good review of the case for HF's authorship of what
Baker thinks "may well be the best parody in English literature." In spite of such enthusiasm, he is especially instructive on the religious debate from which much of the
parody grows.

402 Davis, Joe Lee. "Criticism and Parody." Thought,
  26 (1951), 180-204.
  A general discussion of parody as a criticism without
malice that constructs more than it destroys. In a glance
at Shamela, Davis notes that HF's best achievement is his
correction of Richardson's ethics, psychology, and sociology.
Moreover, he suggests that the creative importance of
Shamela is its preparation for JA.

403 de Castro, J. Paul. "Did Fielding Write Shamela?"
  N&Q, 8 Jan. 1916, pp. 24-26.
  Suggests HF's authorship by a rendering of passages
from his other recognized works set next to parallel passages of Shamela.

404 Doody, Margaret Anne. A Natural Passion: A Study

in the Novels of Samuel Richardson. Oxford, England:
Clarendon Press, 1974. See pp. 71-74.
   Observes that HF upholds the droit de seigneur, the double
sexual standard, and the stationary place of the poor. Doody
consequently claims that in Shamela HF reacts to Pamela because Richardson's novel is subversive: it upsets classical
literary decorum with a low female as heroine; it overthrows
social barriers in the Pamela-Mr. B. alliance; and it questions
the double sexual standard.

404a Hunter, J. Paul. "Historical Registers for the Year
      1740. " In his Occasional Form: Henry Fielding and
      the Chains of Circumstance. Baltimore: Johns Hop-
      kins Univ. Press, 1975, pp. 76-93.
      See No. 198.

405 Jenkins, Owen. "Richardson's Pamela and Fielding's
     'Vile Forgeries. '" PQ, 44 (1965), 200-210.
     Makes an interesting case for reading Pamela II both
as a witty answer to Shamela and a defense of Pamela I.
By dramatizing his retorts to HF in the plot of the sequel,
Richardson, however diffusely, answers HF's charges and
attacks him in Turner (Turn-her; i. e. , turn Pamela to
Shamela), a witty lawyer who poses as a parson (i. e. , Tickletext and Oliver).

405a Jenkins, Ralph E. "A Note on Hogarth and Fielding's
      'Shamela.'" N&Q, Sept. 1971, p. 335.
      Perceives the influence of Hogarth's two 1736 engrav-
ings, Before and After, in Letter VI of Shamela. Both Hogarth and HF depict a master's seduction attempt of a servant girl, both imply the girl's willingness, and both juxta-
pose theological and pornographic titles in the girl's library.

406 Jensen, Gerard E. "An Apology for the Life of Mrs.
     Shamela Andrews, 1741. " MLN, 31 (1916), 310-311.
     Claims that Shamela can be positively ascribed to HF
on the basis of word-usage (frequently of hath, doth, durst,
etc. , all considered passé by his contemporaries) and by a
notice of parallel phrasings in Shamela and The Covent-
Garden Journal and The Champion.

407 Johnson, Maurice. "The Art of Parody: Shamela. "
     In his Fielding's Art of Fiction. Philadelphia: Univ.
     of Pennsylvania Press, 1961, pp. 19-46.
     A useful and workmanlike juxtaposing of passages from
Pamela and Shamela to demonstrate HF's art of parody, his

provoking laughter by recognition. But the chapter is finally disappointing. Though it illustrates the "how" of the parody closely, the chapter retreats into an unexplained cliché to answer its "why": that the parody results from HF's desire to satirize the false pretensions of life and literature. See No. 206.

408   Kreissman, Bernard. "From Pamela Andrews to Joseph Andrews." In his Pamela-Shamela: A Study of the Criticisms, Burlesques, Parodies, and Adaptations of Richardson's "Pamela." Lincoln: Univ. of Nebraska Press, 1960, pp. 3-22.
An advocacy of HF's satire at Richardson's expense that produces only a simplified reading of Pamela and a summary of HF's attacks on it. Assuming with HF that Pamela expounds "the business view of morality," Kreissman regards Shamela as an attack on "the concealed eroticism of Pamela" and JA as an attack on its ethical outlook.

409   Olivier, Theo. "Pamela and Shamela: A Reassessment." ESA, 17 (1974), 59-70.
Asserts that Shamela is overvalued as an exposé of Pamela. Olivier also claims that there is more humor in Pamela than Richardson is usually credited with, for Richardson maintains a "constant duality of intention toward Mr. B."

410   Rothstein, Eric. "The Framework of Shamela." ELH, 35 (1968), 381-402.
Contends that the framework of Shamela foreshadows and complements a main theme in the novel proper. That framework sets up hits at the Church (Middleton), the state (Hervey), and the arts (Cibber). By imputing a prostitution to each--a self-selling to Walpole--HF fashions a link to the story line. The obscene puns (e. g., Fanny, etc., Conny) all refer to the female sexual organ and highlight the prostitution theme. Moreover, the Tickletext-Oliver debate is a bridge to the narrative satire on Pamela. Arguing textual issues, Tickletext is the consummate Methodist whose pronouncements virtually establish Pamela as a Biblical substitute, while Oliver is the voice of common sense.

411   Shepperson, Archibald Bolling. "Richardson and Fielding: Shamela and Shamelia." In his Novel in Motley: A History of the Burlesque Novel in England (1936). Rpt. New York: Octagon, 1967, pp. 9-38.
Notes the main attacks on Pamela and explains Shamela as a full-scale parody-burlesque, a genre that ridicules a

specific work rather than a type. Shepperson shows that
the framework, the characters, and the scenes all parody
Richardson's novel in a coarse but not vulgar way. He concludes by highlighting the history of a similar reaction to
Shamela, TJ, and Amelia to suggest that the parody-burlesque was a popular and potent type of the 1740s and 1750s.

412   Watt, Ian. "Shamela." Introduction to his edition of
      An Apology for the Life of Mrs. Shamela Andrews.
      Augustan Reprint Society, No. 57. Los Angeles:
      Clark Memorial Library, 1956, pp. 1-11. Rpt. in
      Paulson (No. 239).
      A clear review of the topical literary, moral and re-
ligious satire in Shamela. Watt especially stresses the
book's chief polemical purposes of attacking both the fulsome
praise of Pamela and Richardson's interpretation of his heroine's character. Moreover, Watt calls attention to HF's
rarely noticed and close stylistic parody, e. g., his hitting
off Richardson's juxtaposition of high sentiment and trivial
detail. In all, Watt regards Shamela as one of the best
products of HF's long experience with the burlesque genre.

413   Wood, Carl. "Shamela's Subtle Satire: Fielding's
      Characterization of Mrs. Jewkes and Mrs. Jervis."
      ELN, 13 (1976), 266-270.
      Believes that HF noticed some redeeming traits in
Richardson's Mrs. Jewkes and some less than admirable
actions in Mrs. Jervis. By reversing their names and
characters, HF achieves a subtle turn of satire to be
savored only by the most careful reader of Pamela and
Shamela.

414   Woods, Charles B. "Fielding and the Authorship of
      Shamela." PQ, 25 (1946), 248-272.
      Believes that HF's authorship is likely because Sham-
ela's satiric targets are men HF might well have attacked
in 1741: Middleton, Cibber, Walpole, and Richardson. But
one of the most recurring targets is the despicable priest,
for sentimental clergy were among the most ardent admirers
of Pamela. A minor character in that novel, Parson Williams, is elevated by HF to a rank equal with Shamela.
Williams's rationalization on the sanctity of adultery is one
hit at hypocritical preachers. And the framework of the
Oliver-Tickletext correspondence sets up the clerical satire.
Woods concludes that if HF made a travesty of Pamela in
Shamela, he then was ready for the next step: to provide
an ethical contrast to it in JA.

VI

JOSEPH ANDREWS

415 Alter, Robert. "The Design of Character" and "The Architectonic Novel. " In his Fielding and the Nature of the Novel. Cambridge, Mass.: Harvard, 1968, pp. 61-98, 99-140. See No. 121.

416 Baker, Sheridan. "Henry Fielding's Comic Romances. " PMASAL, 45 (1960), 411-419.
Argues that JA and TJ are closer to the romance than to the epic in language, characters, and motifs. Yet HF's novels "deal with romance in two opposite ways, often managing a synthesis: they accept courtly love and much of its romantic sublimity, and they mock heroic adventure with the picaresque scuffling of low life. " Baker notes that it is Scarron who seems to have suggested HF's term "comic romance. "

417 Banerji, H. K. "First Efforts in Fiction. " In his Henry Fielding: Playwright, Journalist, and Master of the Art of Fiction (1929). Rpt. New York: Russell & Russell, 1962, pp. 98-133. See No. 131.

418 Battestin, Martin C. "Fielding's Joseph Andrews: Studies Toward A Critical and Textual Edition. " Diss. Princeton. DA, 19 (1959), 2080.

418a Battestin, Martin C. "Fielding's Changing Politics and Joseph Andrews. " PQ, 39 (1960), 39-55.
Presents circumstantial evidence for HF's abandoning the Opposition and going into Walpole's pay. Battestin contends that HF's reasons were the ingratitude and hypocrisy of the Patriots as well as his own financial problems that were aggravated by a dying daughter and an ill wife. After satirizing the Patriots in his 1741 pamphlet, The Opposition, he mocks them in JA in the characters of the Man of

Courage, Squire Fickle, Sir Oliver Hearty, and Sir Thomas Booby.   The importance of this article is its suggestion that HF was a political realist and not a paragon of political integrity.

419 _____ . "Fielding's Revisions of Joseph Andrews. " SB, 16 (1963), 81-117.
A rare demonstration of HF's habits of composition. This article features a table collating 128 of the more than 600 textual variants in the five lifetime editions of JA.   Battestin concludes that HF was a careful craftsman, meticulously shaping and sharpening his first novel.

420 _____ . "Introduction. "   In his edition, Joseph Andrews.   Riverside Edition.   Boston: Houghton Mifflin, 1961, pp. v-xl.
The best short discussion of the circumstances of composition, the implications (and limitations) of HF's comic theory, the intellectual backgrounds of his thought, and the characters of Adams and Joseph.   Especially valuable is Battestin's explanation of the neo-Augustinian-Pelagian controversy in terms of HF's concept of the nature of man.

421 _____ . "Lord Hervey's Role in Joseph Andrews. " PQ, 42 (1963), 226-241.
Suggests that HF identifies Beau Didapper with John, Lord Hervey, deserter of the Opposition and Walpole's favorite agent.   HF worked various of Hervey's traits into Didapper, e. g. , his shortness, effeminacy, Frenchified airs, difficulties with Latin, and moderate philandering. Allusions to Pope's work in HF's treatment of Hervey suggest a meeting of the poet and the novelist in 1741.   Yet above all, Hervey's role is important because it illustrates HF's use of the real world in his fiction.

422 _____ . The Moral Basis of Fielding's Art: A Study of Joseph Andrews.   Middletown, Conn. :   Wesleyan Univ. Press, 1959.   195 pp.
An essential background study of JA.   Battestin's aim is threefold: to identify its main themes, to relate its ethics to the contexts of 17th- and 18th-century Latitudinarian Christianity, and to examine the novel as an artifact given pattern by its ethics.   Battestin carefully specifies the benevolist writings of the Low Church divines--Barrow, Tillotson, Clarke, and Hoadly--as influential on HF's moral thought, especially their beliefs in the essential goodness of human nature and in the doctrine of salvation by good works.

Indeed, Battestin claims, HF's Latitudinarian picture of the
good man as charitable (selfless) and chaste (temperate)
raises him to the status of a Christian hero.

Battestin further suggests that HF deepends his ethical
characterization by associating Joseph with his Old Testament prototype, who withstands the seductive advances of
Potiphar's wife, and by associating Adams with the patriar-
chal Abraham. By such symbolism, HF renders JA a moral
allegory, the Christian heroes on a pilgrimage from corruption (the city) to innocence (the country). In terms of that
structure, Battestin reads the Wilson episode as an epitome
of the novel in its treatment of the main themes of morality,
vanity, rural retirement, and providence versus fortune.

Chapters on HF's ethics and his attitude toward the
clergy's plight round out Battestin's thesis. Though HF did
not admit in any absolute sense the innate goodness of man,
he did allow that through wholesome education and religion,
man could achieve a high degree of moral excellence. Battestin likewise shows that one of HF's main concerns was
the contemporary contempt for the clergy, their poverty,
and their ignorance. So in the novel HF shows reasons for
the general scorn in which the clergy was held: The six
clergymen contrasted with Adams reflect HF's belief that
though no other type of person could be so effective for social good, too often the priest was remiss.

If Battestin seems to make HF more a moralist than
a comic novelist, the result is nevertheless worthwhile, for
it details a side of HF and his art that has often been
glossed over. No one ever doubted the comedy of JA, but
the case had to be made for its morality.

Reviews: MLN, 76 (1961), 464-467; RES, n. s. 12
(1961), 211-212; SAQ, 59 (1960), 299-300; TLS, 25 Dec.
1959, p. 756; YR, 49 (1960), 454-457.

423 _____. "On the Contemporary Reputations of Pamela, Joseph Andrews, and Roderick Random: Remarks
by an 'Oxford Scholar,' 1748." N&Q, Dec. 1968, pp.
450-452.

A report on the laudatory reception of JA by a contemporary anti-Pamela pamphleteer. Seeing HF's first
novel as a masterpiece, the author, an "Oxford Scholar,"
compares it favorably with Scarron's Roman comique (1651-
1657) and Le Sage's Gil Blas (1715-1735). Discovery of the
pamphlet corrects the belief that JA had an indifferent to
hostile reception.

424 Bissell, Frederick Olds, Jr. "The Theory of Joseph

Andrews. " In his Fielding's Theory of the Novel
(1933). Rpt. New York: Cooper Square, 1969, pp.
24-37.
See No. 139.

425   Bosdorf, Erich. "Entstehungsgeschichte von Fieldings
Joseph Andrews. " Diss. Berlin, Humboldt Universität,
1908.

426   Braudy, Leo. "Joseph Andrews: The Relevance of
Facts. " In his Narrative Form in History and Fiction:
Hume, Fielding, and Gibbon. Princeton, N. J.: Prince-
ton Univ. Press, 1970, pp. 95-121.
See No. 143.

427   Brooks, Douglas. "Abraham Adams and Parson Trulliber: The Meaning of Joseph Andrews, Book II, Chapter
14. " MLR, 63 (1968), 794-801.
Reveals HF's allusive method of characterization by
noting the relationship between this section of JA and the
Odyssey. E. g. , Brooks notes that Trulliber is ironically
allusive of both Circe (who turns Ulysses into a hog) and
Eumaeus (who offered him grand hospitality). Playing off
Circe's beauty and Eumaeus' charity, HF makes Trulliber
hoglike and greedy. Besides such classical allusions, HF's
references to the Bible and the Faerie Queene further deepen
the episode's meaning. Brooks offers as well a full interpretation of Trulliber's name (entrails, a corpulent person).

428   _____. "Fielding: Joseph Andrews. " In his Number and Pattern in the 18th-Century Novel. London,
Routledge, 1973, pp. 65-91.
An interesting but strained attempt to explain the
novel's structure. Brooks argues that the structural chias-
mus, number symbolism, Christian-epical and Biblical associations, and internal repetitions and parallels all render
JA "fundamentally baroque. " Moot.

429   _____. "The Interpolated Tales in Joseph Andrews
Again. " MP, 65 (1968), 208-213.
Contends that the interpolated tales of "The Unfortunate
Jilt" (II, 4 and 6) and "The History of Two Friends" (IV,
10) are closely related to the narrative proper. In the first
Leonora's concern for Bellarmine parallels Slipslop's for
Joseph, and both are contrasted with Fanny's genuine love
for Joseph. Also the duel in the tale echoes Adams's de-
fense of Joseph. Likewise, the second tale functions in the

"marriage spectrum" of the novel, composed of the Tow-
wouses, Trullibers, Adamses, Wilsons, and, prospectively,
Joseph and Fanny. As the tale's main concern is with the
relationship between marriage and friendship, so the marriages in the novel take up the correlative marriage-charity
theme.

430 _____. "Introduction." In his edition, Joseph An-
    drews and Shamela. Oxford English Novels. London:
    Oxford Univ. Press, 1971, pp. vii-xviii.
    In the main, a reproduction of the standard comments
on the genesis and themes of the two books. But Brooks
also offers a perceptive suggestion that the echoes of Pamela
and the Bible in JA are reinforced by allusions to Hercules
and the Odyssey (VI and XIV) that deepen the themes of virtuous strength and hospitality.

431 _____. "Richardson's Pamela and Fielding's Joseph
    Andrews." EIC, 18 (1967), 158-168.
    Overstresses Pamela's influence on the structure of
JA. Brooks claims that in his novel HF rewrote Pamela in
his own mode. He notes some interesting parallels but
others are in themselves ludicrous and taken together, unconvincing. E. g., he associates Joseph with Mr. B. (Mr.
B's clothes fit Joseph); Adams with Mr. B. (At one point
each confuses someone's sex); and Pamela's animal imagery
with JA's. (The animal imagery of Pamela is "rewritten"
in the Lion and Dragon inns of HF's novel.)
    A. M. Kearney in EIC, 18 (1968) denies most of
Brooks' parallels on grounds of common sense.
    In EIC, 18 (1968) Brooks repeats his claims before
Kearney issues his rejoinder in EIC, 18 (1968). The final
sally is Brooks' in EIC, 19 (1969).

432 Buck, Gerhard. "Written in the Manner of Cervantes. "
     GRM, 29 (1941), 53-61. [In German.]

433 Cauthen, I. B. , Jr. "Fielding's Digressions in Joseph
     Andrews." CE, 17 (1956), 379-382.
     An important essay demonstrating that the interpolated
stories in the novel are variations on its basic theme and
aesthetic: the exposure of vanity and hypocrisy. The history of Leonora (II, 4 and 6) exposes her vanity and Bellarmine's hypocrisy. Wilson's story (III, 3) depicts him as a
vain wit and hypocritical fop. And the history of the two
friends (IV, 10) dramatizes the vanity of being correct.
Dealing respectively with courtship, a young man's entry

into life, and marriage, they are ultimately exempla complementing three important subjects of the novel proper.

434   Coley, William B.   "Fielding, Hogarth, and Three
       Italian Masters. "   MLQ, 24 (1963), 386-391.
       Recalls that Joseph Andrews's mention of three Italian
painters (III, 6) is a satire on the English predilection for
the foreign.   "Ammyconni" (Jacopo Amigoni), "Paul Varnish" (Paolo Veronese), and "Hannibal Scratchi" (Annibale
Carracci) are included in his list with "Hogarthi, " who alone
among English artists could compete with the foreign mo-
nopoly in the arts.   Coley details the relationship between
Hogarth and Amigoni.

435   de Castro, J. Paul.   "Fielding's Parson Adams. "
       N&Q, 18 March 1916, pp. 224-225.
       Endorses the belief that the Rev. William Young, Dor-
set parson and schoolmaster, is the model for Parson Adams.

436   Digeon, Aurélien.   "Joseph Andrews. "   In his Novels
       of Fielding.   London: Routledge, 1925, pp. 195-248.
       See No. 167.

437   Donovan, Robert Alan.   "Joseph Andrews as Parody. "
       In his Shaping Vision: Imagination in the English
       Novel from Defoe to Dickens.   Ithaca, N. Y. :   Cornell
       Univ. Press, 1966, pp. 68-88.
       Argues that JA derives its form from HF's impulse to
parody Pamela and thus rejects the usual dictum that the
only parodic parts are the first 10 and the last 13 chapters.
Donovan suggests that HF shows Pamela's moral judgments
to be inadequate by transferring them to Adams after putting
him into an expansive, morally complicated world where
such precepts are hard to maintain.   Consequently HF ridicules the notion at the center of Pamela that the choice between good and evil is simple.   By mocking Pamela, JA
asserts its own unity and "autonomy. "   All is convincing
except Donovan's charge that Adams is a hypocrite.

438   Driskell, Leon V.   "Interpolated Tales in Joseph An-
       drews and Don Quixote: The Dramatic Method as In-
       struction. "   SAB, 33, No. 3 (1968), 5-8.
       Sees the three interpolated tales of JA as "essentially
dramatic in function, and their circumstances of narration ... more important than their content. "   E. g. , in lis-
tening to "The Unfortunate Jilt" Mrs. Slipslop identifies with
the heroine and underlines her misconception of herself.

Likewise, Adams reveals his vanity by his comments on
Wilson's story and "The Tale of the Two Friends. " A ten-
able but not essential reading of the function of the tales.

439   Duncan, Jeffrey L. "The Rural Ideal in Eighteenth-
        Century Fiction. " SEL, 8 (1968), 517-535.
    Suggests that JA embodies two of HF's main themes,
social order and moral order. The Wilson family's pristine,
archetypal society establishes these themes of order in the
country as ethical touchstones that recur variously in the
fiction of Smollett, Sterne, and Goldsmith. This rural ideal
counters the values of the new realism of Defoe and Richardson.

440   Eaves, T. C. Duncan, and Ben D. Kimpel. "Two
        Names in Joseph Andrews. " MP, 72 (1975), 408-409.
    Recalls that in 18th-century slang "slip-slop" meant
sexual play and a "tow-wow" meant the female pudendum.
Thus Mrs. Slipslop and the Tow-wouses are vulgar creations.

441   Ehrenpreis, Irvin. "Fielding's Use of Fiction: The
        Autonomy of Joseph Andrews. " In Twelve Original
        Essays on Great English Novels. Ed. Charles Shapiro.
        Detroit: Wayne State Univ. Press, 1960, pp. 23-41.
    A major essay on the unity of the novel. Ehrenpreis
shows how HF masses ironies, exposures, conflicts, and
reversals to form its pattern. By a graphic explanation of
plot movements, he specifies recurring motifs such as rape
attempts and sequential formulae such as unexpected meet-
ings leading to conversation, disagreement, argument, and,
sometimes, mock-heroic scuffle. Moreover, Ehrenpreis
shows how HF adapted traditional devices for unity: the
pedlar, inserted tales, the concealed parent motif, and authorial interventions. His remarks linking HF's use of the
incest and familial motifs in JA with HF's own life are interesting but, even if accurate, fail to improve an otherwise
essential essay.

442   Evans, James E. "Fielding's Community of Fiction:
        Fielding's Supporting Characters in Joseph Andrews,
        Tom Jones, and Amelia. " Diss. Pennsylvania. DAI,
        32 (1972), 4560A.

443.   _____ . "Fielding's Lady Booby and Fenelon's
        Calypso. " SNNTS, 8 (1976), 210-213.
    Suggests that HF's allusions to motifs, tones, and
soliloquies of Calypso in Fénelon's Télémaque increase comic
enjoyment and enhance the comic mythology of JA.

444   Forman, H. B.   "Richardson, Fielding, and the An-
       drews Family. "   Fortnightly Review, 1 Dec. 1901, pp.
       949-959.
       Views Richardson as a milktoast, absurd prude, and
vain little printer, whose Pamela was a "screed of osten-
tatious virtuousness. " Ironically, HF's "manly, " "bracing"
castigation of Pamela in JA did Richardson a service by
prodding him to improve his epistolary technique in Clarissa.
And because of Pamela, Richardson is directly responsible
for sparking HF to invent the modern novel with its narrative realism.

445   Freedman, William A.   "Joseph Andrews: Clothing
       and the Concretization of Character. "   Discourse, 4
       (1961), 304-310.
       Suggests that HF specifies character not only by names,
gestures, conversations, and actions, but also by dress.
Yet Freedman discusses only Adams's dress as a means by
which HF demonstrates the inverse relationship between his
tattered clothing and his ideal character and between appearance and reality.   Freedman neglects mentioning the use of
the clothing motif in fixing character in such instances as
the great coat in the coach episode, Joseph's livery, and
Didapper's frippery.

446   _____.   "Joseph Andrews: Fielding's Garden of
       the Perverse. "   TSL, 16 (1971), 35-46.
       Claims that HF defines good nature as essentially hu-
man nature.   Seeing ill nature thus as a distortion of humanity, he associates ill-natured characters with beasts.   Slipslop has affinities with a cow, Didapper with a bird, Mrs.
Tow-wouse with a dragon, Trulliber with a pig, and the
hunting squire with a cur.   By treating others as beasts,
they reveal their own beast-like or distorted natures.   Freedman's theory is interesting, but it does not account for HF's
highly selective use of this Jonsonian method, as ill-natured
characters such as Peter Pounce, Lawyer Scout, the coach
passengers, and the surgeon all go without bestial insignia.

447   Goldberg, Homer.   The Art of Joseph Andrews.   Chi-
       cago: Univ. of Chicago Press, 1969.   292 pp.
       Mainly a source study of JA.   Carefully specifying
HF's use of his avowed models--Cervantes, Scarron, Lesage,
and Marivaux--Goldberg attempts to account for his artistry.
The ten chapters aim at reconstructing HF's reasoning in
his choice of these models and to assess their influence on
his presentation of character, dialogue, the interpolated
stories, and the narrator's function.

There are faults. Goldberg spends time finding continental sources even for commonplaces (e. g. , the motif of
the exchanged twin) while overlooking the importance of such
native models as the English comic drama, Hogarth, and
Pamela. To argue for artistry from an accumulation of
sources may be mechanical anyway, but then to omit essential ingredients from the blend is finally self-defeating.
Goldberg's dogged extradition of both the obvious and the
esoteric from the continent is conveyed in a largely graceless prose style as well.
    Ultimately this book is important more as a reference
tool than as a carefully reasoned and complete argument.
Its detailed index is invaluable in leading the user to the
European sources of JA.
    Reviews: CE, 32 (1971), 817-822; PQ, 49 (1970), 349-
350; RES, n. s. 22 (1971), 89-93.

448   . "Comic Prose Epic or Comic Romance:
       The Argument of the Preface to Joseph Andrews. "   43
       (1964), 193-215.
    A tedious explanation of HF's own explanation of the
form of JA in the Preface to the novel. Goldberg insists
that HF's conception of the new form derives from genuinely
comparative reflection on the other species of fiction available to him and not from a facile a-priori reasoning from
literary doctrine.

449   . "The Interpolated Stories in Joseph Andrews
       or 'The History of the World in General' Satirically
       Revised. " MP, 63 (1966), 295-310.
    Claims that Don Quixote so pervaded HF's thinking
that he bases his interpolated tales in JA on models in Cervantes' novel. Far from slavish imitations, however, they
are ironic inversions of ones in the Spanish work. In "The
Unfortunate Jilt" and "The History of Two Friends, " HF
parodies two of Cervantes' romantic tales by depicting a
sterile courtship and marriage which reduces love to vanity
and passion to domestic bickering. Such parody by contrast
heightens the Joseph-Fanny romance. Likewise, the Wilson
story satirically imitates one in Don Quixote extolling the
literary life. In each of the three interpolated stories HF
flattens the romantic point, turning Cervantes' ideal to
reality, and thereby denigrates the quality of life in his own
society.

450 Gottfried, Leon. "The Odysseyan Form: An Explora-
       tory Essay. " In Essays on European Literature in

Honor of Liselotte Dieckmann. Ed. Peter E. Hohen-
dahl et al. St. Louis: Washington Univ. Press, 1972,
pp. 19-44.
Proposes that HF's "new species of writing" involves
using modern materials in classical forms. Gottfried notes
how JA, Don Quixote, and Huckleberry Finn share structural
parallels with the Odyssey. The structures he cites are
(1) the three-part pattern of flight, adventure, return, (2) the
contrasting central figures undergoing ordeals, (3) the gain
of identity or wisdom by the hero, (4) his change of name
or identity, (5) his passage through a symbolic death, (6) the
rescue of the naked hero, and (7) the transmission of values
from an older or wiser figure to his junior.

451 Harder, Kelsie B. "The Preacher's Seat." TFSB, 23
(1957), 38-39.
Notes the similarity between Parson Adams's being
plunged into the vat of water at the home of the rude squire
(III, 7) and a Perry County, Tennessee prank of the early
1930s, "The Preacher's Seat."
Robert G. Cowser, ibid., 40 (1974), 56, recalls the
same party prank of the 1940s in Northeast Texas, though
there it was called "Meeting the Queen."

452 Hartwig, Robert J. "Pharsamon and Joseph Andrews."
TSLL, 17 (1972), 45-52.
Suggests Marivaux's Pharsamon (1737) as a main technical influence on JA, one ultimately more important than
the details and incidents HF borrowed from the Frenchman's
other novels. Minor likenesses include the avowedly Cer-
vantesian manner, the picaresque structure, and details of
phrasing and character portrayal. But most important is
HF's use of Marivaux's intruding narrator. With it, both
novelists digress to address the reader on character motivation, to offer diverse essays, and to discuss compositional
problems. Moreover, the intruding narrator affords them
opportunity both to satirize affectation by ironic exposure
and to apply moral points directly for the reader.

453 Haslinger, Adolf. "Die Funktion des Stadt-Land-
Themas in Henry Fieldings Tom Jones und Joseph Andrews." NS, 14 (1965), 101-109.

454 Hunter, J. Paul. "Some Contexts for Joseph Andrews"
and "The Conquest of Space: Motion and Pause in
Joseph Andrews and Tom Jones." In his Occasional
Form: Henry Fielding and the Chains of Circumstance.

Baltimore: Johns Hopkins Univ. Press, 1975, pp. 94-
117, 142-165.
See No. 198.

455   Irwin, Michael. "Joseph Andrews. " In his Henry
Fielding: The Tentative Realist. Oxford, England:
Clarendon Press, 1967, pp. 65-83.
See No. 199.

456   Iser, Wolfgang. "The Role of the Reader in Fielding's
Joseph Andrews and Tom Jones. " In his Implied
Reader: Patterns of Communication in Prose Fiction
from Bunyan to Beckett. Baltimore: Johns Hopkins
Univ. Press, 1974, pp. 29-56. Originally pub. in
German, 1972.
Avers that HF's innovation in JA and TJ is his method
of letting the reader produce the meanings of the novels.
E. g. , Iser suggests that by associating JA with the familiar
form of biography and then by diverging from it, HF forces
the reader to recognize the generic ramifications of his
"new species of writing. " Likewise, by his announcement
of human nature as the general subject of TJ, HF allows
the reader to ponder specific character contrasts and thereby to arrive at an understanding of his theme.
Iser's largely epistemological approach argues that the
reader's perception commands the novels' meanings. Yet
he shows also that HF's direct instructions and comments
to the reader prevent too subjective an interpretation.

457   Jacobson, William S. "The Rhetorical Structure of
Fielding's Epic Joseph Andrews. " Diss. Stanford.
DA, 27 (1966), 1057A.

458   Jason, Philip K. "Samuel Jackson Pratt's Unpublished
Comedy of Joseph Andrews. " N&Q, Nov. 1967, pp.
416-418.
Asserts that Pratt's 1778 adaptation of the novel to
the stage is extremely good theater. A comic afterpiece,
the production dramatized some main incidents of Books I
and IV with brilliant alterations of Slipslop, Didapper, and
Lady Booby.

459   Johnson, Maurice. "The Art of Comic Romance:
Joseph Andrews. " In his Fielding's Art of Fiction.
Philadelphia: Univ. of Pennsylvania Press, 1961, pp.
47-60.
Suggests that JA grows from a burlesque to a genuine

romance.   By an overview of the four books, Johnson shows
that the burlesque section, Book I, satirizes Pamela but
also importantly establishes the themes of chastity and charity that are amplified in the "true romance" of the last three
books.   Johnson also explains that HF's art of characterization becomes clear when we realize that the burlesque butts
of Book I have become complex human beings by Book IV.
    See No. 206.

460 _____. "A Comic Mythology: Joseph Andrews."
    In his Fielding's Art of Fiction.   Philadelphia: Univ.
    of Pennsylvania Press, 1961, pp. 73-82.
    Analyzes HF's comic use of two Biblical myths for
thematic purposes.   His association of the title character
with the Old Testament Joseph strengthens Joseph Andrews's
exemplary virtue.   And his linking of Parson Abraham Adams
with the Biblical Abraham allows HF to reveal not a duty-
bound, resigned-to-Providence patriarch, but a compassionate
father.   Though we laugh both at the parodies and at the
other comical treatment of Joseph and Adams, HF reveals
their essential humanity through the trials they undergo.
    See No. 206.

461 _____.   "The Poet and the Player: Joseph An-
    drews." In his Fielding's Art of Fiction.   Philadel-
    phia: Univ. of Pennsylvania Press, 1961, pp. 61-72.
    A careful explanation of the juxtaposed tenth and
eleventh chapters of Book III.   In the tenth, the vain poet
and player discourse on drama, while in the eleventh, the
virtuous Adams and Joseph, pondering Fanny's abduction,
discourse on life.   Adams's preachments on Joseph's inability to accept ill-fortune, like the poet's criticism of
actors' ineptitude, is focussed from an ideal perspective.
By the juxtaposition, HF underlines the discrepancy between "reasonable" codes of conduct and man's psychological
reality, between Adams's doctrine and Joseph's feeling of
grief, between Providence and human nature.
    See No. 206.

462 Johnston, Arthur.   "Fielding, Hearne and Merry-An-
    drews." N&Q, Aug. 1960, pp. 295-297.
    Presents circumstantial evidence that HF's digression
on the "Merry-Andrews" in JA (I, 2) is a hit at verbose
biographical practice, especially that of Thomas Hearne.
The digression is followed by a possible reference (autoko-
pros) to the "hard-word" style of Andrew Borde (d. 1549),
supposed founder of this school of laughing philosophers.

463   Jones, Howard Mumford. "Introduction." In the edi-
       tion, The History of the Adventures of Joseph Andrews
       and of His Friend Mr. Abraham Adams. Modern Li-
       brary College Edition. New York: Random House,
       1950, pp. v-xxii.
    Restates the routine facts about the genesis, influences,
characters, and humor of JA. Interesting, however, is
Jones' allowance that "it would be possible ... to make out
an excellent case for Henry Fielding and the Class Struggle.
On the whole his sympathies are on the side of the dispos-
sessed." Perhaps. But it is also interesting that all of
HF's heroes ultimately become men of property.

464   Jordan, Robert M. "The Limits of Illusion: Faulkner,
       Fielding, and Chaucer." Criticism, 2 (1960), 278-305.
    Suggests that HF purposely separates form from con-
tent in JA to achieve a double illusion: the story of the
narrator--a foolish, naive historian--and the story of Adams,
Joseph, and Fanny. Jordan thinks that HF expects the
reader to perceive the gap between the narrator's truth and
the real truth, apparently to show the illusory nature of
historiography.

465   Karl, Frederick R. "Joseph Andrews." In his Reader's
       Guide to the Eighteenth-Century English Novel. New
       York: Noonday, 1974, pp. 149-161.
    Shows HF puzzling over whether his characters are
satiric butts or human beings and whether he should diminish
or develop them. Ultimately, Karl claims, the novel reveals a twofold resolution. The dialectic between Christianity
and the World supersedes the satiric effect. And the media-
tion between romance and farce produces "dignified picaresque."

466   Kurrelmeyer, W. "A German Version of Joseph An-
       drews." MLN, 33 (1918), 469-471.
    Locates a 1765 German version entitled Fieldings
komischer Roman in vier Theilen. Though the story is un-
altered, characters are renamed and allusions to English
characters redacted. Thus Parson Adams is Noel Moles-
worth; Lawyer Scout is Sachwalter La Mouche, etc.

467   Macallister, Hamilton. "Joseph Andrews: 1. Sources
       and Structure." and "Joseph Andrews: 2. Characters,
       Themes." In his Fielding. New York: Arco, 1971,
       pp. 53-66, 67-85.
       See No. 223.

468   MacAndrew, M. Elizabeth. "Fielding's Use of Names
        in Joseph Andrews. " Names, 16 (1968), 362-370.
        A useful article showing that three classes of names
occur in JA as signals of characterization. Parodic names
from Richardson (Andrews, etc.) and the Bible (Joseph,
Abraham, Barnabas, etc.) deepen thematic resonance. Type-
names sharpen the comedy (Goodwill, Slipslop, Pounce,
Suckbribe, etc.). And "romance" names (Leonora, Bellarmine, etc.) point the satire on contemporary fiction.

469   McCullen, J. T.   "Fielding's Beau Didapper. "   ELN,
        2 (1964), 98-100.
        Notes that Agrippa's Dictionary, probably known to HF,
defines didapper as a water fowl "equivocally produced. "
Thus HF's mockery of Beau Didapper acquires a sharper
point when HF describes him as "no hater of women ... yet
so little subject to lust. " Appropriately, he is motivated by
a desire for self-assertion yet frustrated by his incompetence
with Fanny.

470   McDowell, Alfred. "Fielding's Rendering of Speech in
        Joseph Andrews and Tom Jones. " Lang&S, 6 (1973),
        83-96.
        A rare subject selectively but closely analyzed. Mc-
Dowell explains HF's use of "free indirect speech, " the
lexical, syntactical, and punctuational methods by which he
transforms direct into indirect speech. This essay is important not only because it touches an area of HF's rhetoric
previously unnoticed, but also because it calls into question
the commonplace opposition of HF's forte of "telling" and
Richardson's of "showing. " Throughout McDowell stresses
the dramatic in HF's rendering of speech.

471   Mack, Maynard. "Introduction. " In his edition,
        Joseph Andrews. Rinehart Edition. New York: Holt,
        1948, pp. ii-xxiv. Rpt. in Paulson (No. 239).
        An important essay that defines JA generically as a
comedy (and not a satire) by reference to its static characters and imposed plot. First, Mack explains that Parson
Adams and Lady Booby, because they expose but do not dis-
cover themselves, are essential comic types. And second,
he shows that HF's "calculated tripartite system--country,
road, and city" is essentially a comic form in which HF
can fix, exhibit, and expose a wide range of static characters.

472   Maxwell, J. C.   "Hazlitt and Fielding. " N&Q, Jan.
        1964, p. 25.

Notes Hazlitt's use of a passage praising Adams (IV, 5) in The Spirit of the Age and an 1829 paper of the Edinburgh Review.
Cf. S. R. Swaminathan (ibid., May 1964, p. 180), who notes that Lamb also uses the passage in "The South-Sea House."

473   Oda, Minoru. "Joseph Andrews as a Literary Experiment." Memoirs of Osaka Kyoiku University, 17, ser. 1 (1968), 69-80.

474   Olsen, Flemming. "Notes on the Structure of Joseph Andrews." ES, 50 (1969), 340-351.
Random--and commonplace--notes on the novel's themes, characters, and compositional techniques. This article serves best as a checklist of conventional critical points.

475   Palmer, E. T. "Fielding's Joseph Andrews: A Comic Epic in Prose." ES, 52 (1971), 331-339.
A caution that Latitudinarian doctrine is not the only root of morality in JA. Palmer suggests that HF's conscious conformity to epic and comic conventions helps produce the morality of the novel. Epic conventions, e. g., required the depiction of manners and customs; thus HF's exposure of the hypocrisies of society and the vanity and naiveté of his heroes allows both moral analysis and laughter.

476   Paulson, Ronald. "Models and Paradigms: Joseph Andrews, Hogarth's Good Samaritan, and Fénelon's Télémaque." MLN, 91 (1976), 1186-1207.
A noteworthy assessment of HF's reworking of the Good Samaritan parable popularized by Hogarth in 1737 and of the Telemachus myth popularized by the 1699 translation of Fénelon's Télémaque. By these precedents Paulson explains HF's typological mode of rendering the themes of charity and the search-for-father.

477   _____. "The Pilgrimage and the Family: Structures in the Novels of Fielding and Smollett." In Tobias Smollett: Bicentennial Essays Presented to Lewis M. Knapp. Ed. G. S. Rousseau and P. -G. Boucé. New York: Oxford Univ. Press, 1971, pp. 57-78.
Suggests that by using the family and the journey as structural principles in JA and TJ, HF helps to establish the structure which dominated the English novel into the 19th century. Separated for a time from a complex familial

relationship, the hero makes a spiritual journey to identification and fulfillment.

478   Penner, Allen R.   "Fielding and Cervantes: The Con-
       tribution of Don Quixote to Joseph Andrews and Tom
       Jones. "   Diss. Colorado.   DA, 26 (1966), 6720A.

479   _____.   "Fielding's Adaptation of Cervantes' Knight
       and Squire: The Character of Joseph. "   RLC, 41
       (1967), 508-514.
       Specifies some parallels between the characters of
Cervantes and HF.   Though Adams plays generally the
quixotic idealist to Joseph's realist, Joseph nonetheless embodies much of the Spanish knight: He is the proponent of
male chastity and he is extravagant in his love for Fanny.
Yet Penner claims that, unlike the Don, Joseph is finally
a credible lover.   By the end of the novel, he has changed
from a burlesque of false virtue to "a semi-naturalized
Quixote ... and archetype of the good-natured hero to
emerge again in Tom Jones. "

480   Priestly, J. B.   "Parson Adams. "   In his English
       Comic Characters (1925).   Rpt. New York: Phaeton,
       1972, pp. 91-110.
       An appreciative but unscholarly suggestion that the
humorous qualities of Adams--his absent-mindedness, appearance, pedantry, gullibility, childlike antics, vanity,
etc. --command our love and respect as well as our laughter
because they reveal his vulnerable idealism and humanity.

481   Reid, B. L.   "Utmost Merriment, Strictest Decency:
       Joseph Andrews. "   SR, 75 (1967), 559-584.
       Holds that good will is the chief notion of the novel
and is emblematized in many ways in the plot.   The journey
motif, e. g. , from London mansion to country church, represents a horizontal progression which HF marks by vertical
emblems.   The three kinds of travel on the journey--pedes-
trian, equestrian, and vehicular--are further emblems of
moral distinction.   True good will is close to the earth
(the walking Adams) and is characterized both by proper
joy and proper discipline.   In the final scenes, Adams is
duly decent at the marriage, duly merry at the marriage
feast.

482   Renwick, W. L.   "Comic Epic in Prose. "   E&S, 32
       (1946), 40-43.
       A literal analysis of the 18th-century meaning of HF's

definition to remind us that "comic epic in prose" implies pleasure, realism, serious narrative, and ethical content. Renwick notes that though the doctrine of literary kinds was inescapable for HF, he nevertheless found his power in it.

482a   Richardson, Tony, dir. Joseph Andrews. With Ann-
Margret, Peter Firth, and Jim Dale. Screenplay by
Allan Scott and Chris Bryant. Paramount Pictures,
1977.
Reviews: America, 6 May 1978, p. 366; New Republic,
13 May 1978, p. 27; New York Times, 14 April 1978, Sec.
3, p. 9, col. 2; New Yorker, 24 April 1978, pp. 145-46;
Theatre Crafts, March 1978, pp. 32-34.

483   Schilling, Bernard N. "Fielding's 'Preface' and Joseph
Andrews" and "Slipslop, Lady Booby, and the Ladder
of Dependence." In his Comic Spirit: Boccaccio to
Thomas Mann. Detroit: Wayne State Univ. Press,
1965, pp. 43-70, 71-97.
Explains HF's comic method by showing how Adams
acts as a contrast to vain and hypocritical characters who
are ridiculous. Schilling illustrates the tenets of HF's
Preface by showing how his exposure of affectation in such
characters as Trulliber and Barnabas becomes comic, humane, and moral.
Schilling's next chapter shows how Mrs. Slipslop and
Lady Booby's vanity and hypocrisy mask their utter helpless-
ness. Schilling suggests that HF uses gradations and ladders
as figures for condemning what is artificial.

484   Sherbo, Arthur. "Fielding's Dogs." N&Q, N. S. 17
(1970), 302-303.
Designates Thomas D'Urfey's "Solon's Song" from the
Marriage-Hater Match'd as the source of names for five of
the dogs in Adams's mock-epic battle (III, 6): Jowler,
Ringwood, Rockwood, Thunder, and Wonder. Moreover,
HF constructed two names (Plunder and Blunder), invented
one (Fairmaid), and borrowed one popular canine name
(Caesar).

485   _____. "The 'Moral Basis' of Joseph Andrews."
In his Studies in the Eighteenth-Century English Novel.
East Lansing: Michigan State Univ. Press, 1969, pp.
104-119.
See No. 267.

486   _____. "Naked Innocence in Joseph Andrews." In

his Studies in the Eighteenth-Century English Novel.
East Lansing: Michigan State Univ. Press, 1969, pp.
120-127.
See No. 267.

487   Shesgreen, Sean.   "Joseph Andrews." In his Literary
Portraits in the Novels of Henry Fielding.   DeKalb:
Northern Illinois Univ. Press, 1972, pp. 72-105.
See No. 270.

488   Shipley, John B.   "Ralph, Ellys, Hogarth, and Fielding: The Cabal against Jacopo Amigoni." ECS, 1
(1967), 313-331.
Shows that HF's friends used Ralph's Weekly Register
to attack the current Italian favorite, Amigoni. Yet Amigoni left England in 1739 with wealth and fame.   The ignorant Joseph Andrews' complimentary linking of "Ammyconni,
Paul Varnish, Hannibal Scratchi, or Hogarthi" (III, 6)--names
parroted from dinner talk overheard at the Booby house-
hold--is HF's barbed comment that only Italian artists
amounted to anything, at least in the judgments of boobies
and their footmen.

489   Sokolyansky, Mark G.   "Poetics of Fielding's Comic
Epics." ZAA, 22 (1974), 251-265.
Attempts to illustrate HF's system of novel-writing in
JA and TJ by linking his critical precepts with elements of
his narrative practice.   A worthy attempt, but Sokolyansky
only repeats familiar dicta about HF's use of low people,
realism, generalized character, contrasts, and plot.

490   Spilka, Mark.   "Comic Resolution in Fielding's Joseph
Andrews." CE, 15 (1953), 11-19.
A close examination that shows the night adventures at
Booby Hall to be more than just picaresque antics.   Indeed,
Spilka claims that they yield HF's main theme while revealing the comic mechanism of the novel at large.   "By sending his beloved parson from bed to bed, Fielding has put a
kind of comic blessing on the novel." He resolves the lust-
chastity theme through benevolent humor.

491   [Stead, P. J.]   "The Trial of Mary Blandy." Police
College Magazine, 7 (1963), 433-444.
Identifies Henry Cranstoun as the original of Beau
Didapper.   He became the suitor of Mary Blandy, tried in
1752 for the murder of her father, who opposed the match.

492   Tave, Stuart M.   The Amiable Humorists: A Study in

the Comic Theory and Criticism of the Eighteenth and Early Nineteenth Centuries. Chicago: Univ. of Chicago Press, 1960. See pp. 140-145.

Argues that in his portrait of Parson Adams, HF helps establish the humorous character as lovable but not laughable. HF's usage marks a change from the tradition that employed the innocent as a satiric butt.

493   Taylor, Dick, Jr. "Joseph as Hero in Joseph Andrews." TSE, 7 (1957), 91-109.

A cogent minority opinion that sees Joseph as the hero of the novel because of his growth and maturity. Taylor specifies Joseph's ardour, his common sense, his willingness to argue with Adams (yet his respect for him), his knowledge of the world, his courage, and his sense of balance.

494   Warner, John M. "The Interpolated Narratives in the Fiction of Fielding and Smollett: An Epistemological View." SNNTS, 5 (1973), 271-283.

Suggests that the opposition of the interpolated stories to the main narrative produces an "epistemological uncertainty." Neither inductive nor deductive, HF's theory of knowledge informs his fiction by showing an ironic tension between precept and reality. E. g., Wilson's inductive conclusions about retirement from a world of knavery counter Adams's deductive precepts about the active Christian. But Warner does not attempt to develop his argument in TJ-- where it might apply--or in Amelia.

495   Weinbrot, Howard. "Chastity and Interpolation: Two Aspects of Joseph Andrews." JEGP, 69 (1970), 14-31.

Two random looks at JA, the second cogent, the first not quite. First, Weinbrot suggests that Joseph's chastity is not silly, priggish, or laughable. Instead, it is normative in its prudence, control, self-respect, and virility. Indeed, the women who try to seduce Joseph are dangerous and his rebuff of them is thereby sensible. Lady Booby's attempt would destroy a social order (mistress-servant hierarchy); Mrs. Slipslop's would smack of incest (she is a "bovine mother figure"), and Betty's would endanger health (she is promiscuous and diseased). Weinbrot implies that HF values prudence over passion, which he may, but that is not to say that prudence in some situations is still not laughable. Second, he shows that the interpolated stories-- of Leonora, Wilson, and Leonard and Paul--contrast the comic world of the novel with an unhappy one of violence, loneliness, and separation.

496 Whittuck, Charles. "The Good Man--Human. " In his
    "Good Man" of the XVIIIth Century. London: George
    Allen, 1901, pp. 69-92.
    Suggests that whereas on the Continent the recurring
figure of the good man is philosophical, abstract, and intellectual, in England it is literary, individual, and ethical.
JA is an apt expression of the good man as human rather
than heroic, beneficent rather than wise. Parson Adams's
goodness is defined by his charitable works, his enjoyment
of life, his recognition of future retribution, his loftiness
of aims, and his unworldliness. Yet if his view of life is
simple, it is also strict. He declaims against the theater
and the luxury of the established church and argues for
proper human resignation and submission.

497 Wiesenfarth, Joseph. "'High' People and 'Low' in
    Joseph Andrews: A Study of Structure and Style. "
    CLAJ, 16 (1972-73), 357-365.
    Reworks the obvious in HF's satire on social superior-
ity in JA: that the highest socially are the lowest morally.
Yet Wiesenfarth lays out specific detail to show how the
structure of satiric reversal is strengthened by words that
elevate HF's low people (e. g. , by epic conventions) and re-
duce his characters of fashion and the professions (e. g. , by
animal imagery).

498 Williams, Murial Brittain. "Marriage in the Early
    Novels. " In her Marriage: Fielding's Mirror of
    Morality. University: Univ. of Alabama Press, 1973,
    pp. 43-70.
    See No. 301.

499 Wilner, Arlene Fish. "Henry Fielding and the Uses of
    Language: A Study of Joseph Andrews and Tom Jones. "
    Diss. Columbia. DAI, 37 (1976), 3656A.

500 Wright, Andrew. Henry Fielding: Mask and Feast.
    Berkeley: Univ. of California Press, 1965.
    Various subsections on JA. See No. 304.

VII

JONATHAN WILD

501 Braudy, Leo. "Jonathan Wild: The Varieties of Historical Explanation." In his Narrative Form in History
and Fiction: Hume, Fielding, and Gibbon. Princeton,
N. J.: Princeton Univ. Press, 1970, pp. 121-143.
See No. 143.

502 Digeon, Aurélien. "Jonathan Wild the Great...." In
his Novels of Fielding. London: Routledge, 1925, pp.
96-128. Originally pub. in French. Paris, 1923.
Rpt. in part in Paulson (No. 239).
Explains the vogue of criminal biography in England to
indicate why and how HF parodies the genre. But mainly
Digeon regards JW as a turning point in HF's development.
In it the old HF is present in the cynical irony and satire
on Wild. And concurrently the new HF appears in his
grafting of the novel on the satire, specifically in the story
of Heartfree. Digeon's chapter lays the groundwork for Irwin's expanded study of JW (No. 510).

503 Dircks, Richard J. "The Perils of Heartfree: A So-
ciological Review of Fielding's Adaptation of Dramatic
Convention." TSLL, 8 (1966), 5-13.
Counters general opinion on JW by calling the political
satire centered on the Walpole-Wild identification less important than the social implications of the Heartfree story.
More concerned with depicting the plight of innocent victims
caused by successful criminals, HF adopts techniques of the
popular sentimental drama to focus his criticism. E. g.,
he construes the Wild-Snap relationship as sentimental burlesque, renders Wild and Heartfree as the typical sentimental
villain and idealized merchant, and uses varied sentimental
motifs such as the tortured conscience, repentance, twists
of fate, and plot manipulation.

504 Evans, David L. "The Theme of Liberty in Jonathan
Wild." PLL, 3 (1967), 302-313.

Questions the usual critical notice of the goodness-greatness opposition in JW by suggesting that another polarity controls the book--the tension between moral imprisonment and moral freedom. Evans observes that JW is finally a drama pitting moral anarchy (Wild's "instability") against moral order (Heartfree's "moderation" and acceptance of the law). To refuse the law is to enslave oneself; to accept it is to attain true moral freedom.

505   Farrell, William J. "The Mock-Heroic Form of Jonathan Wild. " MP, 63 (1966), 216-226.
      Suggests that the structural form of the novel is not the criminal biography but rather the mock-heroic and the panegyric. Popular in contemporary satire, the mock form in JW is tantalizingly close to serious topoi in Plutarch's Life of Alexander, viz. , the genealogy, tableaux, character juxtapositions, and evaluative comparison. Further, the panegyric oration as a form associates Wild with "greatness. " Both vehicles help support HF's ethical thought in the novel, that bombast structure complements bombast greatness.

506   Harrison, Bernard. "Jonathan Wild: The Logic of Self-Sufficiency. " In his Henry Fielding's Tom Jones: The Novelist as Moral Philosopher. Sussex, England: Sussex Univ. Press, 1975, pp. 127-138.
      Suggests JW to be an index of HF's "indignant pessimism" about the goodness of men and society that runs even beneath TJ. With no ties to others, Wild disallows himself the motives that spring from such ties--friendship, civic pride, etc. Ultimately his self-interest becomes self-sufficiency with its fruits of loneliness and vacuity, and HF's final vision for a society dominated by such characters is of a terrifying nothingness.

507   Hatfield, Glenn W. "Puffs and Pollitricks: Jonathan Wild and the Political Corruption of Language. " PQ, 46 (1967), 248-267.
      Demonstrates HF's attitudes toward political rhetoric as a corruptive perversion of language. His use of the "great man" phrase in JW is a continuation of political satire he began in the "Puffs" notices of the Champion, an ironic column aimed usually at hitting Walpole and the panegyrics devoted to him.
      See No. 188.

508   Hopkins, Robert H. "Language and Comic Play in Fielding's Jonathan Wild. " Criticism, 8 (1966), 213-228.

An estimate of HF's satire based on dictional patterns
in JW. By ascribing a language of materialism to Wild and
his associates and a language of naive literalism and abstraction to the Heartfrees, HF burlesques bestial criminal
values as well as trite bourgeois prudery. E. g., such words
as ravish, liberty, and jewel are used by each group dif-
ferently and by HF in a third or ironic sense.

509   Irwin, Michael. "Jonathan Wild and A Journey from
       this World to the Next. " In his Henry Fielding: The
       Tentative Realist. Oxford, England: Clarendon Press,
       1967, pp. 41-49.
       See No. 199.

510   Irwin, William Robert. The Making of Jonathan Wild:
       A Study in the Literary Method of Henry Fielding
       (1941). Rpt. Hamden, Conn.: Archon Books, 1966,
       156 pp.

A detailed examination of HF's manufacture of JW from
the biographical, philosophical, and literary forms available
to him. Irwin's first chapter, "Biographical and Historical
Background, " presents the few facts known about the criminal
and then reviews his reputation as recorded in the popular
literature of the day. In much of that ephemeral literature,
Irwin shows, the parallels between Wild the criminal and
Walpole the prime minister were frequent, especially in the
emphasis on their mutual arbitrariness and corruption.
       Chapter II, "The Ethical Problem, " reconstructs the
milieu for the ethical conflict of the book that is sounded in
HF's epigram, "Greatness consists in bringing all means of
mischief on mankind, goodness in removing it from them. "
Essentially, Irwin shows the background to be dual: the
didactic literature of popular morality and the speculative,
learned literature of morality. The contemporary popular
literature usually pitted the "great man" as a statesman,
conqueror, or rogue against the "good man. " In this literature Wild was commonly cited as a "great man. " But Irwin
shows that this popular literature usually emerged from the
learned ethics that debated the essential nature of man, a
debate that featured the Hobbesian-Mandevillian view of man
as selfish against the Latitudinarian doctrine of man as
benevolent.
       Irwin then demonstrates that HF's writings before JW
forecast the morality of his novels. Both in the plays and
in the Champion HF used greatness as a satiric butt and
attacked the mere appearance of honor, wisdom, and piety
in such characters as Lord Place, Col. Promise, and Quidam.

Throughout these writings HF's ideal is good nature, "no more than a simplified, informal, common-sense version of the elaborate doctrine of benevolism." In JW, Heartfree is the moral symbol for goodness as Wild is for greatness. A simplification of the ethical debate opposing unregenerate man and benevolent man, JW is ultimately a popular allegory of this fundamental moral problem.

Irwin's third and final chapter, "Literary Forms and Traditions," specifies HF's use of the prevailing literary modes. He reveals HF parodying the popular Newgate biography in JW's straightforward detail, mock genealogy, shortness, etc. Next, he shows that HF satirizes the rogue story and deepens it with a moral purpose. Irwin also reveals HF's debt to low-life writing in his use of details of atmosphere and setting, minor background characters, and satire on fashionable morals and manners. And last, Irwin specifies the influence of the comic prose epic on JW in its low and unworthy hero and manners, its ludicrous sentiments and diction, its digressions, and its use of the marvelous.

511   "Jonathan Wild." TLS, 14 Aug. 1943, p. 396.
Suggests that because of its crude irony, JW may have been written before 1743.
Cf. Brian Downs, ibid., 11 Sept. 1943, p. 444, who thinks that JW was written not long before 1743.

512   Kishler, Thomas C. "Heartfree's Function in Jonathan Wild." Satire Newsletter, 1 (1964), 32-34.
A reminder that Heartfree's function is not to be a realistic character but rather a counter-symbol to complete HF's ethical contrast of the "great man" (Wild) with the "good man" (Heartfree).

513   Miles, Kathleen. "A Note on Richardson's Response to Fielding's Felon." SNNTS, 1 (1969), 373-374.
Claims that though Richardson did not publicly acknowledge HF's JW, he rejected its thematic distinctions between goodness and greatness by having Clarissa say of herself, "Goodness, I thought, was greatness."

514   Newton, William. "The Poetics of the Rogue-Ruined: An Essay in Formal Analysis." Oklahoma A&M Coll. Bull., 48 (1951), 1-15.
Identifies the genre of the "Rogue-Ruined" with reference to JW, Barry Lyndon, and "Haircut." Newton's interest centers on how the genre provokes the reader's antipathy for the main character. He specifies, e.g., the

motifs of the rogue's progression from petty vice to great
vice, his designs against the innocent, and his remorseless-
ness.

515   Plumb, J. H.   "Henry Fielding and Jonathan Wild."
       In his Men and Places.   London: Cresset, 1963, pp.
       281-287.
       Recalls the main outlines of HF's life and repeats the
usual critical dicta on JW.   Plumb sees HF's own attitudes
honestly infused in his fiction: "Haunted by a sense of life's
injustice ... his work underlined the truth of his attitude
time and time again."   Thus, Plumb notes, HF claims
heroic stature for those characters who remained cheerful
and brave in adversity.   It was his own love of life coupled
with a conventional Christianity and "a philosophy sincerely
stoic" that let him both admire Wild's gusto for living and
criticize Wild's savage instincts.

516   Preston, John.   "The Ironic Mode: A Comparison of
       Jonathan Wild and The Beggar's Opera."   EIC, 16
       (1966), 268-280.
       A subtle and valuable distinction between the irony of
Gay and of HF.   Preston shows that though both authors
share the same theme--the selfish impulse in man--Gay's
irony is structural, HF's, rhetorical.   For Gay, irony is
a way of thinking; for HF, it is a way of speaking.   Both
start by linking high life and low life.   But in JW the irony
of the linking is a verbal trick.   HF simply reverses the
terms of moral judgment and the thief becomes a great hero.
The Beggar's Opera is more complex, for Peachum's "greatness" is revealed in the whole action of the play.   By making virtues ambiguous, Gay's irony threatens our faith in
them.

517   Rawson, C. J.   "Epic vs. History: Jonathan Wild and
       Augustan Mock-Heroic."   In his Henry Fielding and the
       Augustan Ideal under Stress: Nature's Dance of Death
       and Other Studies.   London: Routledge & Kegan Paul,
       1972, pp. 147-170.
       See No. 255.

518   _____.   "Fielding's 'Good' Merchant: The Problem
       of Heartfree in Jonathan Wild (With Comments on Other
       'Good' Characters in Fielding)."   MP, 69 (1972), 292-
       313.
       An intelligent but overlong essay that sees Heartfree
as the novel's main failure.   Rawson suggests that though

HF seems genuinely to want to praise Heartfree, his uncon-
scious humor subverts any such sentimental tribute.   E. g.,
he often presents Heartfree as stuffy and reveals tones of
moral sarcasm and direct ridicule in his presentation.
See No. 255.

519 _____. "The Hero as Clown: Jonathan Wild, Felix
Krull and Others." In Studies in the Eighteenth Cen-
tury. Vol. II (Papers Presented at the Second David
Nichol Smith Memorial Seminar, Canberra, 1970).
Toronto: Univ. of Toronto Press, 1973, pp. 17-52.
See No. 255.

520 _____. "The World of Wild and Ubu." In his Henry
Fielding and the Augustan Ideal under Stress: Nature's
Dance of Death and Other Studies. London: Routledge
& Kegan Paul, 1972, pp. 171-227.
See No. 255.

521 Rinehart, Hollis. "Fielding's Jonathan Wild: Form
and Intention." Diss. Chicago, 1966.

522 _____. "Jonathan Wild and the Cant Dictionary."
PQ, 48 (1969), 220-225.
Suggests that HF used A New Canting Dictionary (1725)
for his underworld lexicon in JW. This use of cant aids
characterization, deflates "greatness," and ironically becomes "true language."

523 Robbins, Alfred F. "Jonathan Wild the Great: Its
Germ." N&Q, 1 Oct. 1910, pp. 261-266.
A dubious speculation that HF may have written an
account of Wild as early as 1725 in two issues of Mist's
Weekly Journal. In them are allusions to Wild as "great,"
an attack upon Walpole, and a promise of a biographical
study of Wild; these elements, Robbins claims, suggest HF's
authorship.

524 Seamon, R. G. "The Rhetorical Pattern of Mock-
Heroic Satire." HAB, 17 (1966), 37-41.
Uses JW as an example in placing mock-heroic satire
on a taxonomic spectrum between comedy and the novel.

525 Shea, Bernard. "Machiavelli and Fielding's Jonathan
Wild." PMLA, 72 (1957), 55-73.
An implausible suggestion that JW is an imitation,
parody, and criticism of Machiavelli. Shea claims that the

Life of Castruccio is HF's model for the biographical sections of JW and that in them HF draws heavily on the Dis-
courses and The Prince for language and ideas, e. g. , the
Nature-Fortune pattern that governs the individual. Moreover (and most improbably), Shea thinks that the "prime
target" of JW's satire is Machiavelli himself. The chief
flaw of this last charge is that Shea establishes neither motive nor means for HF's making an Italian, dead for over
200 years, the butt of his satire.
        Review: PQ, 37 (1958), 328-333.

526   Shesgreen, Sean.   "Cibber in Fielding's Jonathan Wild. "
        AN&Q, Feb. 1974, pp. 88-90.
        Suggests that in the second edition of JW, HF revised
the description and appended a footnote to his picture of the
former soldier/cheat in the Snap household (Book I, 12 and
13) to satirize Colley Cibber and his Apology once again.

527   _____.   "Jonathan Wild. "   In his Literary Portraits
        in the Novels of Henry Fielding.   DeKalb: Northern
        Illinois Univ. Press, 1972, pp. 45-71.
        See No. 270.

528   Smith, Raymond.   "The Ironic Structure of Fielding's
        Jonathan Wild. "   BSUF, 6 (1965), 3-9.
        Sees JW as the 18th-century debate between benevolence
and self-interest: Is the benevolent man the natural prey of
the self-interested man?   HF dramatizes this debate by use
of the classical eiron versus alazon pattern to reveal Heartfree's good nature as finally superior to Wild's selfishness.

529   Smith, Robert A.   "The 'Great Man' Motif in Jonathan
        Wild and The Beggar's Opera. "   CLAJ, 2 (1959), 183-
        184.
        A simplification of the obvious in short form.   Smith
does little more than recall that both HF and Gay criticized
the "Great Man" before noting that "the major characters
are symbols of evil, of mismanagement, of tyrannical rule,
of ambition, and of cruelty. "   Causing puzzlement is Smith's
unsupported claim that HF also satirizes Mrs. Heartfree,
who "symbolized ... universal 'badness. '"

530   Ulanov, Barry.   "Sterne and Fielding: The Allegory
        of Irony. "   In his Sources and Resources: The Literary
        Traditions of Christian Humanism.   Westminster, Md. :
        Newman Press, 1960, pp. 206-277.
        Argues that beneath the cool, consistent irony of JW,
there lies a deep stream of moral indignation.

531   Wells, John Edwin. "Fielding's Political Purpose in
      Jonathan Wild. " PMLA, 28 (1913), 1-55.
      A seminal article that specifies Sir Robert Walpole as
the satiric butt of the book. After a comprehensive massing
of external evidence, Wells analyzes three chapters wholly
political in point and with no other bearing on the story:
Book II, 6; Book III, 9; and Book IV, 3. Still, Wells concludes that JW is not a consistent and unified political satire,
nor does he think HF intended it to be such. Indeed, Wells
sees no evidence of HF's personal feeling against Walpole,
for what HF thought about him was typical of public opinion.
For Wells, Walpole is only an emblem of political baseness
in the novel.

532   Wendt, Allan. "The Moral Allegory of Jonathan Wild. "
      ELH, 24 (1957), 306-320.
      An important article that views Heartfree in terms of
18th-century ethical thought. Wendt contends that in the
moral allegory, both Wild and Heartfree are examples of
unsatisfactory temperament. Like Hoadly, HF regards
passivity as a limitation of good nature and consequently is
critical of Heartfree. Like Shaftesbury, he finds virtue to
be the correct balance of self-interest and benevolence. As
Wild is mainly self-principle and Heartfree mainly benevolence, neither is complete or commendable. In accordance
with general 18th-century belief, HF shows the ultimate justice of the universe: Heartfree's final success is due not
to his own goodness but to Wild's hanging. Heartfree's
benevolence is potentially as harmful to himself and society
as is Wild's self-interest.

533   Williams, Murial Brittain. "Marriage in the Early
      Novels. " In her Marriage: Fielding's Mirror of
      Morality. University: Univ. of Alabama Press, 1973,
      pp. 43-70.
      See No. 301.

TOM JONES

534 Allott, Miriam. "A Note on Fielding's Mr. Square."
MLR, 56 (1961), 69-72.
Challenges the usual identification of Square with
Thomas Chubb (1679-1747), a self-taught Salisbury tallow-
chandler. Instead, Allott suggests that Square's origins lie
in the complexities of the deist-orthodox controversy. Not
only does Square counter Thwackum in this debate, but also
his own deistic arguments embody both Christian and non-
Christian principles. Thus HF warns how easily Christian
rationalist ideas could be appropriated by freethinkers intent
on impugning orthodoxy.

535 Alter, Robert. "The Design of Character" and "The
Architectonic Novel." In his Fielding and the Nature
of the Novel. Cambridge, Mass.: Harvard Univ.
Press, 1968, pp. 61-98, 99-140.
See No. 121.

536 _____. "The Picaroon Domesticated." In his
Rogue's Progress: Studies in the Picaresque Novel.
Cambridge, Mass.: Harvard Univ. Press, 1965, pp.
80-105.
A generalized yet provocative chapter relating TJ to the
picaresque novel. Like it, TJ espouses an ethic of fidelity
to conscience and uses its hero as a touchstone to illustrate
the shortcomings of other characters. But HF's novel is a
redaction of the picaresque in a number of ways: Its hero
is neither narrator nor rogue, its world is neoclassically
ordered, and its purpose is moral. HF had reshaped--
"domesticated"--the picaresque for use in new times.

537 Anderson, Howard. "Answers to the Author of Clarissa: Theme and Narrative Technique in Tom Jones and
Tristram Shandy." PQ, 51 (1972), 859-873.
Argues that HF and Sterne create their narrators in
conscious answer to Richardson's Clarissa. Indeed, the

narrators of HF and Sterne bespeak their authors' common thought on the importance of the shared perspective of reader and narrator in arriving at a true understanding of human experience, the theme of the novels. Clarissa as narrator, on the other hand, is individual and solitary. Throughout TJ, HF's narrator works to establish a mutual dependence of reader and himself (figured in his host-guest, ruler-subject, and fellow-traveller metaphors). Thus HF leads the reader to suspect the reliability of the individual judgment.

538   Arnold, Allen D.   "A Social Ethic in Tom Jones."
      Horizontes, 26 (1971), 53-65.
      A somewhat obvious essay suggesting that though Tom compromises his integrity in the affair with Lady Bellaston, the reader can still esteem him for his freeing himself from her, for his regret of his actions, and for his good deeds and resolutions. Arnold concludes that Tom's redemption reflects the novel's self-contained social ethic--benevolence, integrity, honor, and prudence.

539   Baker, Sheridan.   "Bridget Allworthy: The Creative
      Pressures of Fielding's Plot." PMASAL, 52 (1967),
      345-356.
      A useful explanation of how the plot of TJ generates character. Distinguishing between plot (story) and plotting (storytelling), Baker shows how in Bridget the plot demands a passionate, lonely woman while the plotting necessitates a comic old maid above suspicion. By concealing her plot traits, HF extends the mystery of Tom's mother, while by his plotting he adds to the comedy. Only at the story's end is Bridget revealed as more than a comic type, for then she is seen as a complex woman--loving, love-starved, motherly, and calculating. A hint of the Freudian appears in her earlier relations with Tom: implied incest in her favoritism and sadism in punishing him for the psychic strain he has caused her. By suppressing and lightening evidence in the plotting, HF allows a type to become a person.

540   _____.   "Henry Fielding's Comic Romances."
      PMASAL, 45 (1960), 411-419.
      See No. 416.

541   _____.   "Textual Appendix." In his edition, Tom
      Jones. Norton Critical Edition. New York: Norton,
      1973, pp. 763-768.
      Sketches the textual history of TJ to argue for the fourth edition (published 1749, dated 1750) as the authoritative text.

542   Banerji, H. K. "The Masterpiece." In his Henry
       Fielding: Playwright, Journalist, and Master of the
       Art of Fiction (1929). Rpt. New York: Russell &
       Russell, 1962, pp. 187-215.
       See No. 131.

543   Barnes, John L. "Lady Bellaston: Fielding's Use of
       the Charactonym." South Central Names Institute Pub-
       lications, 1 (1971), 114-116.
       Imagines that Lady Bellaston's name is charactonymic.
Asserting that "bell ass" is central to the name, Barnes concludes that "the noble woman has a large derrière."

544   Battestin, Martin C. "Fielding's Definition of Wisdom:
       Some Functions of Ambiguity and Emblem in Tom
       Jones." ELH, 35 (1968), 188-217. Rpt. in his Provi-
       dence of Wit: Aspects of Form in Augustan Literature
       and the Arts. Oxford, England: Clarendon Press,
       1974, pp. 164-192.
       A brilliant essay showing how HF's ambiguity and em-
blematizing define Wisdom as the novel's chief theme. Seek-
ing wisdom, Tom is exposed to three kinds of ambiguous
prudence--practical wisdom, malevolent cunning, and self-
protective expediency. By presenting complex characterizations of each type, HF provides object lessons for Tom's
final graduation to true Wisdom. He further achieves this
theme by use of the emblem. The scene at Mazard Hill,
e. g., occurring midway in Tom's journey, depicts Tom's
view of his past (the south prospect) and his future (the vast
northward woods) in his quest for Sophia, or true Wisdom.

545   . "General Introduction." In his edition, The
       History of Tom Jones, a Foundling. The Wesleyan
       Edition of the Works of Henry Fielding. Oxford, Eng-
       land: Clarendon Press, 1974, pp. xvii-lxi.
       Presents in full detail the historical facts about the
circumstances, date, and history of publication. Non-critical.

545a   . "Introduction." In his edition, Twentieth-
       Century Interpretations of "Tom Jones." Englewood
       Cliffs, N. J.: Prentice-Hall, 1968, pp. 1-15.
       See No. 133.

546   . "Osborne's Tom Jones: Adapting a Classic."
       VQR, 42 (1966), 378-393.
       A sensitive review of the 1963 film, Tom Jones.
Though Battestin faults the production for not dramatizing
the maturation of Tom and for neglecting the moral basis of

the novel, he lauds it highly as "one of the most imaginative of comic films, a classic in its own right." Focusing on cinematic rhetoric, Battestin shows how Osborne translated HF's fictional techniques to the screen to capture not only the spirit but also the body of the novel as well.

547 _____. "Tom Jones and 'His Egyptian Majesty': Fielding's Parable of Government." PMLA, 82 (1967), 68-77.
Recalls that contemporary sources associated Gypsies with Jacobites. Battestin reads the Gypsy episode of TJ (XII, 11-12) as an emblem of the dangers of absolute monarchy espoused by Jacobites and many Tories. For HF, a Stuart reign was as nostalgic a fantasy as the happy, simple world of the Gypsies. Yet in the winter of 1745 such fantastic political hopes posed as diabolic a danger as the dark night and Gypsy meeting that frightens Partridge.

548 _____. "Tom Jones: The Argument of Design."
In The Augustan Milieu: Essays Presented to Louis A. Landa. Ed. Henry Knight Miller, Eric Rothstein, and G. S. Rousseau. Oxford: Clarendon, 1970, pp. 289-319. Rpt. in his The Providence of Wit: Aspects of Form in Augustan Literature and the Arts. Oxford, England: Clarendon Press, 1974, pp. 141-163.
A source-filled essay contending TJ to be the consummate achievement of the Augustan Age because of its superb design. Battestin sees its design as more than a technique, however. It has symbolic value, for it stands as an artistic analogue to the Design of God in the universe, and the novel's main theme--Providence--stands as cause and effect of the design. The form of TJ is its final triumph; its symmetry of design, its artful contrivance of plot, its intrusive, omniscient narrator, and its final miraculous resolution. Its design, Battestin concludes, is an emblem of HF's coherent and Christian view of life.

549 Bell, Michael. "A Note on Drama and the Novel: Fielding's Contribution." Novel, 3 (1970), 119-128.
A close reading of Tom's proposal to Sophia (XVIII, 12) that analyzes it as a sportive ritual with a debt to Molière, Etheridge, and Congreve. The apparent artificiality of the scene is in fact an implicitly agreed-upon ritual by the lovers to reveal their feelings. Bell suggests that HF's transplanting of the comic ritual from drama to fiction worked its influence on Jane Austen and the novel form in general.

550 Bennett, James O'Donnell. "Fielding's Tom Jones."

In his Much Loved Books: Best Sellers of the Ages.
New York: Liveright, 1927, pp. 236-242.
A piece more useful for a study of antique prose than
for its understanding of HF. Essentially Bennett sees TJ as
a "treasure ... because it is one of the supreme works of
instruction. It helps the man who would understand mankind.... It is more than a gallery. It is a pageant, for
HF's figures hang not flat and lifeless upon a wall, but stride
swearing and storming along, like Squire Western, Falstaff's
heir...." Such impressionism explains the welcome emer-
gence of the New Criticism.

551   Bensly, Edward. "Fielding's 'Tom Jones': Its Geogra-
       phy." N&Q, 10 Oct. 1914, 292-293.
Suggests some parallels for the war prophecy Partridge
speaks of in TJ (VIII, 9).

552   _____. N&Q, 7 Nov. 1914, p. 372.
Asserts that when HF mentions the battle of Tannieres
(TJ, VII, 12), he means what we now call the battle of Mal-
plaquet, 11 Sept. 1709.

553   Bissell, Frederick Olds, Jr. "The Theory of Tom
       Jones." In his Fielding's Theory of the Novel. 1933;
       rpt. New York: Cooper Square, 1969, pp. 38-66.
       See No. 139.

554   Blake, Warren Barton. "Tom Jones in France." SAQ,
       8 (1909), 222-233.
Shows that though the Fielding vogue was great in 18th-
century France, HF's reputation was never as high as Richardson's. Many worthless novels were attributed to HF; besides numerous direct forgeries, works from his sister's
David Simple to Smollett's Roderick Random were called his.
Because few readers took fiction seriously, critical and
scholarly standards were shaky.
       The popularity and superficial imitations of TJ aside,
the effect of the novel was slight. Perhaps French critics
resented its association with the Anglomania then rampant in
France, or perhaps the novel offended Gallic notions of
"form." Perhaps, too, the greatness of TJ defies true
imitation. In any case, HF's influence is hard to trace in
18th-century French fiction.

555   Bliss, Michael. "Fielding's Bill of Fare in Tom
       Jones." ELH, 30 (1963), 236-243.
Shows that in the introductory chapters, HF involves

the reader in the novel's moral universe.   The reader's
identification with the "value universe" of these chapters
"proves the philosophical theme of the novel, which is lo-
cated in and around the concept of mutuality. " As HF establishes his narrator's empathy for Tom, the reader develops an empathy for the narrator for his good heartedness
and likewise for Tom.   Somewhat facile.

556   Bloch, Tuvia.   "Bamfylde-Moore Carew and Fielding's
        King of the Gypsies. "   N&Q, May 1967, pp. 182-183.
        Denies that HF's King of the Gypsies (TJ, XII, 12) is
modeled on Carew's own character in his 1745 autobiography.
Rather, Bloch suggests that it was TJ that exerted an influence on the 1750 edition of the Carew autobiography.
        Cf. Angus M. Fraser, ibid., Nov. 1967, p. 424, who
notes that HF was familiar with Gypsies' broken speech and
would not confuse Gypsies with "maunders" like Carew.

557   Booth, Wayne C.   "Fielding in Tom Jones. "   In his
        Rhetoric of Fiction.   Chicago: Univ. of Chicago Press,
        1961, pp. 215-218.
        The locus classicus of work on the intrusive narrator
or "implied author. "   Booth suggests that the narrator (HF's
dramatic version of himself) fashions an intimacy with the
reader and acts as a chorus to set a wise and comic tone.
But mainly HF produces a harmony between the drama of
Tom's story and that of the narrator's intrusive commentary,
for Tom is always in concert with the most important norms
of the narrator.

558   Bort, Barry D.   "Incest Theme in Tom Jones. "   AN&Q,
        3 (1965), 83-84.
        Holds that Tom's fright at the thought of incest with
his mother is a burlesque of the Oedipus myth.   Oedipus
thought himself innocent but was guilty; Tom thinks himself
guilty, but events prove him innocent.

559   Braudy, Leo.   "Tom Jones: The Narrative Stance. "
        In his Narrative Form in History and Fiction: Hume,
        Fielding, and Gibbon.   Princeton, N. J. :   Princeton
        Univ. Press, 1970, pp. 144-180.
        See No. 143.

560   Brogan, Howard O.   "Fiction and Philosophy in the
        Education of Tom Jones.   Tristram Shandy, and Rich-
        ard Feverel. "   CE, 14 (1952), 144-149.
        Observes that fiction provides a trial run for educa-

tional theory.   E. g. , in TJ, HF offers a critique of Lockean
educational thought.   The novel suggests that character is
determined by parental love and passion as well as by human
associations.   TJ also implies that guidance can orient
character but cannot determine it.

561   Brooks, Douglas.   "Fielding: Tom Jones and Amelia."
      In his Number and Pattern in the Eighteenth-Century
      Novel.   London: Routledge & Kegan Paul, 1973, pp.
      92-122.
      An overly ingenious argument that HF patterned TJ on
an intricate numerological system derived conceptually from
Shaftesburian Platonism.   Brooks also contends that while
Amelia is not constructed on a numerological system, its
narrative symmetries are essential to its artistry.

562   Brophy, Brigid, et al.   "Tom Jones."   In their Fifty
      Works of English and American Literature We Could
      Do Without.   New York: Stein & Day, 1968, pp. 19-
      22.
      The sophomore's Leavis (No. 219).   This is a wry
squib charging the novel with dullness.   Tom is "a tom-cat
of remarkable passivity, " the other characters are "characters only on the sandwich-flag system, " and the narrator, if
vigorous himself, leaves the reader exhausted from his
wordy monologue.

563   C. , A. C.   N&Q, 10 Oct. 1914, p. 293.
      Notes a document speculating the model of Allworthy's
estate to be at Prior Park near Bath.

564   Carroll, John J.   "Henry Fielding and the 'Trunk
      Maker.'"   N&Q, June 1959, p. 213.
      Explains an allusion to the "famous Trunkmaker" in
TJ (IV, 6) by reference to Addison's Spectator.   Paper 235
told of a drama fan who applauded by knocking on the wain-
scot or benches.   Because of his habit, audiences dubbed
him the "trunk-maker in the upper gallery. "

565   Carver, Wayne.   "The Worlds of Tom and Tristram. "
      WHR, 12 (1958), 67-74.
      Impressionistic and uncritical.   Carver ranks Sterne
over HF in realism and comedy.   First, he regards the
world of Tristram Shandy to be more "real, " i. e. , modern,
than that of TJ.   For Carver, HF's world assures us of
its order and stability while Sterne's "quivers with the threat
of annihilation. "   And second, Carver values Sterne's nervous

humor over HF's urbane wit.   He sees TJ as the novel of
a judge,   Tristram Shandy of a dreamer.

566   Cazenave,   Michel.   "A Propos de Tom Jones. "   NRF,
      12 (1964),   891-894.

567   Chandler,   S. B.   "A Shakespeare Quotation in Fielding
      and Manzoni. "   Italica,   41 (1964),   323-325.
      Suggests that in Chapter 7 of I promesi sposi, Manzoni
borrows HF's reference to Julius Caesar in TJ (XV, 3) in
describing Fellamar's "conspiracy" against Sophia.   Chandler
thinks that Manzoni's loan came via an Italian translation of
TJ, in turn based on de la Place's French translation of the
novel.

568   Chesterton,   G. K.   "Tom Jones and Morality. "   In his
      All Things Considered.   New York: John Lane,   1909,
      pp. 259-266.
      A defense of Tom Jones against detractors who call
him immoral.   Chesterton holds that HF depicted a real
young man in Tom, and that, if Tom's practical morality
is bad, HF's theoretical morality is not.   He further suggests that the attacks on Tom's morality grow from the
modern notion that a moral book is about moral people but
claims that in HF's time just the opposite was true.

569   Cleary,   Thomas.   "Jacobitism in Tom Jones: The
      Basis for an Hypothesis. "   PQ,   52 (1973),   238-251.
      An important note on the composition of TJ.   Cleary
suggests that HF may have hastily revised the central books
in light of the threat of the Forty-Five.   First, his introduction of the rebellion is sudden and violates the chronology
established in the first six books.   Moreover, in the first
and last thirds of the novel, characters seem unaware of
the Jacobite threat, even such politically opinionated characters as Western and his sister; the digressive anti-Jacobite
set pieces occur only in the six central books.   Second,
Cleary shows evidence that HF was working simultaneously
on these books and the Jacobite's Journal.   In that organ,
he unfairly equated Country Toryism with Jacobitism, an
equation he works on Western, but only in the novel's central section.   Also, virtually every attack on Jacobitism in
the Jacobite's Journal is thematically paralleled in this
section of TJ.   Cleary concludes that HF probably imposed
the specific historical background of the Jacobite invasion
on these central books during the first half of 1748 while he
was at work on the Jacobite's Journal.

570   Combs, William W.   "The Return to Paradise Hall:
       An Essay on Tom Jones. "   SAQ, 67 (1968), 419-436.
       Confronts the dilemma in TJ of how innocence is to be
maintained while prudence is acquired.   Combs suggests that
HF resolves it by means of the "fortunate fall. "   Tom's expulsion from Paradise Hall at first seems tragic, but he
does return--legitimatized, married, wealthy, and reconciled
with Allworthy.   The model is that of Paradise Lost, a
movement from bliss to misfortune to reconciliation.   At
the end, Fortune's malice is still present--Blifil, Thwackum,
Bellaston--but this partial evil dissolves in the final harmonious vision of Tom and family life.

571   Compton, Neil, ed.   Henry Fielding: "Tom Jones":
       A Casebook.   Casebook Series.   London: Macmillan,
       1970.   272 pp.

572   Crane, R. S.   "The Plot of Tom Jones. "   JGE, 4
       (1950), 112-130.
       A seminal essay that is at once an exposition of plot
in general and of TJ's plot in particular.   Defining plot as
the fusion of action, character, and thought, Crane sees TJ's
plot as one stressing action which effects a change in its
hero's fortune.   Specifically his meticulous analysis shows
how HF's plot attains unity, especially by its "intricate
scheme of probabilities, involving moral choices, mistaken
judgments, and accidents of fortune. "   Throughout the essay
Crane notices the importance of the reader's perception of
reported actions, a perception that becomes an expectation
that HF must fulfill.

573   Cross, Wilbur L.   "The Secret of Tom Jones. "   Book-
       man (New York), 48 (1918), 20-29.
       Detects the prime secret of "the Hamlet of English
fiction" to be "in the manner in which [HF] trained his
imagination to work ... from the individual to the species,
always keeping his mind upon things as they are, and yet
generalizing them to the proper extent. "   In drawing character and setting, e. g. , HF begins with a definite real-life
model but invests it with qualities from other sources.   Thus
people and places in TJ have an actual basis and also a
mythic resonance.

574   DeBlois, Peter.   "Ulysses at Upton: A Consideration
       of the Comic Effect of Fielding's Mock-Heroic Style
       in Tom Jones. "   Thoth, 11 (1971), 3-8.
       Contends that the true comedy of TJ is in our exhilara-

tion as we hear the narrator's elevated language sounded in remarkably prosaic contexts. Indeed, the narrator, laughing at his own delight in mock-heroic diction, becomes the novel's truly comic figure.

575   DeBruyn, John R.   "Tom Jones: A Genealogical Approach, Fielding's Use of Type Characters in Tom Jones." Diss. N. Y. U.   DA, 15 (1955), 1070.

576   de Castro, J. Paul.   "Fieldingiana."   N&Q, 17 June 1916, pp. 483-485.
      Two notes. The first identifies two characters in HF's "To Miss H.... at Bath" as Miss Husband and Thomas Brewster, M. D. A second note identifies "the merriest gentleman in England" (TJ, XVIII, 6) as Odber Knapton, a Lymington lawyer.

577   _____.   "Fielding's Tom Jones."   N&Q, 27 June 1914, pp. 507-508.
      Recalls that in Book VIII, 8, HF writes that the "most vile pettifogger," or pseudo-lawyer, lived in Lidlinch in Somersetshire. But because no Lidlynch is known to exist anywhere but in Dorset, HF may have erred. It may also be possible that as a magistrate he deemed it prudent to veil the personality of the mountebank by misstating his residence to guard against a libel action.

578   _____.   "Fielding's 'Tom Jones': Its Geography."   N&Q, 26 Sept. 1914, p. 253.
      Locates Knoyle (TJ, VIII, 2) in Wiltshire as a village five miles north of Somley Station.

579   _____.   "Gravelot."   N&Q, 1 Feb. 1941, p. 87.
      Notes that "Gravelot" was the professional name of H. F. Bourguignon (1699-1773), illustrator for the French translation of TJ.   The Champion of 15 May 1740 carried an article on his prints.

580   Dickson, Frederic S.   "The Chronology of Tom Jones."   N&Q, 30 May 1914, pp. 425-426.
      Validates HF's chronology and his characters' itinerary after the Upton respite in TJ.

581   _____.   "Errors and Omissions in Tom Jones."   The Library, 3rd series, 9 (1918), 18-26.
      Claims that in such a vast novel as TJ only 14 errors and 10 omissions, all minor, exist. E. g., HF calls the

highwayman Anderson in Book XIII, 8 and then Henderson in
Book XVII, 6. And though he announces Molly's pregnancy
in Book IV, 10, he omits telling of her child anywhere later
in the novel.

582 _____. "Fielding's Tom Jones: Its Geography. "
N&Q, 5 Sept. 1914, pp. 191-192.
Notes that some places named in TJ are inventions,
e. g. , Little Baddington (II, 5) where Partridge lived. Also
questionable are such places as Noyle (VII, 2), the "Red
Lion" (IV, 8), Ox-Cross (VII, 7), and Aldergrove and Wester-
ton (XVIII, 4).

583 Digeon, Aurélien. "La Condamnation de Tom Jones à
Paris." RAA, 4 (1927), 529-531.

584 _____. "Tom Jones." In his Novels of Fielding.
London: Routledge, 1925, pp. 39-90.
See No. 167.

585 Downie, J. A. "Garrick's Hamlet and Tom Jones."
N&Q, Feb. 1978, p. 44.
Recalls that the New Shakespeare edition of Hamlet
(1938, p. lxxviii) noticed that HF changed the sequence of
events of Act III in Garrick's production in TJ.

586 Drew, Elizabeth. "Henry Fielding: Tom Jones." In
her Novel: A Modern Guide to Fifteen English Masterpieces. New York: Norton, 1963, pp. 59-74.
No thesis, but a set of standard comments on random
issues in the novel: HF's benevolence, irony, views of
marriage, use of contrast. Noteworthy is Drew's comment
that the scenes concerning Sophia's pet bird (IV, 3 and 4)
are a compact unit revealing the true characters of the
novel's main figures.

587 Dyson, A. E. "Fielding: Satiric and Comic Irony. "
In his Crazy Fabric: Essays in Irony. London:
Macmillan, 1965, pp. 14-32.
Argues that HF's primary instinct is comic and not
satiric. Too good-humored for satire, HF in TJ "lacks the
misanthropy to carry off the disgust which he must frequently feel to possess. " Consequently, his satiric verbal
irony that is directed at local episodes is finally submerged
by the larger and more gentle situational irony of comedy
which derives from his perception of the incongruous but
realistic juxtaposition of virtue and vice.

588   Eaves, T. C. Duncan. "The Publication of the First
       Translations of Fielding's Tom Jones. " The Library,
       4th Series, 26 (1945), 189-190.
       Notes the French and Dutch translations of the novel
in 1749 and 1750.

589   Ehrenpreis, Irvin. Fielding: Tom Jones. London:
       Edward Arnold, 1964. 78 pp.
       The best introduction to the novel. Five chapters,
sometimes derivative, but always sound. (1) "Author" terms
HF's "obtrusive presence" between story and reader as a
kind of Greek chorus that interprets events. (2) "Story" explains the various designs and paradigms in the novel, the
chronological, spatial, and topical structuring that produces
TJ's highly wrought plot. (3) "Meaning and Form" shows
how HF's planned "externality" (his supposed concern with
the appearance of things) is a device of the stage used to
convey meaning by illustrative events, juxtapositions, and
spectacles. (4) "Doctrine" is a lucid account of HF's moral
imperatives (latitudinarian Christianity and Providence) and
of his negation of Stoicism, enthusiasm, Augustinianism,
and the fashionable code of honor. And (5) "Comedy" insists on HF's hopefulness for man because a human being's
contrary impulses--incongruous and therefore laughable--
are finally compatible. Accordingly, HF's satiric honesty
is often softened by his benevolism. Somewhat counter to
modern critical trends, Ehrenpreis concludes that "Fielding
intends character, rather than language, to be the foundation
of his comedy. "

590   Empson, William. "Tom Jones. " Kenyon Review, 20
       (1958), 217-249.
       An important, wide-ranging defense of the novel. Emp-
son argues that HF preaches a moral doctrine in TJ by the
use of "double irony, " a style little understood by his de-
tractors. This double irony allows the narrator and reader
to feel sympathy for two philosophies at once. E. g. , the
concept of honor in the novel is relativistic, for different
characters offer plausible versions of it. A "mutuality of
impulse" thus defines the moral stance of the novel: "If
good by nature, " Empson writes, "you can imagine other
people's feelings so directly that you have an impulse to
act on them as if they were your own; and this is the source
of your greatest pleasures as well as of your only genuinely
unselfish actions. " HF, then, is anything but neo-classic
and neo-Christian; in his ethic he is humanist, liberal, and
materialistic. Not to feel his double irony is not to understand his relativistic doctrine.

Cf. C. J. Rawson ("Professor Empson's 'Tom Jones,'"
N&Q, Nov. 1959, pp. 400-404), who argues that Empson is
misleading because Empson's ascription of irony to HF
makes him more evasive than assertive. Rawson cites HF's
discussion of love (VI, 1) to show that HF asserts his relativistic doctrine directly--and not ironically.
Review: PQ, 38 (1959), 324-325.

591   Faulkner, Peter. "The Rise of the Novel." In his
       Humanism in the English Novel. New York: Barnes
       & Noble, 1976, pp. 9-41.
Denies TJ full status as a humanist novel because of
the number of significant scenes and statements concerned
with repentance. Faulkner believes that though HF's latitudinarian viewpoint differs from Richardson's view of morality,
it is still too Christian to be called humanism--an ethic that
makes human happiness, regardless of the supernatural, the
central concern.

592   Feil, J. P. "Fielding's Character of Mrs. Whitefield."
       PQ, 39 (1960), 508-510.
Reprints a letter of 1749 which, while praising TJ
generally, criticizes HF's laudatory sketch of Mrs. Whitefield (VIII, 8), sister-in-law of the Methodist preacher,
George Whitefield. As HF had praised her character and
appearance, the letter-writer dismisses the landlady of the
Bell Tavern as an aging coquette.

593   Ferguson, Oliver W. "Partridge's Vile Encomium:
       Fielding and Honest Billy Mills." PQ, 43 (1964), 73-
       78.
Identifies the actor of Claudius as the mediocre William
Mills (XVI, 5). This identification underlines Partridge's
simplemindedness when he faults Garrick's realistic Hamlet
while admiring Mills's inept Claudius: "Who would think by
looking in the king's face, that he had ever committed a
murder?"

594   Fleissner, Robert F. "'Kubla Khan' and Tom Jones:
       An Unnoticed Parallel." N&Q, March 1960, pp. 103-
       105.
Suggests that the description of Allworthy's estate (I,
4) is a probable source for some lines in Coleridge's poem.
A close scrutiny of meaning, sound, and rhythm.

595   Folkenflik, Robert. "Tom Jones, the Gypsies, and
       the Masquerade." UTQ, 44 (1975), 224-237.

An intelligent paradigmatic interpretation correcting
the general opinion that the gypsy episode is digressive.
Holding that "the major polarities of the novel are found in
the opposition of open and closed personalities, " Folkenflik
shows that the gypsy episode (XII, 12) forms a highly artistic
contrast with the masquerade (XIII, 1). The "low" gypsy
society is natural, warm, festive, moral, and open, while
the "high" masquerade society is artificial, cold, calculating,
immoral, and closed. Together, the episodes allow Tom a
wide look at the world and structurally figure his opposition
with Blifil.

596   Forster, E. M.   "The Ivory Tower. "   LM, Dec. 1938,
      pp. 119-130. Rpt. in Atlantic Monthly, Jan. 1939, pp.
      51-58.
An essay on the need for escapism during troubled
times with a noteworthy aside on HF. Because Forster regards HF as an extrovert, he views TJ's prefatory chap-
ters--meditative exercises--as failures. They "make detest-
able reading--horrid little leathern receptacles that lead no-
where and keep us away from the gayety, bustle, and decent
carnality that make up the rest of the novel. "

596a Gide, André.   "Notes for a Preface to Fielding's Tom
      Jones. "   In Fielding: A Collection of Critical Essays.
      Ed. Ronald Paulson.   Twentieth-Century Views.   Engle-
      wood Cliffs, N. J. : Prentice Hall, 1962, pp. 81-83.
A rigorous Protestant view of HF's sense of "spontaneous virtue. "   Gide thinks it "curious that Fielding only chose
to portray pious hypocrites and that true virtue is never
associated with real piety in his novels. "

597   Goldknopf, David.   "The Failure of Plot in Tom Jones. "
      Criticism, 11 (1969), 262-274. Rpt. in slightly dif-
      ferent form in Goldknopf's The Life of the Novel.
      Chicago: Univ. of Chicago Press, 1972, pp. 125-142.
A provocative essay.   Suggests that the callow boy-
meets-loses-finds-girl plot is inadequate to express HF's
neo-classic philosophy.   Moreover, the Augustan values of
balance and reciprocation drain the plot of its tensions.   So
HF comes to the plot's rescue in his own person with authorial commentary that instead only dissipates the plot's energy.
Rather than complementing the plot, these supplements only
point up its weakness.   Indeed, the camaraderie between
HF and his reader "is founded on the shared attitude of con-
descension toward the narrative. "

598   Graham, W. H. "Fielding's Tom Jones." The Con-
       temporary Review, March 1946, pp. 164-168.
       A useless glance at the novel's main characters. Be-
cause of the characters, Graham sees TJ as "social and
domestic history of the eighteenth century presented to us
in true comedy manner. "

599   Greenberg, Bernard L. "Fielding's 'Humane Surgeon.'"
       N&Q, Dec. 1962, pp. 456-457.
       Counters general opinion that the "humane surgeon" of
the Man of the Hill's speech is John Ranby. Greenberg
notes that more probably the allusion is to Etienne Ronjat,
Sergeant-Surgeon to King William III.

600   Guthrie, William B. "The Comic Celebrant of Life in
       Tom Jones." TSL, 19 (1974), 91-105.
       Derives from Wright's study (No. 304) that stresses
the comic over the moralist tendency of the novel. Guthrie
argues that the narrator's festive spirit encourages the
reader to join in a celebration of life by appreciating Tom's
positive and healthy sexuality and thus to suspect Allworthy's
preachments against it. The narrator's tone, Tom's animal
spirits and good-natured concern for his women, and the
novel's conclusion in a scene of weddings, drinking, and
feasting all affirm the joy of living over the lessons of prudence.

601   Haage, Richard. "Charakterzeichnung und Komposition
       in Fieldings Tom Jones in ihrer Beziehung zum
       Drama. " Britannica, 13 (1936), 119-170.

602   Harrison, Bernard. Henry Fielding's Tom Jones: The
       Novelist as Moral Philosopher. Sussex, England:
       Sussex Univ. Press, 1975. 140 pp.
       Argues that TJ advances a sophisticated moral theory.
Harrison refutes the truism that HF is philosophically naive
by setting him within his philosophical context, discriminat-
ing his relationship with it, and showing the novel to be a
dramatically crafted moral statement. E. g. , he shows HF
to be no facile Shaftesburian. In his "goodness of heart"
theory (willful concern for another's good), HF stresses
thought as important; indeed, hasty acts of goodness may
finally be injurious. HF constructs a plot so that Tom will
grow into true goodheartedness; he develops from a purely
goodhearted boy to a man, still goodhearted, but chastened
by sober reflection or prudence.
       Structurally, Harrison views TJ as resting on two

central polarities--the willfully moral mind versus the mind
lacking emotional power to obey moral dictates.   All of the
main characters group about one pole or other, and HF continually illustrates their conduct in terms of these groupings,
e. g. , in the varied perspectives of the characters in the
scene of Blifil's release of Sophia's bird (IV, 3).   This general tension helps integrate the novel and allows the reader
to judge the moral issues raised.
   Harrison also provides useful but difficult chapters on
18th-century philosophy and JW.   An important study.

603   Haslinger, Adolf.   "Die Funktion des Stadt-Land-Themas
      in Henry Fieldings Tom Jones und Joseph Andrews. "
      NS, 14 (1965), 101-109.

604   Hatfield, Glenn W.   "'The Serpent and the Dove':
      'Prudence' in Tom Jones. "   MP, 65 (1967), 17-32.
      See No. 188.

605   Herman, George.   "Fielding Defends Allworthy. "   Iowa
      English Yearbook, 10 (1965), 64-70.
      Counters criticism that faults HF's characterization of
Allworthy.   By an analysis of six situations, Herman shows
Allworthy to be a good neighbor, generous host, good brother,
foster-father, and a charitable, chaste, and devout man besides.   HF justifies Allworthy's ill-judgment of Tom by giving him reason to trust the wrong people.   Moreover, by
stressing Allworthy's relations with others than Tom, HF
sets the two apart and thus gives Allworthy less opportunity
to judge Tom directly.

606   Hilles, Frederick W.   "Art and Artifice in Tom Jones. "
      in Imagined Worlds: Essays on Some English Novels
      and Novelists in Honour of John Butt.   Ed. Maynard
      Mack and Ian Gregor.   London: Methuen, 1968, pp.
      91-110.
      A broadside attack on the criticism that sees the
novel's contrivance as its main flaw.   Indeed, Hilles argues
that because of such contrivance HF keeps us from identifying with his characters.   HF "insists upon our remaining
detached so that we can see clearly.   If we were to become
involved we should no longer have that balanced view of
mankind which the highly symmetrical plot presents to
us. ... "   Hilles sees that HF's appeal is to the literate who
will enjoy the story and appreciate the artifice that focuses
his serious intentions.   Includes a useful diagram of the
plot.

607 Hunter, J. Paul. "Some Models for Tom Jones."
     "The Conquest of Space: Motion and Pause in Joseph
     Andrews and Tom Jones, " and "Occasions Large and
     Small: Symmetry and the Limits of Symmetry in Tom
     Jones. " In his Occasional Form: Henry Fielding and
     the Chains of Circumstance. Baltimore: Johns Hop-
     kins Univ. Press, 1975, pp. 118-141, 142-165, 166-
     191.
     See No. 198.

608 Hutchens, Eleanor Newman. Irony in "Tom Jones."
     University: Univ. of Alabama Press, 1965. 190 pp.
     Mainly a study of the connotative irony that reflects
HF's moral-comic view. Hutchens defines irony as "the
sport of bringing about a conclusion by indicating its opposite. " Her central chapters then discuss HF's mastery of
the two basic methods, substantial irony (achieved through
action, statement, or symbol) and verbal irony (effected by
the choice and arrangement of words).
     "Substance, " Chapter III, is a seemingly exhaustive
catalogue of the larger ironies of TJ, e. g. , ironies of plot,
character, reader's perceptions, and symbols (e. g. , Sophia's
muff as symbolic of both union and disunion). Hutchens's
analysis of the bird adventure (IV, 3 and 4) illustrates the
workings of these various types of substantial irony so that
she labels the episode "Tom Jones in miniature, with all its
ironies concentrated. "
     The remainder of this book consists of Hutchens's dis-
cussion of verbal irony. In Chapter IV, "Denotation, Tone,
and Reference, " she offers a sensitive reading of passages
revealing three types of ironic artistry. First, she illustrates his denotative irony, which simply signifies the opposite of what is really meant (e. g. , Squire Western as wise,
a hag as fair, etc.). Next she discusses HF's tonal irony,
which he achieves by the arrangement of words (e. g. , prosaic phrases following a flowery passage). And last Hutchens
explains HF's use of referential irony, a type by which he
mockingly compares a subject to something more dignified
to emphasize the subject's triviality (e. g. , Aunt Western's
machinations described in terms of high statesmanship).
     The next chapters consider the most polished type of
verbal irony, the connotative. Defining it as "the use of a
word with its literal meaning intact but its connotation strip-
ped away, " Hutchens details the working of connotative irony
on the crucial word prudence. A main theme of the novel,
prudence has both positive and negative connotations. Many
of TJ's characters, Tom excepted, are described as prudent,

but Hutchens shows that HF's implication is that while prudence is desirable, it should not get in the way of more important qualities. E. g. , Blifil's prudence is calculation, Partridge's cowardice, and Sophia's basic caution. Hutchens suggests that HF, by asking the reader to discriminate among such variations, deepens the meaning of the theme of prudence. Chapter VI, "Connotation," reviews the many voices of the novel and HF's use of irony to show the positive and negative alternatives in his moral vision.

Hutchens's final chapter, "Verbal Irony in the Later Comic Novel," argues for HF's influence on Austen, Dickens, and Thackeray. She concludes that by his irony, "the great transition accomplished by HF was the coupling of the technique of the persona with that of the straightforward narrator and expositor in the novel. He taught the writers of English fiction to assume and remove the mask at will. "

609   _____ . "O Attic Shape! The Cornering of Square. "
       In A Provision of Human Nature: Essays on Fielding
       and Others in Honor of Miriam Austin Locke. Ed.
       Donald Kay. University: Univ. of Alabama Press,
       1977, pp. 37-44.
       Suggests that the geometrical design of TJ--its balances,
parallels, and symmetries--is a mock formalism in which
the novel's true spirit of spontaneous, natural, and organic
humanity is housed. Hutchens opines that Square's crouching
to hide in the triangle that is Molly's attic while Tom stands
freely in its center is an apt emblem of the constriction of
systems versus the openness of true humanity. Likewise
she sees Allworthy's Gothic (non neo-classical) estate as an
image of unsystematic and naturally good nature.

610   Huxley, Aldous. "Tragedy and the Whole Truth. " In
       his Music at Night. London: Chatto & Windus, 1931,
       pp. 3-18.
       An allusion to TJ. Huxley suggests that HF portrays
the trite irrelevancies that render his novel life-like or
"Wholly Truthful. " This rendering is impossible in tragedy,
for it can deal only with concentrated and important experience, a limitation that leaves it only "partly truthful. "

611   Imbert, Henri-François. "Stendhal et Tom Jones. "
       RLC, 30 (1956), 351-370.

612   Irwin, Michael. "Tom Jones. " In his Henry Fielding:
       The Tentative Realist. Oxford: Clarendon Press,
       1967, pp. 84-112.
       See No. 199.

613   Iser, Wolfgang. "The Role of the Reader in Fielding's
       Joseph Andrews and Tom Jones. " In his Implied
       Reader: Patterns of Communication in Prose Fiction
       from Bunyan to Beckett. Baltimore: Johns Hopkins
       Univ. Press, 1974, pp. 29-56. Originally pub. in
       German, 1972.
       See No. 456.

614   Iyengar, K. R. Srinvasa. "Fielding's Tom Jones. "
       JUB, 8 (1939), 29-44.
       Directionless and shallow. Iyengar first offers the
standard defense of TJ against the standard charges (immorality, extraneous chapters, etc.). Then he exudes over
the novel's "good story, " expansiveness, and insights before
curiously labeling it a novel of character.

615   Jennings, Edward Morton, III. "Reader-Narrative Re-
       lationships in Tom Jones, Tristram Shandy, and
       Humphrey Clinker. " Diss. Wisconsin. DA, 26 (1965),
       3303-04.

616   Jensen, Gerard E. "Proposals for a Definitive Edition
       of Fielding's Tom Jones. " The Library, 4th series,
       18 (1937), 314-330.
       Holds that the definitive edition of TJ must be based
on the third edition of HF's lifetime, the last of three in
1749. The fourth edition--or last lifetime edition--in 1750
shows evidence that the revisions were not HF's. Such a
claim has been disallowed by more recent editors, who rely
on the fourth edition.

617   Johnson, Maurice. "The Art of the Novel: Tom
       Jones. " In his Fielding's Art of Fiction. Philadelphia:
       Univ. of Pennsylvania Press, 1961, pp. 83-94.
       A useful but uninterpretative list of HF's dicta on the
novel culled from the 18 prefaces of TJ. Johnson locates
15 main prescriptions that he cites under three headings:
qualifications for the novelist, the craft of fiction, and the
art of reading fiction. Concluding that the prefaces have
interest in their own right, Johnson further shows their major importance to be HF's demonstration of the "working
machinery" of TJ and their laying out of the future of the
novel.
       See No. 206.

618   _____. "The Device of Sophia's Muff in Tom
       Jones. " MLN, 74 (1959), 685-690.

Explains that the muff is both functional and symbolic in the novel. Serving to generate incident, it is as much a symbol, construed variously, of Tom's and Sophia's persons. Each kisses it and sleeps with it. When it interferes with Sophia's music for her father, a conflict is set up between love of Tom and love of Western. In these ways, its ten appearances aid the full architecture of the novel.

619 _____. "The Foundling and the Prince: Tom Jones. " In his Fielding's Art of Fiction.   Philadelphia: Univ. of Pennsylvania Press, 1961, pp. 95-106.

Claims that HF associates Tom with Hamlet to deepen the significance of the comic plot. Johnson suggests that if the Garrick performance of Hamlet is an analogue of Tom's story (that of a passionate, unheroic hero haunted by his father's spirit and involved in a disastrous chain of events), then HF invites the reader to consider the moral implications of Tom's situation. Perhaps. But Johnson's invitation to see Blifil as Claudius, Mrs. Waters as Gertrude, Mr. Fitzpatrick as Polonius, Partridge as Horatio, etc. seems a bit far fetched.

See No. 206.

620 _____. "Here the Book Dropt from Her Hand: Tom Jones. " In his Fielding's Art of Fiction.   Philadelphia: Univ. of Pennsylvania Press, 1961, pp. 107-114.

A fanciful reading that suggests parallels between Sophia's state and the story of Thomas Southerne's Fatal Marriage that she reads in Book XV, 5.   When Fellamar attempts his reluctant rape of her, Johnson imagines, she weeps and cries out more for sympathy of the "feigned" suffering of the play's lovers than for her own "real" situation.

See No. 206.

621 _____. "Some Minute Wheels: Tom Jones. "   In his Fielding's Art of Fiction.   Philadelphia: Univ. of Pennsylvania Press, 1961, pp. 115-138.

A selected, obvious, and derivative list of HF's rhetorical and symbolic devices that contribute to the novel's "system of action. " Johnson describes but does not evaluate (1) ironic variations of the prudence theme, (2) the recurrent food-love analogy, (3) a cycle of clothes images, (4) a pattern of "bitch" references, and (5) Sophia's muff.

See No. 206.

622 Kaplan, F.   "Fielding's Novel about Novels: The 'Prefaces' and the 'Plot' of Tom Jones. "   SEL,   13 (1973),   535-549.

Submits that the 18 prefatory chapters maintain their own "plot" whose self-conscious theme is the act of composing the novel. Kaplan traces their development to show that the contradiction between the demands of narrative realism and those of the artifices of TJ (rhetoric, contrivances, idealizations, allegorical trappings, and moral and aesthetic paradigms) are explained by and become part of HF's prefaces.

623   Karl, Frederick R.   "The History of Tom Jones: A
       Foundling. " In his Reader's Guide to the Eighteenth-
       Century English Novel. New York: Noonday, 1974,
       pp. 161-179.
       Lists 14 categories of conflict in TJ, all governed by
the theme of primitive "disorder" versus civilized "order. "
Yet the novel transcends the dialectic in characters such as
Western.   "Disorderly" yet "orderly, " he exemplifies both
the duality and individuality of HF's characters in the novel.

623a   Kearney, Anthony.   "Tom Jones and the Forty-Five. "
       Ariel: A Review of International English Literature,
       4, No. 2 (1973), 68-78.
       Maintains that the novel's themes of imposture and
usurpation partly allegorize the 1745 rebellion.   E. g. , Blifil's
intrigues parallel the Pretender's unholy bid for power, and
Tom, through his good qualities, reveals his true right to
inheritance and figures the Hanoverian right to the crown.

624   Kettle, Arnold.   ["Tom Jones. "]   In Vol. I of his In-
       troduction to the English Novel.   London: Hutchinson,
       1951, pp. 76-81.
       A Marxist reading that sees TJ as a panoramic com-
mentary on England in 1745 with Tom and Sophia as rebels
against a conventional society--with its concern for property
and a "good" marriage--personified in Blifil.   Indeed, Kettle
suggests that Tom comes close to the character of the noble
savage or natural man, his strength being in the "revolu-
tionary assertion of the capacity of human nature to change
itself and the world. "

625   Knight, Charles A.   "Multiple Structures and the Unity
       of Tom Jones. "   Criticism, 14 (1972), 227-242.
       Argues for the coherence of the plot by showing how
events are arranged in the middle third, or "road" section,
of TJ.   Knight identifies four main structures: (1) the
linear pattern of causal sequence (analogous to the geographi-
cal movement of the characters), (2) the non-linear pattern

of causation (hidden causes of events), (3) the symmetrical
pattern of narration (the alternating of Tom and Sophia as
central), and (4) the symmetrical pattern of corresponding
events (arranged around the Upton scene).   Recurrent imagery
(e. g. , eating, clothing, hunting) and allusions (chiefly to epic
and chivalric works) allow further coherence.   Thus Knight
cogently illustrates the fusion of the picaresque (dynamic,
linear movements) and the neo-classical (symmetries) in TJ.

626   Lavin, Henry St. C.   "Rhetoric and Realism in Tom
       Jones. "   The University Review (UKCR),   32 (1965),
       19-25.
       Questions why the three exemplary characters--All-
worthy, Tom, and Sophia--often speak an abstract, allusive,
and Latinate diction.   Such speech may be thought to undermine HF's realism, but Lavin answers that HF's avowed
ethical purpose is responsible because all such speeches
are formal expressions of a moral thought that demands dignity.   Lavin suggests that HF is more interested in recom-
mending goodness that in producing integrated art.

627   Leimbach, Burkhard, and Karl-H. Löschen.   Field-
       ings Tom Jones: Bürger und Aristokrat: Sozialethik
       als Indikator Sozialgeschichtlicher Widersprüche.   Bonn:
       Bouvier Verlag Herbert Grundmann, 1974.   68 pp.

628   Lockwood, Thomas.   "Matter and Reflection in Tom
       Jones. "   ELH, 45 (1978), 226-235.
       Argues that the chief quality of TJ is not the story
but HF's reflection about events in the story.   E. g. , Lockwood suggests that the discovery of Square in Molly's bedchamber is a narrative matter of fact eclipsed in importance
by HF's expatiation and universalizing of it.   The novel is
thus "about" HF's mind.   The effects of Lockwood's article
are significant.   First, it redefines the center of interest
of TJ in its meditative (née "meddling") narrator.   And
second, it further establishes TJ in the 18th-century tradition of indigenous commentary reflected in such diverse
other types as the essay, the meditative-descriptive poem,
and the Shandyan novel.

629   Longhurst, John E.   "Fielding and Swift in Mexico. "
       MLJ, 36 (1952), 186-187.
       Prints the letters of two friars who examined Gulli-
ver's Travels and TJ for the Mexican Inquisition in 1803.
They found both books worthy reading, TJ "having nothing ...
which opposes our holy faith or good customs, " though "it
might be very well that some poison is hidden in it. "

630   Longmire, Samuel E.   "Allworthy and Barrow: The
       Standards of Good Judgment."   TSLL, 13 (1972), 630-
       639.
       Challenges general opinion by regarding Allworthy's
role as an artistic achievement rather than as a difficulty.
Longmire shows that the issues involved in Allworthy's
judging the actions of others may be understood by reference
to Issac Barrow's sermon, "Against Rash Censuring and
Judging."   In it, Barrow says that only the knowledgeable
and reasonable man should pass judgment and that the charitable man is slow to find fault and to accept human fallibil-
ity.   But Barrow also says that the good judge is wary; and
this Allworthy is not, for he is duped by relying more on
imputed motive than on actions.   By the novel's end, however, he develops prudence, judges Tom correctly, and
illustrates a main theme: the standards for right judgment.

631   _____.   "Fielding's Tom Jones."   Expl, 33 (1975),
       Item 52.
       Suggests, on slight evidence, that Partridge is a sexu-
ally virile man and finally a worthy match for Molly.

632   _____.   "Partridge's Ghost Story."   SSF, 11 (1974),
       423-426.
       Contends that Partridge's ludicrous ghost story (VIII,
11) serves two functions.   First, it reveals his character
as a sociable but unreliable storyteller who has suppressed
his own personal misery.   And second, it counters and deflates the Man of the Hill's story, which is neither entertaining nor philosophically sound.   The comic Partridge
serves as a foil to the misanthropic Man of the Hill.

633   Loomis, Roger S.   "Tom Jones and Tom-Mania."   SR,
       27 (1919), 478-495.
       An attack on the cardboard characters of the novel,
its plot (implausible resolutions), its scenery (focus on bump-
kins and not on country), and its ideas (medieval attitudes
toward manorial rights and women).   Because of its ideas,
Loomis calls TJ a favorite of the conservative cult, "The
Tom-Maniacs."   Yet he sees the book as a foreshadowing
of the naturalistic novel, indeed, of Hardy.   Its intention as
realistic fiction and its repudiation of the Aristotelian canons
of poetic justice, of "chance as the antithesis of art," and
of propriety in characterization, all mark it as opposing the
fictional tendencies of its time.   Mrs. Waters and Mrs.
Fitzpatrick, e.g., are creatures bludgeoned by fate, not
unlike Hardy's Tess.

634 Lutwack, Leonard. "Mixed and Uniform Prose Styles in the Novel." JAAC, 18 (1959-1960), 350-357.
Labels HF's style in TJ as "mixed," a blend of three narrative modes. The "plain" style is straightforward and objective and is used mainly for storytelling. The "Homerican" style parodies epic narration for comic effect. And the formal, essayistic style is used to comment on the plot. Such a mixture is ideal for the ironic author who wishes his reader to experience variant attitudes toward his fiction.

635 Lynch, James J. "Structural Techniques in Tom Jones." ZAA, 7 (1959), 5-16.
A useful account of the techniques that produce the novel's architectonic precision. Lynch first reviews three larger techniques of plot division, temporal and spatial verisimilitude, and parallelism. He then discerns HF's use of five smaller techniques: the planned reappearance, the undisclosed motive, the blurred consequence, the minute cause, and the alternative interpretation. As the larger elements establish an ordering of narration, the smaller ones establish tight causal relationships.

636 Macallister, Hamilton. "Tom Jones: 1. General Outline, Structure" and "Tom Jones: 2. Characters, Themes." In his Fielding. New York: Arco, 1971, pp. 86-96, 97-122.
See No. 223.

637 McDowell, Alfred. "Fielding's Rendering of Speech in Joseph Andrews and Tom Jones." Lang&S, 6 (1973), 83-96.
See No. 470.

638 McKenzie, Alan T. "The Processes of Discovery in Tom Jones." DR (1974-75), 720-740.
Sees "discovery" as central to the novel and important to every character in it. McKenzie examines some of the several hundred passages in which discovery appears. He classifies the discoverers as manipulative (e.g., Blifil and Honour), instinctual (Tom, Western), and suspicious (Aunt Western, Mrs. Wilkins, Thwackum). Throughout, Lawyer Dowling appears to ask the reader to make discoveries of his own, and HF as narrator regulates many discoveries by "Providence." As a theme, discovery's references to inventiveness, disclosure, and exposure serve HF's narrative and satiric aims.

639   McKillop, Alan D. "An Iconographic Poem on Tom
       Jones." PQ, 17 (1938), 403-406.
       A note on a 1749 poem, The Fan, based on the "advice
to a painter" formula. Fashionable fans were ornamented
with scenes from popular writings, and this poem tenders
advice to the painter of such a fan by suggesting details of
the bird episode, Molly's bedchamber scene, Allworthy's
judgment scene, etc.

640   _____. "Some Recent Views of Tom Jones." CE,
       21 (1959), 17-22.
       Reviews the common concerns of recent criticism of
TJ. This criticism examines the novel's unity, stresses
HF's epic usage, his comic presentation, the plot, and the
self-conscious narrator. McKillop synthesizes the sometimes discordant criticism by suggesting that the novel is
ultimately unified by the comic--and beneficient--tone of its
narrator.

641   Malone, Kemp. "Fielding's Tom Jones." In Literary
       Masterpieces of the Western World. Ed. Francis H.
       Horn. Baltimore: Johns Hopkins Univ. Press, 1953,
       pp. 242-255.
       A disjunct discussion that repeats random clichés about
TJ. Malone also compares HF with Chaucer in that both
are more amused than indignant in their satire.

642   Mandel, Jerome. "The Man of the Hill and Mrs. Fitz-
       patrick: Character and Narrative Technique in Tom
       Jones." PLL, 5 (1969), 26-38.
       Suggests that the tales of these characters include paral-
lels with Tom's and Sophia's situations. Mandel also shows
that the Man of the Hill constructs his narrative by logic
while Mrs. Fitzpatrick fashions hers by digression. In their
narrative techniques, Mandel concludes that HF consciously
parodies two traits of his own style.

643   Maugham, W. Somerset. "The Ten Best Novels: Tom
       Jones." Atlantic Monthly, Dec. 1947, pp. 120-126.
       An error-flecked review of HF's life and a praise of
TJ's gusto, style, story, and basic morality. But Maugham
objects to the introductory essays because they impede the
story and to HF's conversational manner because it hinders
involvement in the story.

644   Meredith, Robert C. "Henry Fielding and the Idea of
       Benevolence: A Study of the Structure of Tom Jones."
       Diss. Wisconsin, 1955.

645 Milburn, D. Judson. "The Psychology of Wit in Henry
     Fielding's Tom Jones and Laurence Sterne's Tristram
     Shandy." In his Age of Wit, 1650-1750. New York,
     Macmillan, 1966, pp. 106-119.
     A superficial glance at HF's ideas about the creative
process in TJ. Milburn claims that he reacts against wit
and fancy (frivolous and wanton powers of imagination). In
their place he posits "genius" and "invention" (powers of
mental penetration) that form judgment, the primary faculty
of the creative process in the novel. Milburn illustrates
HF's judgment only by noting the structural symmetry of TJ.

646 Miller, Henry Knight. "The 'Digressive' Tales in
     Fielding's Tom Jones and the Perspective of Romance."
     PQ, 54 (1975), 258-274.
     Suggests that the tales of the Man of the Hill and Mrs.
Fitzpatrick are not digressive, for they present to Tom and
Sophia very real temptations: to doubt others and to attri-
bute all to fortune. Both tales imply also "that maturity
is not worth the achieving." Thus they represent obstacles,
such as those encountered in the romance tradition, to the
rite de passage to maturity.

647 _____ . Henry Fielding's "Tom Jones" and the Ro-
     mance Tradition. English Literary Studies Monograph
     Series, No. 6. Victoria, B. C.: Univ. of Victoria
     Press, 1976. 112 pp.
     An enlightened warning that judgments about TJ based
on modern concepts of realism and the novel can distort understanding of HF's achievement. Indeed, Miller argues,
"it cannot be adequately interpreted--or 'decoded'--unless
the conventions of romance are imaginatively comprehended."
If this is overly insistent, there still is no better sustained
corrective of the "realistic" criticism of TJ than Miller's
study. Yet it is not negative, for it propounds its own
positive thesis: that HF's book is a romance in all its
major elements. Miller devotes five chapters to an analysis of these elements.
     "Mythos" specifies the controlling plot of TJ as the
archetypal pattern of Exile, Initiation, and Return (or Fall,
Suffering, and Salvation). Values within this pattern are
focused by carefully juxtaposed events, themes, and characters (e. g., the positive lovers, the negative Blifil, and the
wavering senex figures of Allworthy and Western). In "Time
and Place" Miller shows that, as in the romance, time in
TJ is not "evolutionary." Instead, Tom's movement from
youth to maturity is marked by settings that mirror his

moral situation at each stage of that movement (e. g. , in
the bushes with Molly, at Upton Inn, in the Gatehouse).
"People" demonstrates that HF's view of character is typological. Moral and social values represented by the characters are more important than individual motives; thus
characters do not develop in the "realistic" sense, though
a process of moral education does occur with a radical conversion common to romances. In "Ethos" Miller designates
the force of the didactic and allegorical in TJ and the romance tradition to show that the image of a providential
universe dominates the book's meaning. And in "Logos"
Miller notices HF's use of stylistic devices of the romances
in TJ (e. g. , the dominant narrator and his easy, elegant
language). Miller's is an elegant and important piece of
scholarship.

648 _____. "Some Functions of Rhetoric in Tom Jones. "
    PQ, 45 (1966), 209-235.
    Explains the dominant rhetorical devices. Miller shows
that throughout the novel, the narrator and the characters
argue, exhort, praise, dispraise, and judge. The techniques the characters use aim to persuade on many scores,
but it is the narrator who persuades his reader that the
world is ultimately ordered and harmonious.

649 _____. "The Voices of Henry Fielding: Style in
    Tom Jones. " In The Augustan Milieu: Essays Pre-
    sented to Louis A. Landa. Ed. Henry Knight Miller,
    Eric Rothstein, G. S. Rousseau. Oxford, England:
    Clarendon Press, 1970, pp. 262-288.
    A brilliant commentary on HF as a character in TJ
by a subtle discrimination of his many voices. Miller
specifies the voices of humor, of poetical and moral eleva-
tion, of Homeric epic, of medical, legal, and hunting jar-
gons, and of his "hypothetical reader, " the Institutional
Moralist and the Impressionable Young Lady (the skeptic
and the sentimentalist).

650 Miller, Susan. "Eighteenth-Century Play and the Game
    of Tom Jones. " In A Provision of Human Nature:
    Essays on Fielding and Others in Honor of Miriam
    Austin Locke. Ed. Donald Kay. University: Univ.
    of Alabama Press, 1977, pp. 83-93.
    Regards TJ in view of recreational theory. Miller
reviews 18th-century preindustrial recreational activities
and attitudes and then shows how the novel's plot, characters, setting, and narration bear traits of actual or meta-

phoric games.   E. g. ,   Miller suggests that HF uses games
(poaching,   storytelling,   hide-and-seek at Upton,   masquerade,
play-going,   etc.) to define Tom's development.   And she
concludes that the novel itself is a game for HF's readers,
for he demands that they "play" TJ to find a solution to its
puzzle and an awareness of themselves.

651   Mitani,   Norio.   "The Narrator in Tom Jones. "   SELit,
       49 (1973),   185-198.   [In Japanese.]
The English synopsis relates that the article shows
how HF's narrator manipulates the reader into accepting his
views of causality and morality.

652   Mundy,   P. D.   "Fielding's Tom Jones. "   N&Q,   28
       Dec. 1935,   p.   456.
Includes a 1749 letter of Joseph Spence in which he
notes that 2500 copies of TJ were sold before it was published,   "an unheard-of case. "   Spence notes also that HF
sold the copy for £100 each volume "and might probably
have got five times as much by it,   had he kept the right
in his own hands. "

653   Murray,   Peter B.   "Summer,   Winter,   Spring,   and
       Autumn in Tom Jones. "   MLN,   76 (1961),   324-326.
A strained argument that HF clarifies some characters' relationships with one another by associating them
with the seasons.   Tom's father is summer,   Bridget Allworthy winter,   Tom and Sophia spring,   and Lady Bellaston
autumn.

654   Murry,   J. Middleton.   "In Defense of Fielding. "   In
       his Unprofessional Essays.   London: Jonathan Cape,
       1956,   pp.   25-39.
Rejects the criticism that sees TJ as "low" by showing that,   quite the contrary,   the novel is founded on a
philosophy of good nature,   characterized by a sympathy and
generosity toward others and exhibited by Tom.   Even the
"sexual ethic" in the novel is part of this moral philosophy,
for it is as much Tom's idealism about women as his appe-
tite that leads him into three entanglements,   none of which
he initiates.

655   Nassar,   Eugene Paul.   "Complex Irony in Tom Jones. "
       In his Rape of Cinderella: Essays in Literary Con-
       tinuity.   Bloomington: Indiana Univ. Press,   1970,   pp.
       71-84.
One of the best explanations of HF's irony.   Nassar

argues that "the continuity of the book is in the drama of irresolution" fostered by the narrator as he views his characters both sentimentally and skeptically.   HF regards Bridget as good-natured yet prudishly hypocritical, Western as loving yet egotistical, Mrs. Fitzpatrick as an injured wife but an intriguing adulteress.   HF even regards himself as narrator as dull but witty.   Such ironies reveal a dualism in HF's mind and a consequent irresolution mirrored in his shifts between sentimental and skeptical tones.

655a   Osborne, John.   Tom Jones: A Film Script.   New
      York: Grove, 1964.

656   Palmer, E. Taiwo.   "Fielding's Tom Jones Recon-
      sidered. "   English, 20 (1971), 45-50.
      More a useful review of the Christian reading than a reconsideration.   Palmer sees the heart of the novel in the Genesis myth, i. e. , in Tom's banishment from both Paradise Hall and the deus-figure, Allworthy.   In spite of the devil (Blifil) and the temptress (Molly), Tom's fall is his own doing, brought about by his "basic lustfulness. "   Palmer traces Tom's fall from grace and his subsequent reformation and redemption to reaffirm "the Christian hope of pardon and eventual victory over the forces of evil. "

657 _____ .   "Irony in Tom Jones. "   MLR, 66 (1971),
      497-510.
      Little new here.   Palmer's review specifies five types of irony but fails to distinguish all of them clearly: (1) "praise/blame inversion, " (2) tonal irony, (3) linguistic irony, (4) rhetorical irony, and (5) double irony.

658   Park, William.   "Tom and Oedipus. "   HSL, 7 (1975),
      207-215.
      Argues that a pervasive incest theme figures importantly in Tom's attaining wisdom and in HF's comic patterning of the novel.   Park lists numerous examples--some strained-- of Tom's sexual (and figurative) relationships with mother-figures and of his "hostile" behavior toward father-figures. In the sexual ambience of the novel, Tom is an Oedipus figure who, when faced with the horror of his having committed incest, assumes responsibility for his behavior and thus attains prudence and wisdom.   HF's exorcising of this horror by the turn of events approaches a comic catharsis.

659   Parker, A. A.   "Fielding and the Structure of Don
      Quixote. "   BHS, 33 (1956), 1-16.

Contrasts Don Quixote and TJ on grounds of technical
unity to find Cervantes' novel superior. Cervantes builds a
close pattern of cause and effect between the episodes and
the moral rise and fall of Don Quixote. But HF, intent on
observing the fixed neo-classic epic precepts, achieves only
external symmetry because he allows no causal connection
between Tom's moral conduct and his social fortunes: "On
the plane of cause and effect which binds the incidents together, Tom's fall from favour would have happened just the
same if he had been a wholly virtuous young man, and his
restoration to favour would have happened just the same if
he had remained a scapegrace."

660 Passler, Susan Miller. "Coleridge, Fielding, and Ar-
     thur Murphy." The Wordsworth Circle, 5 (1974), 55-
     58.
     Suggests that Coleridge owes a twofold debt to Arthur
Murphy's Life of Fielding (1762). First, Passler claims
Murphy's influence on Coleridge's criticism of TJ. Both
men praise HF's descriptive powers, his portrayal of characters in action, his plot (in terms of moving water), and his
overall talents (in terms of warmth and sunlight). (Passler
also claims Murphy to be a source for Coleridge's distinctions between the primary and secondary imagination.) And
second, Passler isolates a passage in Murphy's Life--itself
derived from HF's description of Allworthy's estate--that
she calls the source of Coleridge's underground river in
"Kubla Khan." The phrasings are remarkably similar.

661 _____. "Theatricality, the Eighteenth Century and
     Fielding's Tom Jones." Diss. North Carolina at
     Chapel Hill. DAI, 32 (1972), 6941A.

662 Paulson, Ronald, "Fielding in Tom Jones: The His-
     torian, the Poet, and the Mythologist." In Augustan
     Worlds: Essays in Honour of A. R. Humphreys. Ed.
     J. C. Hilson, et al. Leicester: Leicester Univ.
     Press, 1977, pp. 175-187.
     An interesting speculation that TJ is based on the his-
torical nexus of the Rebellion of '45. Paulson recalls that
as rumor and myth passed for truth in an England under
Scottish threat, so rumor dominates opinion about Tom in
the novel. Indeed, Paulson regards "false history" to be
a subject of the book. He wonders, moreover, if Tom re-
minded 1749 readers of Prince Charles Edward, for both
heroes are exiles wandering to find their true homes.

663 Poirier, Roger. "Tom Jones." In his La Bibliothèque

universelle des romans.   Geneva: Librarie Droz,
1977, pp. 83-89.

664   Poovey, Mary.   "Journeys from This World to the
        Next: The Providential Promise in Clarissa and Tom
        Jones. "   ELH, 43 (1976), 300-315.
        Contends that HF suggests providential design in meta-
phors that reflect spiritual states.   E. g. , HF intimates that
Tom's prison is a spiritual dungeon and that his winning of
Sophia (or wisdom) is the fulfillment of the promise of
Providence.

665   Powers, Lyall H.   "Tom Jones and Jacob de la Vallée. "
        PMASAL, 47 (1962), 659-667.
        Cites Marivaux's Le Payson parvenu (1735) as the basic
pattern for TJ by noting various parallels: the picaresque
form, the benevolent and humanistic themes, and the digressions that comment on the main fable.   Powers observes
likenesses between Jacob and Tom as well.   Both have
"noble savage" traits; both are attractive to women; and
both follow similar careers.   Yet for all the likeness, HF's
novel transcends the education sentimentale type, for his
course is a pursuit of wisdom.

666   Preston, John.   "Tom Jones (i):   Plot as Irony, "
        "Tom Jones (ii):   The Pursuit of True Judgment. "   In
        his Created Self: The Reader's Role in Eighteenth-
        Century Fiction.   London: Heinemann, 1970, pp. 94-
        132.
        Defines the "created self" as "the reader invented by
the author in order to make his fictional world work" and
suggests that HF tries to change his reader's way of perceiving.   By broadening the reader's viewpoint to let him
validate a number of subjective judgments, HF makes his
plot "a vehicle for what is self-contradictory, what is emo-
tionally as well as intellectually confusing in human experience. "   Preston thinks the subject of TJ, then, to be the
reader's judgment; its plot is more epistemological than
moral.   A bit overstated.

667   Price, John Valdimir.   "Sex and the Foundling Boy:
        The Problem in Tom Jones. "   REL, 8 (1967), 45-52.
        Claims that Tom's sexual adventures were regarded by
both HF and his age as guiltless.   In a century that quibbled
little about a double standard (Richardson notwithstanding),
Tom's behavior is typical.   Moreover, the philosophical
stress by Locke and Hume on the goodness of the passions

provides an intellectual context accommodating that behavior.
And finally, because Tom is never the seducer, his actions
are further mitigated. Throughout, Price suggests, HF's
irony is pointed to defend Tom's actions.

668   Randall, David A. , and John T. Winterich. "One
       Hundred Good Novels. " Publishers' Weekly, 21 March
       1942, pp. 1200-1202.
       Collations by Randall of title pages of TJ's first edi-
tion and sparse textual notes by Winterich.

669   Rawson, C. J. "Tom Jones and Michael: A Parallel. "
       N&Q, Jan. 1967, p. 13.
       Notes a textual relationship between TJ (VIII, 2) and
Wordsworth's Michael (vv. 448-450) on the strength of love.

670   Rexroth, Kenneth. "Tom Jones. " Saturday Review,
       1 July 1967, p. 13.
       A disjointed piece of metaphorized generality. Rex-
roth calls TJ a realistic Märchen, terms its characteristics
"Chinese" (decorum, lectures on good nature), and sees
Tom's likeness to Moses in the Bullrushes, Huck Finn, and
Thomas Jefferson. Still, such curiosities do not divert
Rexroth from uttering the obvious: that the minor charac-
ters are stereotypes, that Tom is not, that the thesis is
Tom's humanity, that HF intrudes into his story and de-
fines a gentleman in it.

670a   Richardson, Tony, dir. Tom Jones. With Albert
       Finney, Susannah York, and Hugh Griffith. Screen-
       play by John Osborne. United Artists, 1962.
       Winner of Academy Awards for best motion picture
and best direction of 1963.
       Reviews: America, 2 Nov. 1963, p. 532; Common-
weal, 25 Oct. 1963, p. 141; Esquire, Feb. 1964, p. 32;
Nation, 30 Nov. 1963, p. 374; National Rev. (New York),
25 Feb. 1964, p. 165; New Republic, 19 Oct. 1963, pp. 27-
28; New Yorker, 7 Sept. 1963, p. 98 and 12 Oct. 1963, pp.
169-70; Saturday Rev. , 5 Oct. 1963, p. 52; VQR, 42 (1966),
378-93.

671   Robert, Frédéric. "Tom Jones. De Fielding à
       Philidor. " In Roman et lumières au XVIIIe siècle.
       Colloque. Paris: Editions Sociales, 1970, pp. 360-
       365.

672   Robinson, Roger. "Henry Fielding and the English

Rococo. " In Studies in the Eighteenth Century II, ed.
R. F. Brissenden. Toronto: Univ. of Toronto Press,
1973, pp. 93-111.
An ingenious look at HF's discursive style that produces
a literary rococo.   Besides the lavish texture of calculated
digressiveness, Robinson points to HF's development of
themes (that of merciful judgment) as tendrils off the main
Tom-Sophia narrative that eventually wind back into it.   Likewise, his putting a story within a story (the Old Man of the
Hill) and of accumulating analogical imagery about an incident (rutting animals about Tom and Molly) are not peripheral
embellishments but are part of a definite pattern.   Such
copious detail finally produces an exuberant unity that can be
called Augustan rococo.

673   Roddelston, J. D.   "Revivals of Fielding's Plays. "
      N&Q, 25 Jan. 1941, p. 70.
Recalls the staging of Sophia, an adaptation from TJ,
at one of the Strand theaters in the 1880s.

674   Roscoe, Adrian A.   "Fielding and the Problem of All-
      worthy. "   TSLL, 7 (1965), 169-172.
Argues oversimply that HF's aim is to show Allworthy
as a blunderer to expose the shortcomings of his social
world, especially its legal system.   This claim rests only
on Allworthy's judgment of Partridge (II, 6), in which the
squire both prejudges him and admits Mrs. Partridge's testimony against her husband, an admittance contrary to pro-
cedural law.   Yet Roscoe concludes that if Allworthy is not
admirable, he is "a good man in a particularly bad system ...
which makes landlords like Allworthy and Western into small
kings. ... "

675   Rothschild, Nathaniel Mayer Victor, comp.   The His-
      tory of Tom Jones, A Changeling.   Cambridge, Eng-
      land: Lord Rothschild, 1951.   160 pp.
Contains the summons, complaint, response, and court
transcripts in a lawsuit brought by Lord Rothschild in 1942
against a rare book dealer.   Rothschild alleged that the New
York dealer had sold him a faked first edition of TJ (with
some Pope mss.) for £3500 in 1937.   The suit for £1650
($8, 151) in damages was settled out-of-court.

676   Roy, G. Ross.   "French Stage Adaptations of Tom
      Jones. "   RLC, 44 (1970), 82-94.
Cites the main French stage adaptations of TJ.   The
most important were Poinsinet's musical version, Tom

Jones (1765) and Desforges's Tom Jones à Londres (1782),
a five-act comedy, and its sequel, Tom Jones et Fellamar
(1787). Rage for the novel was so great that interest in
its author called forth Le Portrait de Fielding and Fielding,
one-act plays of 1800 and 1823 respectively.

677   Rundus, Raymond J. "The History of Tom Jones in
      Adaptation." Diss. Nebraska. DA, 30 (1969), 1535A.

678 _____. "Tom Jones in Adaptation: A Chronology
and Criticism." BNYPL, 77 (1974), 329-341.
    Evaluates 17 authenticated adaptations and cites a dozen
unauthenticated adaptations of TJ from 1761 to 1963.

679   Ruthven, K. K. "Fielding, Square, and the Fitness
      of Things." ECS, 5 (1971), 243-255.
    Extends Allott's idea (No. 534) that the Latitudinarian
divine Samuel Clarke is the original of Square. Ruthven
suggests that HF satirizes the deistic strain in Clarke by
parodying his use of cant rationalistic phrases, especially
the mathematics-morality analogy to assert the "fitness of
things." The tableau of Tom's discovery of Square in
Molly's bedchamber satirizes Square's "unfitness." Yet "although Clarke's ineptitudes are caricatured in Square, the
bulk of the novel corroborates Clarke's rational supernatural-
ism."

680   Schneider, Daniel J. "Sources of Comic Pleasure in
      Tom Jones." ConnR, 1 (1967), 51-65.
    Argues that the novel's comedy springs from the clash
between the principles of Life-Affirmation and Life-Denial.
E. g., the essentially charitable and out-going characters of
Tom and Sophia are checked at every point by Property and
Propriety. Schneider notes that even HF's narrator revels
in the exuberance of his own style, which produces self-conscious pleasure. Factual errors and neglect of the favorable
qualities of prudence in TJ weaken the impact of Schneider's
essay.

681   Schonhorn, Manuel. "Fielding's Digressive-Parodic
      Artistry: Tom Jones and the Man of the Hill." TSLL,
      10 (1968), 207-214.
    Argues that the Man of the Hill digression is important
to an appreciation of HF's achievement for three reasons.
It parodies the Wilson episode of JA (by surprising the expectations of the reader of both novels); it forms the structural and philosophic center of the novel (by comparing Tom

and the Old Man on specific themes); and it illustrates HF's use of epic convention to control picaresque looseness (by its parody of Aeneas' descent to the underworld) at the midpoint of TJ.

682 _____. "Heroic Allusion in Tom Jones: Hamlet and the Temptations of Christ." SNNTS, 6 (1974), 218-227.
An imaginative suggestion that Tom gains mythic significance by embodying traits of both Hamlet and Christ. The 18th-century critical and dramatic view of Hamlet (Tom watches Garrick's production in Book XVI) stressed the Prince's filial piety as essential to his character. And Tom's concern for Black George, Allworthy, Partridge, and Summer, each a sort of father to Tom, shows this same virtue. Moreover, Tom has Christlike associations not only in his 40 days in the wilderness beyond Paradise Hall, but also in his experiencing the three temptations of Jesus: the flesh (Molly), the world (Mrs. Waters), and the devil (Lady Bellaston).

683 Shaw, E. P. "A Note on the Temporary Suppression of Tom Jones in France." MLN, 72 (1957), 41.
Notes that the first French edition of TJ was suppressed merely to punish its bookseller, Jacques Rollin, who had printed the novel without permission from an official censor. Printed copies were recalled and Rollin was fined 500 livres.

684 Sherburn, George. "Introduction." In the edition, The History of Tom Jones, a Foundling. Modern Library College Edition. New York: Random House, 1950, pp. v-xiv.
Includes routine information on HF's life. Noteworthy, however, are Sherburn's brief comments on two not-so-usual introductory subjects. First, he connects TJ with the mid-18th century vogue of charity to foundlings. And second, in reference to Tom's good nature, he asserts that HF's "view of goodness is at times curiously ... confused by a notion of psychological determinism."

685 Shesgreen, Sean. "The Moral Function of Thwackum, Square, and Allworthy." SNNTS, 2 (1970), 159-167.
A paradigmatic reading suggesting that HF dramatizes motives for benevolence in TJ by a formula consisting of three allegorical characters. Thwackum represents the inducements of religion and Square the philosophic love of virtue. But neither represents true benevolence. That is to

be found in Allworthy's active sympathy, the via media to
benevolence between Thwackum and Square's positions.

686   . "Tom Jones. " In his Literary Portraits
in the Novels of Henry Fielding. DeKalb: Northern
Illinois Univ. Press, 1972, pp. 106-153.
See No. 270.

687 Sokolyansky, Mark G. "Poetics of Fielding's Comic
Epics. " ZAA, 22 (1974), 251-265.
See No. 489.

688 Solomon, Stanley J. "Fielding's Presentational Mode
in Tom Jones. " CEA, 31, No. 4 (1969), 12-13.
Counters criticism that sees HF's treatment of Tom's
psychology as a failure. Solomon shows instead that HF
made it plausible by inventing a double mode of external,
indirect characterization: he reveals Tom as active and as
reflective. Tom's speeches are not corny or insincere, but
virtuous. In them HF lets Tom express his ideals in an
Allworthian way. The speeches tell us of Tom's reflection
on "right" behavior after his "wrong" actions. HF's juxtaposition of Tom's ignoble actions with his virtuous speeches
thus allows a revelation of Tom's psychology as well as the
development of his character.

689 Spacks, Patricia Meyer. "Young Men's Fancies:
James Boswell, Henry Fielding. " In her Imagining a
Self: Autobiography and Novel in Eighteenth-Century
England. Cambridge, Mass.: Harvard Univ. Press,
1976, pp. 227-263.
By turns a fluent and lumpish discussion of the recipro-
cal relationship between the London Journal and TJ. Spacks
locates their power in their merging the act of writing with
the act of living. That is, both authors perceive the imagination's dual role as a literary and personal resource in
the characterization of young men. Thus Boswell's imagin-
ings are both subject and structure in a work [that defines
himself for himself] in which he attempts to "know himself. "
In TJ, HF uses Tom's imaginative participation in others'
situations to allow Tom to "know the world. " For Boswell
imagination is an act of illusion for the purpose of self-
discovery. For HF it is an act of penetration for the purpose of self-reformation.

690 Spearman, Diana. "Fielding. " In her Novel and Society. New York: Barnes & Noble, 1966, pp. 199-213.

A loose assessment of the documentary value of TJ
and Amelia as a reflection of 18th-century society. Spearman concludes that on the whole, HF's presentation of society is accurate, especially in his depiction of the justice
system, politics, and thought about illegitimacy. Yet she
suggests that his own attitudes impede an accurate depiction
of the squirearchy and Methodism and cause him to neglect
the abnormal and eccentric. Spearman calls Amelia the
first novel of social criticism that appeals not to the individual heart for sympathy but to Parliament for legislation.

691   Stanzel, Franz. "The Authorial Novel: Tom Jones."
       In his Narrative Situations in the Novel: Tom Jones,
       Moby Dick, The Ambassadors, Ulysses. Trans. from
       the German by James P. Pusack. Bloomington: In-
       diana Univ. Press, 1971, pp. 38-58.
       An important analysis of the narrator's presence in the
novel. Stanzel discusses TJ as an "authorial novel," one
in which the narrator stands far above the fictional reality
and achieves credibility in his presentation of it. He shows
HF solving such presentational problems as narrative distance, the merging of narrative and action time, the com-
pression of events, and direct interpolation. For Stanzel,
HF "symbolizes the epistemological view held since Kant
that we do not apprehend the world as it is in itself, but
as it has passed through the medium of an observing mind."

692   _____. "'Tom Jones' und 'Tristram Shandy.' Ein
       Vergleich als Vorstudie zu einer Typologie des Romans."
       EM. Ed. Mario Praz. Rome: Edizioni di Storia e
       Letteratura, 1954. Vol. 5, pp. 107-148.

693   Stevick, Philip. "On Fielding Talking." CollL, 1
       (1974), 19-33.
       Argues that HF's conversational commentary in TJ be-
comes an epistemological exercise for the reader. In this
exercise the reader comes to know and judge characters
and events within a universal human experience.

694   Stitzel, Judith G. "Blifil and Henry Fielding's Con-
       ception of Evil." WVUPP, 17 (1970), 16-24.
       Suggests that in HF's ethical purpose, Blifil's hypocrisy
is less important than his inability to respond to love and
life. While his scheming and evil instincts obviously make
him Tom's foil, Blifil best shows his perversity in his latent
sadism--his desire to possess Sophia even though she hates
him. Here again, Tom's (and HF's) healthy passion counter-
point and comment ethically on Blifil's perversity.

695 Stumpf, Thomas A. "Tom Jones from the Outside. "
     In The Classic British Novel. Ed. Howard M. Harper,
     Jr. and Charles Edge. Athens: Univ. of Georgia
     Press, 1972, pp. 3-20.
     A thoughtful essay holding that HF's "anti-psychologism,"
an unwillingness to enter the minds of his characters, allows
him to develop their motives through their actions and his
commentary on them. Stumpf contends that for HF "judicious
observation [of actions] is more important than psychological
speculation" in perceiving motive.

696 Suerbaum, Ulrich. "Das Gasthaus zu Upton: zur
     Struktur von Fieldings Tom Jones. " In Festschrift
     für Edgar Mertner. Ed. Bernhard Fabian and Ulrich
     Suerbaum. Munich: Fink, 1969, pp. 213-230.

696a Swingewood, Alan. "Fielding, Tom Jones, and the
      Rise of the Novel. " In Diana T. Laurenson and Alan
      Swingewood's Sociology of Literature. New York:
      Schocken, 1972, pp. 175-206.
      A broad reading of TJ in its social contexts. Swinge-
wood maintains that the novel asserts the ethos of a vanish-
ing traditional rural England over the dynamic bourgeois and
capitalistic world of London. Consequently he regards the
displaced Tom as "the hero of a declining gentry whose
prestige and power were steadily being undermined. ... This
factual loss of status is the condition for social marginality
and for the marginal hero, the first 'superfluous man', the
first modern anti-hero. "

697 Tabbs, Bernard L. "Fielding's Oedipal Fantasy: A
     Psychoanalytic Study of the Double in Tom Jones. "
     Diss. American. DAI, 37 (1976), 1524A.

698 Tannenbaum, Earl. "A Note on Tom Jones and the
     Man of the Hill. " CLAJ, 4 (1961), 215-217.
     A useful detailing of the parallels between Tom and the
Old Man. They have in common Somerset origins, animal
spirits, sibling problems, forgiving fathers, and experiences
with love, misery, and the army. Yet Tannenbaum recalls
that the novel's main moral lesson is in their dissimilarity:
the Old Man thinks mankind to be evil and corrupt, while
Tom believes man to be basically good.

699 Taube, Myron. "Tom Jones with French Words and
     Music. " Southern Speech Journal, 26 (1960), 109-117.
     Notes that after TJ was adapted as a comic opera in

1764, it became a mainstay on the French musical stage for 40 years.   Taube avers that TJ capitalized on the Parisian demand for things English, rustic, and pathetic.   Yet he notes that the three-act adaptation suffers in translation: crucial episodes are dropped, characters are dropped or cleansed, and all is moralized.

700   Tillett, Nettie S.   "Is Coleridge Indebted to Fielding?" SP, 43 (1946), 675-681.
Strongly suggests three borrowings of Coleridge from HF.   All seem to be loans from the introduction to Book VIII of TJ, the most important of which is the "willing suspension of disbelief" passage of the Biographia Literaria, Chapter XIV.

701   Tillyard, E. M. W.   "Tom Jones." In his Epic Strain in the English Novel.   Fair Lawn, N. J.:   Essential Books, 1958, pp. 51-58.
Asserts that though TJ is impressive in its "Englishness," it is not a prose epic as is Robinson Crusoe because it reflects only the manners and not the soul of its times. Further, Tom is more a knight errant than a great hero, and HF's vision is less broad than that of an epic author. Tillyard thinks that it is better to think of TJ more as a romance than as an epic.

702   Van Doren, Carl.   "Tom Jones and Philip Carey: Heroes of Two Centuries."   Century Magazine, 110 (1925), 115-120.
Illustrates the importance of cultural milieu to an author's rendering character by comparing HF's and Maugham's heroes.   He suggests that the settled pattern of life and thought of the 18th century make Tom a creature more of will than of understanding; because roles and goals are fixed, only volition is needed.   But the changes wrought over 150 years make Philip Carey a more reflective youth who must puzzle with problems of hope and expectation.   In his unconfused world, such pains of doubt are spared Tom. In him HF could neatly generalize all men.   Maugham could not do so with his hero because his troubled times had destroyed the possibility of such universals.

703   Van Ghent, Dorothy.   "On Tom Jones." In her English Novel: Form and Function (1953).   Rpt. New York: Harper, 1961, pp. 65-81.
An essential reading of the novel that interprets TJ in terms of its comic curve.   Noting "form versus feeling" to be

the main thematic contrast, Van Ghent analyzes the structure
of the plot to reveal a network of oppositions that produce
the novel's aesthetic tension. She sees the comic curve
validated by a belief in the intelligibility and rightness of
nature that allows Fortune to favor Tom with wife and wealth
at the end, and to see form punished and feeling rewarded.

704   Vogel, Dan.   "A Lexicon Rhetoricae for 'Journey'
      Literature. "   CE, 36 (1974), 185-189.
      Distinguishes six sub-types of "journey" literature.
Vogel incorrectly terms TJ a picaresque fiction and the most
unsophisticated of the sub-types. His seeing its plot as implying no significance runs counter to the better current
scholarship.

705   Vopat, James B.   "Narrative Technique in Tom Jones:
      The Balance of Art and Nature. "   JNT, 4 (1974), 144-
      154.
      A useful illustration of artifice in TJ. Vopat suggests
that its main narrative principle is "to demonstrate the
necessity of applying the control of art to nature. " Thus,
Paradise Hall controls its landscape, Tom's self-control
comes to regulate his good nature, and the narrator's artifice imposes control on fictional events and historical time.

706   Waldschmidt, Karl.   "Die Dramatisierungen von Tom
      Jones. "   Diss. Rostock, 1906.

707   Warren, Leland E.   "Henry Fielding and the Search
      for History: The Historiographical Context of Tom
      Jones. "   Diss. Illinois at Champaign-Urbana.   DAI,
      37 (1977), 2905A.

708   Watt, Ian.   "Fielding as Novelist: 'Tom Jones. '"   In
      his Rise of the Novel: Studies in Defoe, Richardson,
      and Fielding.   Berkeley: Univ. of Calif. , 1957, pp.
      260-289.
      A seminal essay. Watt interprets four elements of
TJ in terms of HF's social and philosophical thought. First,
the lack of an inner life and personality development for his
characters suggests HF's Aristotelian view that a stable human nature precludes individual development. Next, HF's
plot reflects the neo-classic principle of an author imposing
harmony and order on events. The plot corroborates the
actual social order as well: Tom can only be rewarded by
virtue of his birth and class. Third, HF's definition of virtue as a natural tendency to goodness broadens our moral

sense; thus he sees sexual excesses as ludicrous rather than wicked and his morality is more normative than prescriptive. And last, HF's authorial intrusions make the novel a social and sociable literary form. His comments to the readers both entertain them and distance them from the action so as to allow an objective view. Good contrasts with Richardson as well.

709   Weisgerber, Jean. "Nouvelle Lecture d'un livre ancien: L'Espace dans l'Histoire de Tom Jones, enfant trouvé. " MLA Abstracts, 5 (1975), 96. Pub. in full in CREL, 1 (1975), 69-86.
Asserts the importance of some motifs in the novel: spatial polarities, social gatherings, homecomings, the rejection of solitude, allusions to food and domestic pleasures, and the superiority of country over city life. Weisgerber contends that all such emphases point to the central image of the "home" in TJ.

710   Wess, Robert V. "The Probable and the Marvelous in Tom Jones. " MP, 68 (1970), 32-45.
Explains the coincidences in TJ by reference to HF's own argument that characters should not exceed their capacities. Wess shows that though it may seem a "marvelous" coincidence that two characters meet, if their actions or reasons for journeying are plausible consequences of their natures, probability is not strained. Wess suggests that solutions to the problem of coincidence are found in the characters' plausibility.

711   Williams, Murial Brittain. "Marriage in the Later Novels: Tom Jones. " In her Marriage: Fielding's Mirror of Morality. University: Univ. of Alabama Press, 1973, pp. 71-94.
See No. 301.

712   Williams, Orlo. "Tom Jones. " In his Some Great English Novels: Studies in the Art of Fiction. London: Macmillan, 1926, pp. 1-25.
Disjunct and oversimple. Williams makes six main points. (1) Western is TJ's most impressive character. (2) HF's irony is confined to the comic illustration of self-interest. (3) HF's interest in scene is greater than that in motive. (4) HF's morality is based on an innate consciousness of worth. (5) HF's happy spirit dominates the book. And (6) TJ is fundamentally related to the British temperament.

713   Woodcock, George.   "'Colonel Jack' and 'Tom Jones':
         Aspects of a Changing Century."   WascanaR, 5 (1970),
         67-73.
         An oversimple attempt at illustrating the "altered social
atmosphere" from a dynamic to a stable age by contrasting
Defoe's and HF's novels.   Woodcock contrasts Defoe's world
of perpetual movement with the stability of HF's, Defoe's
matter-of-fact style with HF's grace, and his desire to
"teach by good and bad example" with HF's inclination to
satire and parody.   Besides exhibiting basic misconceptions,
all Woodcock succeeds in doing is to assert that the two
novelists are different.   He fails dismally to connect them
with their separate times.

714   Wright, Andrew.   Henry Fielding: Mask and Feast.
         Berkeley: Univ. of California Press, 1965.
         Various subsections on TJ.   See No. 304.

715   Yardley, E.   "Fielding and Shakespeare."   N&Q, 8
         June 1907, pp. 445-446.
         Two speeches in TJ (IV, 9 and V, 7) allude to Hamlet
and Othello.   Also, the Blifil-Sophia marriage suit scene is
an imitation of one in Romeo and Juliet.

716   Yskamp, Claire E.   "Character and Voice: First Per-
         son Narrators in Tom Jones, Wuthering Heights, and
         Second Skin."   Diss. Brandeis.   DA, 32 (1972), 6948A.

717   Zakaras, Laura V.   "Love and Morality in Tom Jones."
         Diss. Washington.   DA, 34 (1973), 2585A-86A.

IX

AMELIA

718 Alter, Robert. "Fielding's Problem Novel." In his
Fielding and the Nature of the Novel. Cambridge,
Mass.: Harvard Univ. Press, 1968, pp. 141-178.
Sees Amelia as a recreation of the Christian hero, a
social protest novel, and an experiment in new techniques,
especially in irony (reader-directed) and in subtle characterization ("progressive discovery"). Alter avers that the novel
pioneers "the masterful interlocking of separate lives through
shared experience that gives Middlemarch such remarkable
coherence." Still, he shows Amelia's didacticism to be a
main weakness that undermines realism and character.

719 Baker, Sheridan. "Fielding's Amelia and the Materials
of Romance." PQ, 41 (1962), 437-449.
Argues provocatively that HF could not forego the framework of romance despite his avowedly realistic intention because romance was too inherent in his literary climate.
Thus the romance elements are at odds with the realistic
materials in Amelia. Without the distancing effect of comedy,
e. g., his romantically happy ending renders the whole novel
sentimental.

720 Banerji, H. K. "Amelia." In his Henry Fielding:
Playwright, Journalist, and Master of the Art of Fiction (1929). Rpt. New York: Russell & Russell, 1962,
pp. 216-240.
See No. 131.

721 Bevan, C. H. K. "The Unity of Fielding's Amelia."
RMS, 14 (1970), 90-110.
A fourfold argument: that Amelia is a refutation of
the Mandevillian moral psychology of the dominant selfish
passion; that HF unified the novel by the contrast of his own
benevolist vision with that of Mandeville; that Amelia derives
its rhetorical force from these contrasts (e. g., between con-
structive and destructive passionate activity); and that HF

successfully unifies his various intentions, especially the
promotion of virtue and the exposure of evil. Bevan sen-
sibly admits, however, that if the unity of Amelia is dominant it is neither flawless nor complete; he cites lapses
such as authorial intrusion, digressive segments, and Booth's
unconvincing conversion.

722   Bloch, Tuvia.   "Amelia and Booth's Doctrine of the
        Passions. "   SEL, 13 (1973), 461-473.
        An important essay showing that HF subscribes to
Booth's theory that men act according to the dictates of the
passion "uppermost" in their minds, regardless of reason,
will, or good nature.   In Booth, Col. James, the Noble
Lord, Mrs. Ellison, Miss Bath, Mrs. Bennet, Col. Bath,
and Elizabeth, HF first establishes their good nature before
showing their vicious behavior caused by their dominant
passion.   Bloch also suggests that HF had arrived at this
conclusion because of his experience as a magistrate who
frequently saw "good-natured" people guilty of crimes produced by passion.   The biographical importance of this article is to show that HF largely abandoned his doctrine of the
dominance of good nature established in TJ.

723   _____.   "The Prosecution of the Maidservant in
        Amelia. "   ELN, 6 (1969), 269-271.
        Challenges the notion that Booth is curel for his prose-
cution of Betty (XI, 5 and 7).   Rather, Bloch notes the
maid's dishonesty, ingratitude, and cruelty for stealing from
a woman who was like a mother to her.   Bloch also calls
attention to HF's thoughts on gratitude and needless tender-
heartedness.

724   Braudy, Leo.   "Amelia: The Primacy of Private His-
        tory. "   In his Narrative Form in History and Fiction:
        Hume, Fielding and Gibbon.   Princeton, N. J. : Prince-
        ton Univ. Press, 1970, pp. 180-212.
        See No. 143.

725   Brooks, Douglas.   "Fielding: Tom Jones and Amelia. "
        In his Number and Pattern in the Eighteenth-Century
        Novel.   London: Routledge & Kegan Paul, 1973, pp.
        92-122.
        See No. 561.

726   C. , T. C.   "Fielding and Bentley. "   N&Q, 2 May
        1944, pp. 245-246.
        Explains an esoteric allusion to an emendation of
Horace by Bentley in Amelia (X, 1).

727   Coolidge, John S.   "Fielding and the 'Conservation of Character.'"   MP, 57 (1960), 245-259.
A close reading of HF's development of character in Amelia as distinct from that in TJ.   Essentially, Coolidge shows that in TJ HF presents character deductively, but that in Amelia he follows a pattern of "observation and discovery."   That is, in the later novel HF allows personality to emerge by an accumulation of traits so that continual revelations of character are possible.

728   Digeon.   Aurélien.   "Amelia."   In his Novels of Fielding.   London: Routledge, 1925, pp. 195-248. See No. 167.

729   Eaves, T. C. Duncan.   "Amelia and Clarissa."   In A Provision of Human Nature: Essays on Fielding and Others in Honor of Miriam Austin Locke.   Ed. Donald Kay.   University: Univ. of Alabama Press, 1977, pp. 95-110.
Postulates that HF's great admiration for Clarissa led him to write the consciously serious Amelia in hopes that it would be compared favorably with Richardson's novel. But, Eaves suggests, in creating a heroine without faults who neither changes nor develops, HF produced his least successful novel.

730   Erzgräber, Willi.   "Das Menschenbild in Henry Fieldings Roman Amelia."   NS, 6 (1957), 105-116.

731   Folkenflik, Robert.   "Purpose and Narration in Fielding's Amelia."   Novel, 6 (1973), 168-174.
Challenges Hassall's reading (No. 733).   Folkenflik argues that because the novel reveals HF's "perception of the problematic nature of life," its mainly dramatic mode of presentation is a strength and not a weakness.   If Amelia takes the possibility of a tragic outcome seriously, a reassuring narrator would be a liability.   Indeed, HF's extensive allusions to Othello suggest that he is evoking a tragic world, the intensity of which would be weakened by a dominantly omniscient narrator.

732   Foster, James R.   "Sensibility among the Great and Near-Great."   In his History of the Pre-Romantic Novel in England (1949).   Rpt. New York: Kraus, 1966, pp. 104-138.
Acknowledges the satirical in Amelia but states the case for the sentimental as well: Fielding's dedication in-

viting the reader to "a tender sensation, " his respect for
"natural feeling that springs from the good heart, " the
novel's mellow and somber tones, and its distressing situations, romantic ordeals, and typical characters. Indeed,
because it is a "mixed" novel, old HF admirers and senti-
mentalists alike are uneasy with it.

733   Hassall, Anthony J. "Fielding's Amelia: Dramatic
      and Authorial Narration. " Novel, 5 (1972), 225-233.
      An explanation of the artistic failure of the novel.
Hassall argues that HF's inability to commit himself to
either a dramatic or a narrative mode, to showing or telling,
impairs the unity of presentation and disconcerts the reader.
Besides offering no introductory chapters to establish an in-
timate author/reader relationship, the narrator appears and
withdraws fitfully, abandons the dramatic stories and potentially complex characters of Miss Matthews and Mrs. Bennet,
and substitutes the didactic preachments of Harrison for what
had been HF's own philosophical but ironic voice in JA and
TJ. (Cf. No. 731).

734   Hunter, J. Paul. "Flight into the Interior. " In his
      Occasional Form: Henry Fielding and the Chains of
      Circumstance. Baltimore: Johns Hopkins Univ. Press,
      1975, pp. 192-217.
      See No. 198.

735   Irwin, Michael. "Amelia. " In his Henry Fielding:
      The Tentative Realist. Oxford: Clarendon Press,
      1967, pp. 113-134.
      See No. 199.

736   Johnson, Maurice. "The Art of Life: Amelia. " In
      his Fielding's Art of Fiction. Philadelphia: Univ. of
      Pennsylvania Press, 1961, pp. 165-172.
      Contends that in Amelia more insistently than in the
other novels, HF "seems predominantly to want to instruct
the reader in living. " His direct commentaries on "the art
of life" in Amelia are plainly stated and unvarnished by a
waggish or mock-heroic tone.
      See No. 206.

737   _____. "The Noble Model: Amelia. " In his Field-
      ing's Art of Fiction. Philadelphia: Univ. of Pennsyl-
      vania Press, 1961, pp. 139-156.
      A usefully detailed citing of the parallels between the
12 books of Amelia and the Aeneid, HF's model. Johnson

suggests that HF's use of Virgil's narrative in local terms implies that "epic heroism may show itself in human nature around us."
See No. 206.

738 _____. "The Sermon at the Masquerade: Amelia."
In his Fielding's Art of Fiction. Philadelphia: Univ.
of Pennsylvania Press, 1961, pp. 157-164.
Suggests that the incident of Dr. Harrison's letter-sermon at the masquerade (X, 2) is both amusing in its development and serious in its exhortation against adultery directed to the public and private conscience.
See No. 206.

739 Karl, Frederick R. "A Note on Amelia." In his
Reader's Guide to the Eighteenth-Century English
Novel. New York: Noonday, 1974, pp. 179-182.
Calls Amelia a failure because of HF's idealization of his heroine. As a throwback to the lady of courtly love, her goodness and selflessness shatter credibility. The novel's realism of detail does not lessen its "devotional-tract" mode.

740 LePage, Peter. "The Prison and the Dark Beauty of
Amelia." Criticism, 9 (1967), 337-354.
Claims that the unity of the novel rests in the prison, its main symbol. The prison reflects the chief theme--"the universal struggle between the [tyrannical] social [will] and individual will, London versus the Booths." It also generates the various plots, for every major character is introduced in a prison (Newgate, the Verge of Court, Bailiff Bondum's jail, and London).

741 Longmire, Samuel E. "Amelia as a Comic Action."
TSL, 17 (1972), 67-80.
Claims Amelia's happy ending to be consistent with the rest of the novel because HF prepares us for it by three narrative and "comic" patterns. First, Booth's three escapes from disaster after arrest ready the reader for a happy ending. Second, HF's revelation of the comic frustration and blundering of the chief hindering characters, James and the anonymous lord, mitigates their threat. And last, because Booth's character contains much that is good and generous, his happiness at the end proves satisfying for the reader.
One must balk, however, at Longmire's thesis. If HF does prepare us for a happy ending, as Longmire contends, we must question the effectiveness of that preparation. After

all, in the course of the novel, two characters are hanged, two die of venereal disease, one dies in a duel, and another dies abroad "in a most miserable manner." Hardly comic actions.

742 _____. "Booth's Conversion in Amelia." SAB, 40, No. 4 (1975), 12-17.
Suggests that Booth's conversion is in accordance with Isaac Barrow's views on spiritual change: that the individual be good, that his conversion be rational (and not miraculous), that he believe in moral freedom, and that he recognize Christianity's powerful incentive to virtue. Still, neither Barrow nor Longmire makes Booth's conversion probable.

743 _____. "The Narrative Structure of Fielding's Amelia." Diss. Indiana. DA, 29 (1969), 3103A.

744 McCutcheon, Roger P. "Amelia, or the Distressed Wife." MLN, 42 (1927), 32-33.
Rejects any possibility of this book's influence on HF's Amelia, though it was published six months before HF's novel.

745 Nathan, Sabine. "The Anticipation of Nineteenth Century Ideological Trends in Fielding's Amelia." ZAA, 6 (1958), 382-409.
Contends that a "new bourgeois ideal" reflected in Harrison and Amelia foreshadows social and literary trends a century later. Harrison is the militant missionary living with the people to rouse them to a sense of their own importance. And Amelia evinces the new bourgeois qualities in her sentimentalism, sincerity, singleness of purpose, high morality, and simple way of life. Both characters are types created at the start of the Industrial Revolution and epitomize the new bourgeoisie and its struggle for power.

746 Nisbet, Janice A. "The Art of Life as Represented in Henry Fielding's Amelia." Diss. Ball State. DA, 35 (1974), 1057A.

747 Oakman, Robert L. "The Character of the Hero: A Key to Fielding's Amelia." SEL, 16 (1976), 473-490.
Suggests that the manipulated ending is necessary because HF has already fulfilled his fictional goals--the promotion of personal virtue and the exposure of public evil. By showing that HF uses Booth in four ways to effect these goals, Oakman reasons that to allow a corrupt society to

reward him finally would be inconsistent with HF's version. Hence the deus ex machina. This conclusion is forced, but Oakman provides an excellent account of Booth's character and characterization before pressing it.

748   Palmer, Eustace. "Amelia--The Decline of Fielding's Art." EIC, 21 (1971), 135-151.
Discusses Amelia's artistic flaws. HF's use of many of the same techniques of JA and TJ--irony, juxtaposition, burlesque, and mock-epic--is neither as frequent nor as effective. Failing to demonstrate morality, he must resort to preaching it blatantly.

749   Poston, Charles D. "The Novel as 'Exemplum': A Study of Fielding's Amelia." WVUPP, 18 (1971), 23-29.
Counters critical opinion that Amelia represents a decline in HF's artistry. Rather, Poston suggests that the novel's artistry is that of the exemplum set within the context of life itself, as the exempla of Wilson and the Man of the Hill are set within the larger art forms of JA and TJ. As an exemplum, Amelia illustrates life with all the injustices that may often only be resolved by providence. A questionable thesis for Poston makes it rest on the life-as-art analogy which HF uses more as metaphor than fact.

750   Powers, Lyall H. "The Influence of the Aeneid on Fielding's Amelia." MLN, 71 (1956), 330-336.
A cogent argument for Fielding's use of Virgil's epic in the structure of Amelia. Not only do the characters approximate their classical models (Booth-Aeneas, Miss Matthews-Dido, etc.), but also the plot and the action of the 12 books parallel those of Virgil's poem.

751   Rawson, C. J. "Nature's Dance of Death: Part II. Fielding's Amelia (with Some Comments on Defoe, Smollett and George Orwell)." ECS, 3 (1970), 491-522.
See No. 255.

752   Rothstein, Eric. "Amelia." In his Systems of Order and Inquiry in Later Eighteenth-Century Fiction. Berkeley: Univ. of California Press, 1975, pp. 154-207.
A most intelligent reading of Amelia that judges it on epistemological grounds and not by the comic criteria of JA and TJ. Rothstein shows how the withdrawal of the narrator

and his central intelligence leaves the reader on a plane
with the novel's characters where all must stumble blindly,
as in life, after truth about others and the world. The
reader is at ground level with Booth's "system of inquiry"
as it progresses from false philosophy to faith, a system of
order.

753 Sherbo, Arthur. "Fielding's Amelia: A Reinterpreta-
      tion. " In his Studies in the Eighteenth-Century English
      Novel. East Lansing: Michigan State Univ. Press,
      1969, pp. 85-103.
      See No. 267.

754 _____ . "The Time Scheme in Amelia. " Boston
      Univ. Studies in English, 4 (1960), 223-228.
      Explains the novel's chronology. Sherbo shows that
although HF erred in coordinating the time scheme in his
exposition with that in his plot, the plot chronology is as
exact as that of TJ.

755 Sherburn, George. "Fielding's Amelia: An Interpre-
      tation. " ELH, 3 (1936), 1-14. Rpt. in No. 239.
      Argues that Amelia is not a decline in HF's powers by
explaining his intentions. First, Sherburn notes HF's conscious effort at imitating the Aeneid. And second, he identifies the themes of the dominant passion and of aristocratic
callousness as products of HF's social, psychological, and
moral assumptions.

756 Shesgreen, Sean. "Amelia. " In his Literary Portraits
      in the Novels of Henry Fielding. DeKalb: Northern
      Illinois Univ. Press, 1972, pp. 154-176.
      See No. 270.

757 Smith, Leroy W. "The Doctrine of Passions as It
      Appears in the Works of Henry Fielding, Particularly
      in Amelia. " Diss. Duke, 1956.

758 Sokolyansky, Mark G. "Genre Evolution in Fielding's
      Dramaturgy. " ZAA, 20 (1972), 280-295.
      A good review of HF's development as a playwright.
The article shows how he outgrew his earlier tendencies to
Restoration dramatic manner by turning to farce with its
comical-eccentric element. Subsequently he attained the
dramatic realism of pointed political satire--actual people
and actual situations lightly disguised--that makes him
unique.

759   Spacks, Patricia Meyer. "Laws of Time: Fielding
       and Boswell. " In her Imagining a Self: Autobiography
       and Novel in Eighteenth-Century England. Cambridge,
       Mass.: Harvard Univ. Press, 1976, pp. 264-299.
       An intelligent but sometimes muddled comparison of
Boswell for the Defence and Amelia. Spacks shows how the
two "dramatize the increasing tension of the effort to pre-
serve selfhood in maturity. " In the autobiography and the
novel, the characters' sense of time's passage contributes
to a complex psychic drama in which the characters uncon-
sciously color their past in order to understand their present.

760   Stephens, John C., Jr. "The Verge of the Court and
       Arrest for Debt in Fielding's Amelia. " MLN, 63
       (1948), 104-109.
       Explains two 18th-century legal concepts at work in
Amelia. (1) The law allowed a debtor, such as Booth, to
immunize himself from arrest by staying within "the Verge
of Court"--in Middlesex--a vestige of the prevailing of
Royal over civil jurisdiction. (2) One could be arrested for
debt either by a writ of execution (for a debt of any amount)
or by mesne process (for a debt of 40 shillings or more),
as was Booth's case.

761   Thomas, D. S. "Fortune and the Passions in Field-
       ing's Amelia. " MLR, 60 (1965), 176-187.
       Believes the central issue of Amelia to be the wise
man's answer to the shifts of Fortune. Though HF provides
no systematic explanation, he does suggest, via contemporary
theology, that neither surrender to the passions nor resignation to Fortune will suffice. Rather, he sees the answer in
the "Christian Stoicism"--patience and hope--that Harrison
and Amelia espouse.

762   _____. "The Publication of Henry Fielding's
       Amelia. " The Library, 5th series, 18 (1963), 303-
       307.
       Records the details of Millar's publishing and of Stra-
han's part in printing the novel in 1751 and 1752.

763   Todd, William B. "Press Figures. " The Library,
       5th series, 7 (1952), 283.
       Suggests that if--as is said--four presses printed
Amelia, it is reasonable to assume that some nine printers
worked at the job.

764   Towers, A. R. "Amelia and the State of Matrimony. "
       RES, n. s. 5 (1954), 145-157.

Oversimply regards Amelia as a conduct-book for good
marriage. Towers suggests that HF responds to the great
middle-class interest in the subject to exalt love, parental
consent, motherly instruction, and wifely fidelity and obedi-
ence as cardinal virtues. Towers concludes that HF's contrast of the Booths' marriage with the novel's three other
main marriages is cautionary.

765   . "Fielding and Dr. Samuel Clarke. " MLN,
     70 (1955), 257-260.
Notes that HF's descriptive terminology of Robinson,
the Hobbesian determinist, in Amelia (I, 3) is indebted to
the Latitudinarian divine Samuel Clarke. Terming Robinson
variously as freethinker, a deist, and an athiest, HF recalls
Clarke's classifications in the Boyle Lectures of 1705.
     Ralph W. Rader, ibid. , 71 (1956), 336-338, allows
that HF borrows just as much from Ralph Cudsworth's True
Intellectual System as from Clarke.

766   . "An Introduction and Annotations for a
     Critical Edition of Amelia. " Diss. Princeton. DA,
     14 (1954), 351-52.

767 Wendt, Allan. "The Naked Virtue of Amelia. " ELH,
     27 (1960), 131-148.
     An important article arguing that Amelia is the ethical
center of the novel. "Those who love her goodness are
worthy of salvation; those who harm her and those who lust
after her person are only damned. " Through Amelia as
person and symbol, HF affirms his belief in God's providence, in the benevolist doctrine, in virtue as fulfillment
and not denial, and in human desire for the beautiful and
good. Yet Amelia's "naked beauty of virtue" is necessary
but not sufficient for ethical actions, because without heaven's
absolute values, human values cannot exist.

768 West, Rebecca. "The Great Optimist. " In her Court
     and the Castle. New Haven, Conn. : Yale Univ. Press,
     1957, pp. 87-108.
     A discursive essay touching on HF and Amelia to show
his great optimism for humanity. Rejecting the doctrine of
total depravity, HF shows hope always prevalent in everything from his infatuation with the idea of good government
through his portraits of redemptory women to his own effort
to establish law in London. These remarks are submerged
in a discussion of the novel as inferior to the drama in depicting human idealism.

769   Williams, Murial Brittain. "Marriage in the Later
       Novels: Amelia." In her Marriage: Fielding's
       Mirror of Morality. University: Univ. of Alabama
       Press, 1973, pp. 95-120.
       See No. 301.

770   Winterowd, Walter Ross. "The Poles of Discourse:
       A Study of Eighteenth-Century Rhetoric in Amelia and
       Clarissa." Diss. Utah. DA, 26 (1965), 360-61.

771   Wolff, Cynthia Griffin. "Fielding's Amelia: Private
       Virtue and Public Good." TSLL, 10 (1968), 37-55.
       A provocative study that explains Amelia's final am-
biguity by reference to HF's notions about innocence and
human motivation, the function of the legal system, and the
rampant crime he contended with as a magistrate.

772   Wright, Andrew. Henry Fielding: Mask and Feast.
       Berkeley: Univ. of California Press, 1965.
       Various subsections on Amelia. See No. 304.

X

JOURNALISM AND OTHER WRITINGS

773 Amory, Hugh. "Henry Fielding's Epistles to Walpole:
A Reexamination." PQ, 46 (1967), 236-247.
Suggests that in his subtitles HF purposely misdated
two anti-Walpole poems in the Miscellanies.

774 _____. "A Preliminary Census of Fielding's Legal
Manuscripts." PBSA, 62 (1968), 587-601.
Reports the locations of 32 legal manuscripts of HF.
Amory also analyzes a fragment of a volume on criminal
law that HF supposedly had planned to publish.

775 Baker, Sheridan. "Henry Fielding's The Female Husband: Fact and Fiction." PMLA, 74 (1959), 213-224.
Attributes this nearly pornographic pamphlet of 1746
to HF. By a check of contemporary records, Baker suggests that much of the 23-page pamphlet, based on a case
at bar, is fictitious.
See N&Q, Nov. 1959, p. 404, wherein Baker changes
a reference to Tuesday in his PMLA article to Saturday.

776 Banerji, H. K. "The Champion," "The Miscellanies,"
and "Political Journalism." In his Henry Fielding:
Playwright, Journalist, and Master of the Art of Fiction (1929). Rpt. New York Russell & Russell,
1962, pp. 78-97, 134-166, 167-186.
See No. 131.

777 Battestin, Martin C. "Pope's 'Magus' in Fielding's
Vernoniad: The Satire of Walpole." PQ, 46 (1967),
137-141.
Suggests that the venal Magus of Pope's Dunciad (Book
IV) derives from HF's attack on Walpole in the Vernoniad
(1741). In HF's mock-epic Walpole is scored for concilia-
tory policies that mitigated the victories of heroes like
Marlborough and Admiral Edward Vernon. In the final edition of the Dunciad the Magus is seen offering the cup of

self-love, symbolic of the victory of dullness over wit and
civilization.

778   Bloch, Tuvia. "Antedatings from Fielding. " N&Q,
       May 1969, pp. 188-189.
       Notes 17 words and phrases used by HF that antedate
the earliest examples in the OED. The words are mainly
from his journalism.

779   Carter, Charlotte A. "Personae and Characters in
       the Essays of Addison, Steele, Fielding, Johnson,
       Goldsmith. " Diss. Denver. DAI, 30 (1970), 4938A.

780   Chandler, Knox. "Two 'Fielding' Pamphlets. " PQ,
       16 (1937), 410-412.
       Shows that two 1742 satires on Pope, The Cudgel and
Blast upon Blast, bear the name Hercules Vinegar on their
title pages. Yet Ned Ward had written the prototype of the
first in 1728 and Edward Roome that of the second in 1729
during the duncical attack on Pope. Capitalizing on the new
war of the dunces in 1742, the publishers attempted to insure sales by using HF's famous pseudonym. Both Pope
and HF discounted the attacks as HF's.

781   Cleary, Thomas R. "Henry Fielding as a Periodical
       Essayist. " Diss. Princeton. DAI, 31 (1971), 6544A.

782   Coley, William B. "Fielding and the Two Covent-Garden
       Journals. " MLR, 57 (1962), 386-387.
       Declines to ascribe the "first" Covent-Garden Journal,
a single electioneering broadsheet of 1749 to HF. Yet Coley
suggests that because Old England had publically associated
HF with that piece, he ironically chose the title for his own
newspaper, the "second" Covent-Garden Journal of 1752.

783   _____. "General Introduction. " In his edition,
       The Jacobite's Journal and Related Writings. The
       Wesleyan Edition of the Works of Henry Fielding.
       Oxford: Clarendon Press, 1974, pp. xvii-lxxxii.
       A detailed account of the political contexts of (1) A
Dialogue between a Gentleman from London ... and an Honest
Alderman of the Country, (2) A Proper Answer to a Late
Scurrilous Libel, and (3) the Jacobite's Journal.

784   _____. "The 'Remarkable Queries' in the Cham-
       pion. " PQ, 41 (1962), 426-436.
       Questions the ascribing of "The Remarkable Queries"

to HF. Indeed, these insertions in the Champion illustrate
the textual uncertainties, hearsay, and circumstantial evidence that present problems in attributing them to HF.

785   de Castro, J. Paul. "Derham. " N&Q, 15 Feb. 1941,
      p. 123.
      Identifies the "Derham" in the JVL as the Rev. William
Derham, D. D. , Rector of Upminster in Essex, Prebendary
of Windsor, and author of Physico-Theology (1713).

786   _____. "Fieldingiana. " N&Q, 2 Dec. 1916, pp.
      441-443.
      Five random notes on an allusion and a date in HF's
Essay on Conversation, evidence of HF's writing for Mist's
Journal, a source and a date for his Essay on Nothing, and
a correction of the assumption that Maria ("Perdita") Robinson acted in Tom Thumb.

787   _____. "Fielding's Pamphlet: The Female Hus-
      band. " N&Q, 5 March 1921, pp. 184-185.
      HF wrote this 13-page pamphlet in 1746 after the prose-
cution of a woman charged with impersonating a man in marriage.   HF's cousin Henry Gold [Gould?] was involved in the
case, and HF himself probably sat with counsel during it.
Widower and father, he perhaps wrote the pamphlet to re-
imburse himself for the expenses of traveling the circuit.

788   _____. "Fielding's 'Voyage to Lisbon. '" N&Q, 28
      Dec. 1940, p. 461.
      Notes that the drink called wind was popular in 18th-
century England.   Its chief ingredient was turnip juice, fer-
mented with sloes, blackberries, beer, and litharge.

789   De Stasio, C. Henry Fielding e il giornalismo. Bari:
      Adriatica, 1970. 249 pp.

790   Dickson, Frederic S. "The Early Editions of Fielding's
      Voyage to Lisbon. " The Library, 3rd series, 8 (1971),
      24-35. Pollard, Alfred W. "Notes on Old Books. "
      Ibid. , 75-77, 160-162. de Castro, J. Paul. "Henry
      Fielding's Last Voyage. " Ibid. , 145-159.
      Four articles debating the circumstances of the publica-
tion of HF's JVL.   Central to the controversy is Dickson's
contention that John Fielding changed his brother's manuscript to produce the first edition before Andrew Millar
brought out a second edition without John's emendations.

791   Digeon, Aurélien. "Fielding a-t-il écrit le dernier

chapitre de 'A journey from this world into the next.'"
RAA, 8 (1931), 428-30.

792   Dircks, R. J.   "Some Notes on Fielding's Proposal for
the Poor."   N&Q, Dec. 1962, pp. 457-459.
Four random notes on HF's 1753 pamphlet, A Proposal
for Making an Effectual Provision for the Poor.   (1) HF had
been developing his proposal at least since 1751.   (2) He had
planned it to become law.   (3) The Earl of Hillsborough (not
Lord Hardwicke) is one of the "learned Persons" of the pamphlet.   And (4) only two editions of the Proposals appeared
in the 18th century.

793   Eddy, Donald D.   "The Printing of Fielding's Miscellanies (1743)."   SB, 15 (1962), 247-256.
An intricate account of details of publication.

794   French, Robert Dudley.   "The True Patriot by Henry
Fielding."   Diss. Yale.   DAI, 33 (1972), 1140A.

795   Gligor, Emil P.   "A Study of Fielding's The Opposition:
A Vision."   Diss. Case Western Reserve.   DAI, 37
(1977), 7761A.

796   Graham, Walter.   English Literary Periodicals (1930).
Rpt. New York: Octagon, 1966.   References passim.
Descriptions of HF's periodical ventures.   Graham
identifies his Champion as a thrice-weekly organ to make
war on the Walpole administration.   Its features--essays,
verse, and parodies, all practiced by the Vinegar family as
personae--influenced later newspaper methods.   Of real
value, its literary criticism was more approving than condemning.   HF's weekly Jacobite's Journal, while borrowing
its news from other papers, was a throwback to Defoe's
Review, with its Court of Criticism which administered
justice in the "Republic of Literature."   His Covent-Garden
Journal has value today because of HF's essays on diverse
topics.

797   Greason, Arthur LeRoy.   "Fielding's The History of
the Present Rebellion in Scotland."   PQ, 37 (1958),
119-123.
Details publication data of this 1745 pamphlet.

798   _____ .   "The Political Journals of Henry Fielding."
Diss. Harvard, 1954.

799   Grundy, Isobel.   "New Verse by Henry Fielding. "
      PMLA, 87 (1972), 213-245.
      Prints the text of 800 lines of holograph verse of 1729
and 1733, never before published. Grundy analyzes these
verses as mock-epic and polemical epistle; she provides full
textual footnotes as well. The verses reveal HF's relationship with Pope, Robert Walpole, and Lady Mary Wortley
Montagu and specify his support of Whig rule as a guard
against Roman Catholicism and Jacobitism.

800   _____ .   "Some Unpublished Early Verse of HF. "
      NRam, 7 (1969), 2-17.
      A running commentary on two pieces by HF written in
his early twenties.   Each is an attack on Pope for his treatment of HF's cousin, Lady Mary Wortley Montagu.   The
first, a set of three incomplete cantos, is a mock-heroic
parody of the Dunciad, with Pope himself as the favorite of
Dulness.   It attacks Pope's religion, politics, physique, and
[nonsensically] poetic frivolity.   There are hits at other
Scriblerians as well.   The second poem, "Epistle to Lyttleton, " reveals more sobriety.   Indeed, HF praises Pope's
genius but indicts his viciousness.   Interestingly, the first
poem shows favor for Walpole, the second, disenchantment
with him.   Pope saw neither of the poems.

801   Heilman, Robert B.   "Fielding and the First Gothic
      Revival. " MLN, 57 (1942), 671-673.
      Claims that passages in "A Journey from This World
to the Next, " TJ, and JVL link HF tenuously to the Gothic
revival of the 1740s and 1750s.   In each case (the Palace
of the Dead, Allworthy's house, and Belen and Lisbon), HF
praises Gothic architecture--especially its irregularity.

802   Holdsworth, William.   A History of English Law.   17
      vols. London: Methuen, 1938. See Vol. XI, pp.
      563-568.
      Recalls HF's main thoughts on pardons, public execu-
tion, and imprisonment in his Enquiry into the Causes of
the Late Increase of Robbers (1751).

803   Hughes, Helen Sard.   "A Dialogue--Possibly by Henry
      Fielding. " PQ, 1 (1922), 49-55.
      "A Dialogue between a Beau's Head and His Heels" is
more probably by HF than by Timothy Fielding, a comedian
and producer of plays in Smithfield and Bloomsbury.   Its
sophistication and its publication in The Musical Miscellany
of John Watts, HF's play-publisher in 1729-1931, suggest
ascribing it to him.

804   Hunting, Robert S.   "Fielding's Revisions of David
       Simple."   Boston Univ. Studies in English, 3 (1957),
       117-121.
       Recalls that after contemporary critics ascribed Sarah
Fielding's David Simple (1744) to HF he denied writing it
in his preface to the second edition.   But he did acknowledge
that some revisions in the new edition were his.   Hunting
has collated both editions to reveal hundreds of changes made
by HF, among them elevating diction, tightening syntax, correcting fact, and inserting a sharper irony.   While they reveal little more about HF than his concern for style, they
do show the loving interest of a busy man in his sister's
work.

805   Jarvis, R. C.   "The Death of Walpole: Henry Field-
       ing and a Forgotten Cause Célèbre."   MLR, 41 (1946),
       113-130.
       Ascribes The Charge to the Jury on the Sum of the
Evidence on the Trial of A. B.   C. D. and E. F. all M. D. for
the Death of Robert at Orfud to HF.   Dating it 1743 or 1744,
Jarvis refutes the theory that HF was inactive in journalism
during those years.   HF's pamphlet was a hit at physicians
engaged in a pamphlet war with surgeons over the cause of
Walpole's death.   Parodying an inquest, HF mocks the zeal,
theory, and cant of physicians in general.

806   _____ .   "Fielding, Dodsley, Marchant, and Ray:
       Some Fugitive Histories of the '45."   N&Q, 8 Sept.
       1945, pp. 90-92; 22 Sept. 1945, pp. 117-120; 6 Oct.
       1945, pp. 138-141.
       A bibliographic essay that distinguishes the textual
differences among four accounts of the Jacobite Rebellion of
1745.   HF's is but a slight pamphlet, the History of the
Present Rebellion, and may or may not be energetic Whig
propaganda.   It is neither conventional history nor a complete account, for it stops at the battle of Prestonpans.
Much of the pamphlet is a borrowing of facts from anti-papist
pieces in the London Gazette.

807   Jensen, Gerard E.   "An Address to the Electors of
       Great Britain... Possibly a Fielding Tract."   MLN,
       40 (1925), 57-58.
       Suggests HF's authorship of this 1739 or 1740 pamphlet
because of its display of his favorite word-usage (hath, shew,
whilst, etc.), favorite references (Aristotle, Coke, Harring-
ton, etc.), the serious tone of a law student, and the ideal-
istic theme of service to the state.

A. LeRoy Greason, Jr., PQ, 33 (1954), 347-352 and
Thomas R. Cleary, SB, 28 (1975), 308-318 expand on Jen-
sen's arguments to confirm his attribution of the tract to
HF.

But William B. Coley, PQ, 36 (1957), 488-495 questions HF's authorship of the Address by showing that many
of its "Fielding phrases" are commonplace, that its anti-
ministerial satire is stock Opposition journalism, and that
many of its allusions are absent in HF's earlier work.

808 _____ . "The Crisis: A Sermon." MLN, 31 (1916),
     435-436.
Claims this political sermon of 1741 to be HF's on
three grounds of evidence. It opposes Walpole; Nicols and
Lawrence ascribe it to HF; and HF's archaic usages of hath,
doth, etc. recur. Still, the sermon is devoid of HF's
characteristic wit and epigrammatic force.

809 _____ . "Introduction." In his edition, The Covent-
     Garden Journal. 2 vols. New Haven, Conn: Yale
     Univ. Press, 1915. Vol. I, pp. 1-129.
A seven-part survey of HF's 1752 periodical that,
while old, is not dated. More descriptive than critical, it
gives an account of (1) the origin of the Journal, (2) its
general character (contents and themes), (3) the newspaper
war of 1752 (in full detail), (4) HF's word-usage and signatures, (5) his style, (6) texts and editions of the Journal,
and (7) an appendix consisting of three contemporary documents tenuously related to HF's newspaper.

810 Jones, Claude E. "Fielding's True Patriot and the
     Henderson Murder." MLR, 52 (1957), 498-503.
Recounts the shocking murder of his mistress by
Matthew Henderson, a Scottish footman, and HF's letter on
it in The True Patriot of 13 May 1746. In it a footman--
HF's guise--warns of the dangers of servants' imitating
their masters' vices and luxury--a behavior that can lead
only to destruction. Jones reprints both the letter and the
crime report from The Gentleman's Magazine.

811 Kishler, Thomas C. "Fielding's Experiments with
     Fiction in the Champion." JNT, 1 (1971), 95-107.
Allows that HF's use of the Vinegar family framework
in the Champion, notably the device of the impersonated
editor, provided him opportunity for developing the art of
indirection in satire. Kishler also shows HF's use of the
persona, the impersonated letter-writer, the moral exem-

plum, the vision, and the imaginary journey.   Yet as in JW, he used these common narrative techniques in the Champion more to focus satiric attack than to enhance his fiction.

812   Köhler, Friedrich.   "Fieldings Wochenschrift The
         Champion und das englische Leben der Zeit. "   Diss.
         Münster, 1928.

813   Levine, George R.   "Henry Fielding's 'Defense' of the
         Stage Licensing Act. "   ELN, 2 (1965), 193-196.
         Explains HF's use of the ironic narrator in the Champion of 10 Dec. 1739/40.   The persona takes the guise of a citizen outraged at the immorality and sedition of Theophilus Cibber's production of The Rehearsal.   Through the persona, HF attacks the absurdity of stage censorship.   Few direct textual references.

814   McCrea, Brian R.   "Fielding's Political Writings. "
         Diss. Virginia.   DAI, 36 (1976), 4514A.

815   _____.   "Fielding's Role in The Champion: A Reminder. "   SAB, 42, No. 1 (1977), 19-24.
         Provides evidence for Cross' 1918 assertion that James Ralph and not HF was responsible for the main political content of the paper.   In The Champion, HF's essays usually expanded on a classical motto in a witty, learned, and allusive way; they are singularly nonpolitical.   It was Ralph's vituperative leaders and indexes that were directed against the government.   McCrea necessarily concludes, then, that HF's commitment to the Opposition was not as strong as is generally believed.

816   Marr, George S.   "Developments in Journalism of the
         Period, and the Work of Henry Fielding. "   In his
         Periodical Essayists of the 18th Century.   New York:
         Appleton, 1924, pp. 108-114.
         A descriptive mention of HF's periodical work with the Champion (1739), the True Patriot (1745), the Jacobite's Journal (1747), and the Covent-Garden Journal (1752).   Marr concludes that HF's best work in the essay, however, is to be found in the prefatory chapters of TJ.   By drawing the old Spectator-like characters into fiction, "the novel sucked the essay dry. "

817   Miller, Henry Knight.   Essays on Fielding's "Miscel-
         lanies": A Commentary on Volume I.   Princeton, N. J. :
         Princeton Univ. Press, 1961.   474 pp.

A close examination of some of HF's little noticed work. Though Miller refuses to claim great merit for these pieces, he cogently shows the Miscellanies I to be "a microcosm of Henry Fielding's intellectual world."

Besides an introductory chapter on the circumstances of publication and a brief closing one on general observations, Miller offers five densely detailed chapters analyzing the works themselves. Chapter II assesses the 37 poems in the volume. Letting 32 light poems pass in review, Miller then offers close studies of the five verse essays to reveal in them some of HF's favorite themes: true greatness, good nature, liberty, marriage, and the inconstancy of human nature. Chapter III examines the three essays ("On Conversation, " "On the Knowledge of the Characters of Men, " and "Of the Remedy of Affliction") to reveal HF talking directly about root issues such as good breeding (the social virtue of pleasing), hypocrisy and human nature, and consolation. Chapter IV takes up two formal satires, the mock encomium "Essay on Nothing" and a parody of a Royal Society monograph. Chapter V is a consideration of HF's translation of Demosthenes' First Olynthias and Chapter VI of two Lucianic sketches.

This is a valuable book. Miller's detail on the literary gestation of HF's genres and themes and his meticulous rhetorical analyses of many of the Miscellanies are both exemplary. For most students the chapters on the poems and essays will be most useful, for Miller assesses in HF's early work themes that he would develop in the novels. And Miller's explanation of HF's vacillation between acceptance of the orthodox doctrine of human depravity and the Latitudinarian tendency toward basic human goodness should be required supplementary reading. Though his subject concerns some minor work of HF, Miller's book is a major piece of HF scholarship.

Reviews: JEGP, 61 (1962), 413-416; MP, 60 (1963), 290-293; MLR, 57 (1962), 422; RES, n. s. 14 (1963), 88-90; UTQ, 32 (1962), 98-101.

818 _____ . "Fielding and Lady Mary Wortley Montagu: A Parallel. " N&Q, Oct. 1958, pp. 442-443.

Notices a parallel between a travesty of the Aeneid in HF's Miscellanies and an incomplete poem by HF's cousin, Lady Mary. The analogue suggests a literary interest in each other.

819 _____ . "Fielding's Miscellanies: A Study of Volumes I and II of Miscellanies by Henry Fielding

Esq. in Three Volumes, 1743. " Diss. Princeton. DA, 14 (1954), 821.

820 _____. "Henry Fielding's Satire on the Royal Society. " SP, 57 (1960), 72-86.

A useful reminder about the ethical basis of HF's satire. In a 1743 pamphlet, HF parallels a satire on the Royal Society with a satire on Peter Walter, a notorious usurer. Though this witty pamphlet mocks impractical virtuosi, its greater ridicule is directed at avarice, which HF regards as a deliberate crime against society and a direct negation of charity. "This humanistic bias ... was one of the most consistent elements in Fielding's character and thought. "

821 Pagliaro, Harold. "Introduction. " In his edition of HF's Journal of a Voyage to Lisbon. New York: Nardon Press, 1963.

Little on the JVL itself, but this essay offers a review of HF's attitudes with special attention to his "archdemons, " Cibber, Walpole, and Richardson.

822 Peterson, William. "Satire in Fielding's An Interlude Between Jupiter, Juno, Apollo, and Mercury. " MLN, 65 (1950), 200-202.

Shows this brief dramatic sketch included in HF's Miscellanies of 1743 to be a direct satire on the henpecked King George (Jupiter) and his notorious management by Queen Caroline (Juno). Walpole's hesitant military policy and the ministry's hack writers also come under attack.

823 Prideaux, W. F. "Fielding's Journal of a Voyage to Lisbon, 1755. " N&Q, 28 July 1906, pp. 61-62.

Collates the two 1755 editions of the work and notes that passages on the captain and his nephew had been suppressed in the first, or shorter, edition.

Cf. St. Swithin, ibid., 11 Aug. 1906, p. 115, who claims possession of a still shorter 1755 version.

824 R., E. "An Advertisement of Henry Fielding's. " N&Q, 1 Nov. 1930, p. 315.

A reprint from the Daily Journal of 29 Nov. 1730 in which HF denies any involvment in a new act, "The Battle of the Poets, " that had been advertised for his Tom Thumb.

825 Robertson, Olivia. "Fielding as Satirist. " ContempR, 181 (1952), 120-123.

Merely a summary of A Journey from This World to the Next (1743) that calls the work a powerful satire counterpointing the genial humor of JA and TJ. Robertson especially praises HF's portrait of Anne Boleyn for a psychological intensity that approaches tragedy. "In his satire and not in his straight novels HF was carried away into real feeling."

826   Rogers, Pat. "Fielding's Parody of Oldmixon." PQ, 49 (1970), 262-266.

An incisive examination of a 1752 number of the Covent-Garden Journal in which HF produces a mock history of his times viewed from the perspective of A. D. 3000. His persona is Humphrey Newmixon, "profound Critic," whose historiographical style is a parody of that of the 18th-century Whig historian John Oldmixon.

827   Rosenberg, Sondra. "Travel Literature and the Picaresque Novel." EnlE, 2 (1971), 40-47.

A fitful attempt to recommend travel literature as a type worthy of study. After noticing some superficial resemblances between the picaresque tale and the travel genre, Rosenberg lists Smollett's Travels, Sterne's Sentimental Journey, and HF's JVL as three variant types. Then she claims, on the basis of the "sheer monotony and boredom" HF conveys, that he is actually parodying travel literature. Little focus, less substance.

828   S., H. K. St. J. "Poem by Fielding." N&Q, 9 June 1906, p. 446.

Reprints a poem published at Bath in 1782 entitled "An Extempore in the Pump-Room, at Bath, by the Late Henry Fielding, Esq. To Miss H---band."

829   Seymour, Mabel. "Fielding's History of the Forty-Five." PQ, 14 (1935), 105-125.

Incorrectly attributes this political pamphlet to HF on the basis of its summary of evidence and its use of HF's favorite auxiliary, hath.

See Jarvis (No. 806).

830   _____. "Henry Fielding." LM, 24 (1931), 160.

Bibliographical notes on A Compleat and Authentick History of the Rise, Progress, and Extinction of the Late Rebellion.

831   Shepperson, Archibald Bolling. "Fielding on Liberty and Democracy." Univ. of Virginia Studies, 5 (1951), 265-275.

Abstracts HF's views on these topics from his pamphlets and periodical essays. Shepperson reveals HF as consistently Hanoverian and Constitutionalistic, opposed to Republicans and levellers. Because of his concept of imperfectible humanity, HF doubts universal remedies, political or otherwise. Yet from HF's hatred of contempt Shepperson infers his basic sense of democracy.

832   Shipley, John B. "Fielding and 'The Plain Truth' (1740). " N&Q, 22 Dec. 1951, pp. 561-562.
A check of contemporary sources fixing the date of this pamphlet attacking Walpole as 1740.

833   _____. "Fielding's Champion and a Publishers' Quarrel. " N&Q, Jan. 1955, pp. 25-28.
Offers details of a publishers' war in 1741 over the printing of Parliamentary debates. Shipley conjectures that when the Champion became involved, HF may have resigned the editorship.

834   _____. "The 'M' in Fielding's Champion. " N&Q, June 1955, pp. 240-245; Aug. 1955, pp. 345-351.
Ascribes the 16 "M" signatures in the Champion to Fielding with reservations.

835   _____. "A New Fielding Essay from the Champion. " PQ, 42 (1963), 417-422.
Reprints and ascribes to HF a heretofore lost Champion essay. Calling it "On Easy Writing, " Shipley assigns this Baconian piece to HF on stylistic grounds, e. g. , the Ovidian epigraph, allusions to Montaigne, the aphoristic style, the abrupt ending, and the hit at Colley Cibber.

836   _____. "On the Date of the Champion. " N&Q, Oct. 1953, p. 441.
Notes the halts and starts of the Champion from references in other contemporary newspapers. Shipley avers that one of its last issues was on 26 March 1745.

837   Wallace, Robert M. "Fielding's Manuscripts. " TLS, May 18, 1940, p. 243.
Records evidence that a commonplace book of HF may be extant, though several other of his unpublished works were destroyed in the Gordon Riots of 1780.

838   Wells, John Edwin. "The Champion and Some Unclaimed Essays by Henry Fielding. " Englische Studien, 46 (1912-1913), 355-366.

Reviews the dispute over authorship of certain papers in the Champion variously ascribed to either HF or James Ralph. By recognizing recurring themes (falsity of hereditary family honor), targets (Bentley and Cibber), favorites (Dr. South), and antipathy to low words (stupid, sad-stuff), Wells credits HF with unsigned essays of Nov. 1739 and Feb. and May 1740.

839 _____ . "Fielding's Champion and Captain Hercules
Vinegar." MLR, 8 (1913), 165-172.
Notes that Captain Hercules Vinegar was not a fictitious name created for the pseudo-editorship of the Champion, but was instead the name of a popular prize fighter around London. HF's 1739 choice of title and editor of the paper recalls his method in the farces he had stopped writing by 1737.

840 _____ . "Fielding's Champion--More Notes." MLN,
35 (1920), 18-23.
Offers four main, but random, notes about the Champion. (1) Its subtitle and title changed (e. g. , British Mercury, The Impartial Advertiser). (2) Its hours of publication changed from Tuesday-Thursday-Saturday mornings to evenings. (3) Its place of publication changed from Hockley-in-the-Hole to Pall-Mall in 1740. And (4) it encountered subversion and piracy from other London papers. Other useful notes specify its price of three half-pence, its length of four pages of three columns, and its masthead (Hercules slaying the Hydra with Westminster Bridge and St. Paul's in the distance).

841 _____ . "Fielding's Choice of Signatures for The
Champion. " MLR, 7 (1912), 374-375.
Suggests that the C and L with which HF signed a number of his Champion essays were at his bookseller's request that he imitate Addison's practice of signing his Spectator essays with single letters of CLIO Muse of history. Such imitation of the popular Spectator would presumably help sell the Champion.

842 _____ . "Fielding's Miscellanies. " MLR, 13 (1918),
481-482.
Three random notes on the Miscellanies: a substantiation of its publication date (April 1743), a correction of Henley's bibliographer's omission of the subscribers' list to the second edition, and notice of HF's revision of the "Sixth Satire of Juvenal" (originally written about 1720) to include a squib on Pamela.

843 _____. "Fielding's Signatures in The Champion and
the Date of his 'Of Good Nature.'" MLR, 7 (1912),
97-98.
Affirms that the Champion papers signed C and L as
early as 1739 are those of HF because verses in one of
these papers are from a HF poem, "Of Good Nature," later
published in the Champion.

844 _____. "Henry Fielding and The Crisis." MLN,
27 (1912), 180-181.
Ascribes The Crisis, a 1741 political sermon, to HF.
Wells infers HF's authorship from an anecdote by John
Nichols, reviews in two magazines, and HF's interest in
sermons. He includes a useful list of HF's contemporary
publishers.

845 _____. "Henry Fielding and the History of Charles
XII." JEGP, 11 (1912), 603-613.
Suggests the possibility that HF translated the French
version of M. G. Alderfeld's 1060-page History of Charles
XII. If the translation is indeed HF's, we have further
illustration of his persistent energy, for during the period
of translation he also was studying law, writing the Champion,
and planning Shamela and JA.

846 Williams, Ioan. "Introduction." In his edition, The
Criticism of Henry Fielding. New York: Barnes &
Nobel, 1970, pp. xi-xxiv.
A simple review of HF's main interests in his criticism:
comedy, humor, morality, good breeding, genius, etc. Unfortunately Williams provides no analysis of these interests,
nor does he attempt to infer from them a critical theory.

847 Wolfe, George H. "Lessons in Evil: Fielding's Ethics
in The Champion Essays." In A Provision of Human
Nature: Essays on Fielding and Others in Honor of
Miriam Austin Locke. Ed. Donald Kay. University:
Univ. of Alabama Press, 1977, pp. 65-81.
Views HF's Champion essays as the basis for the
ethics of the novels. Wolfe cites HF's concern with human
motive, with man's capacity to sin, and with unscrupulous
political activity, especially ministerial contempt for frail
human virtue. HF's "overriding sense of social responsibility ... requires him always to judge human characteristics in terms of their application to society at large."

848 Woods, Charles B. "Fielding's Epilogue for Theobald."
PQ, 28 (1949), 419-424.

Prints a 38-line epilogue HF wrote for Lewis Theobald's
Orestes: A Dramatic Opera (1731), not appearing in any
edition to date of HF's works.   It includes a disparaging
reference to his own Tom Thumb.   Probably the two playwrights were on friendly terms, at least for a while.   Ironically, too, the play was dedicated to Walpole; HF had the
reputation of being at least a lukewarm admirer of Walpole
in the early 1730s.

849   Zirker, Marvin R. , Jr.   Fielding's Social Pamphlets:
      A Study of "An Enquiry into the Causes of the Late
      Increase of Robbers" and "A Proposal for Making an
      Effectual Provision for the Poor. "   Berkeley: Univ.
      of California Press, 1966.   174 pp.
      Derives from Radzinowicz (No. 99) to question the ro-
mantically liberal picture of HF.   By an examination of his
Enquiry (1751) and Proposal (1753), Zirker reveals not only
HF's deep conservatism as a social thinker, but also his
unoriginal, repressive, and mercantilistic solutions to the
problem posed by the poor.   This monograph is important
in three ways.   First, Zirker shows HF's ideas to derive
from the traditional poor-laws legislation as well as from
numerous other pamphlets on the problem.   Indeed, Zirker
shows that even the language of HF's pamphlets is derivative.   Second, Zirker claims HF to have been anything but
influential in the reforms.   While the Committee of 1750
advocated prison reform and revision of the capital laws,
HF argued for a repressive penal policy.   And last, Zirker
reveals HF's thought first and last to be based on economic
considerations.   Seeing the poor as the wealth of the nation,
he regarded their diversions, drinking, and gambling as im-
pairing their ability to work and defend the nation and thus
upsetting the static socio-economic system.   From the pamphlets Zirker infers that HF thought that the lower-class
poor should be coerced, used, and managed for the sake of
the metaphysical whole society.
      Fixing the pamphlets in their intellectual context, Zir-
ker reveals HF as anything but a humane reformer.   Yet
he admits--as he must--that HF's humanitarianism and sympathy in the novels are unquestionable.   Zirker's answer to
the anomaly is that, faced with the horrible reality of the
poor, only in his fictions could HF "maintain the serenity
and ideality of the classical-Christian virtues. "
      Perhaps.   But there are two problems with Zirker's
conclusions.   First, his account of HF is unbalanced.   By
stressing the pamphlets and neglecting some of HF's humane
measures as a magistrate (e. g. , his dismissals with admoni-

tions and his assignments of lighter penalties than those mandated), Zirker presents a partial picture. And second, his conclusion about HF's lack of influence on reform legislation is moot. In fact, the 16 resolutions of the Committee of 1750 (which Zirker does not mention) do incorporate many of the suggestions, however unoriginal, that HF made. Nevertheless, Zirker's is an important revisionist view.

Reviews: JEGP, 67 (1968), 161-165; MLQ, 28 (1967), 368-377; PQ, 46 (1967), 346.

XI

MISCELLANEOUS

850 Amory, Hugh, ed. Sales Catalogues of Libraries of
Eminent Persons: Poets and Men of Letters. Vol.
VII. London: Mansell Information Publishing, 1973.
246 pp.
Includes enumeration of HF's library. See No. 859.

851 Antal, F. "The Moral Purpose of Hogarth's Art."
JWCI, 15 (1952), 169-197.
Examines parallels between Hogarth and HF. Antal's
account, more accurate than Moore's (No. 229), notes similarities in their realism, their religious attitudes, their
moralizations, comic inclinations, and satiric targets (e.g.,
the French, Jacobites, Catholics, Wesleyans, Deists, lotter-
ies, masquerades, and marriages of interest). Antal also
specifies their high regard for charity and social reform as
motivating features.

852 Balderston, Katherine C. "Goldsmith's Supposed Attack
on Fielding." MLN, 42 (March 1927), 165-168.
Recalls that a passage in Letter LXIII of Goldsmith's
Citizen of the World has often been regarded as an attack
on romances, and possibly on HF's fiction. Balderston,
however, shows that Goldsmith did not write the letter, but
rather borrowed it from a French book on China, which he
acknowledged by quotation marks and an exact footnote.
Moreover, she exonerates Goldsmith by noting that the passage is generalized and allows that if Goldsmith had intended
it as a hit at HF, he most certainly would have pointed it.

853 Beasley, Jerry C. "The Minor Fiction of the 1740's:
A Background Study of the Novels of Richardson,
Fielding, and Smollett." Diss. Northwestern. DAI,
32 (1971), 3242A.

854 Becker, Gustav. "Der Einfluss des Don Quixote auf
Henry Fielding." In his Aufnahme des "Don Quixote"

in die Englische Literatur.   Berlin: Mayer & Müller,
1906, pp. 122-157.

855   Bennett, Robert C.   "Fielding and the Satiric Dance."
Diss. Pennsylvania.   DAI, 30 (1970), 4397A.

856   Bolles, Edwin C.   "Sea Travel from Fielding to Today."   Diss. Pennsylvania, 1931.

857   Borthwick, Mary C.   "Henry Fielding as Critical
Realist: An Examination of the East German Estimate
of Fielding."   Diss. Fordham.   DA, 26 (1965/66),
3945.

858   Burt, David J.   "Henry Fielding's Attitudes toward the
Eighteenth-Century Gentleman."   Diss. Kentucky.   DAI,
33 (1973), 5114A.

859   Catalogue of the Law and Miscellaneous Library of
Henry Fielding, Esq.   A photostatic copy edited and
rearranged by Frederic S. Dickson.   New York, 1913,
135 pp.
An indexed rearrangement of the 1755 auction catalogue
of HF's library.   It numbers 653 titles composed of 228
separate volumes of law and 1070 separate miscellaneous
volumes.   The miscellaneous collection is strong in history
and classical literature and weak in fiction.

860   Chaudhary, Awadesh.   "Henry Fielding, His Attitude
Toward the Contemporary Stage."   Diss. Michigan.
DA, 26 (1965/66), 1642.

861   Clemente, Frances M.   "Social Criticism in the English
Novel: 1740-1754."   Diss. Ohio State.   DA, 28 (1968),
5011A.

862   Coley, W. B.   "Hogarth, Fielding, and the Dating of
the March to Finchley."   JWCI, 30 (1967), 317-326.
Notices numerous anachronisms in Hogarth's March to
Finchley (e. g., an allusion to HF's Jacobite's Journal) to
emend its date from 1746 to 1748-49.   Moreover, Coley
questions Hogarth's having drawn the masthead for HF's
newspaper.

863   Coolidge, Archibald C.   "A Fielding Pamphlet?"   TLS,
9 May 1936, p. 400.
Questions Cross's attribution of Stultus versus Sapien-

tem, an anti-Catholic satire, to HF on stylistic and thematic grounds. Though HF's name appears on the title page, it was no doubt placed there by its publisher to sell copies. Suggests William Chaigneau, a Dublin resident of Huguenot descent, as the likely author.

See Sheridan Baker, N&Q, Aug. 1953, pp. 343-344, who disallows HF's authorship on linguistic grounds (e. g. , the use of northernisms). Baker includes a useful list of HF's gibes at the Irish.

864   Crockett, Harold Kelley. "The Picaresque Tradition in English Fiction to 1770, with Particular Attention to Fielding and Smollett. "   Diss. Illinois at Urbana-Champaign. DA, 14 (1954), 355.

865   de Castro, J. Paul. "Fielding Queries: Sack and 'The Usual Words. '" N&Q, 10 Oct. 1914, p. 293.

Notes that the usual words accompanying a military toast in 1745 (TJ, IX, 4) were "Hip--hip--hurrah!" The note also provides a Dorset recipe for the "cyder-and" that flows through JA: brandy, nutmeg, ginger, and sugar, over all of which smoking hot cider was poured.

866   _____ . "The Printing of Fielding's Works. "   The Library, 4th series, 1 (1 March 1921), 257-270.

Notes on the prices and print runs of HF's works as printed by William Strahan (1715-85) for HF's publisher, Andrew Millar. One interesting note suggests that Sir John Fielding suppressed the edition of the JVL because of his brother's defamatory references to Veal, captain of HF's ship to Lisbon. Such references might have brought about a successful libel action, especially because Isabella Ash, HF's servant on the voyage, was also Veal's fiancée and would doubtless testify for him.

867   Demarest, David P. "Legal Language and Situation in the Eighteenth Century Novel: Readings in Defoe, Richardson, Fielding and Austen. " Diss. Wisconsin. DA, 24 (1964), 2907.

868   Dickson, Frederic S. "Fielding and Richardson on the Continent. " N&Q, 6 Jan. 1917, pp. 7-8.

Establishes that within 50 years of their publication, the continental editions of HF's novels numbered 20 for JA, 46 for TJ, and 15 for Amelia (first ed.). The editions in Great Britain and Ireland during those years totalled 19, 35, and nine respectively.

869   _____. "William Makepeace Thackeray and Henry
       Fielding." The North American Review, 197 (1913),
       522-537.
       Shows that in his 1840 Times review of Roscoe's edi-
tion Thackeray praises HF the author but disparages HF the
man.   First, he continues the scandalous misconceptions
started by Lady Mary Wortley Montagu and Horace Walpole--
the love of low-life, the shady ladies, the spendthrift ways,
the heavy drinking.   And second, Thackeray embellishes
such legends by putting the artist's touch to them.   Moreover, he creates an autobiography of HF's fiction, seeing
the author as Tom Jones and Billy Booth.
       Still, Thackeray admired HF's books and said so fre-
quently.   Dickson shows that, even on cursory examination,
the two authors were remarkably alike in their fates, manners, and morals.   The three pages of parallels that Dickson provides, however, are biographical and do not touch
the fiction.   Throughout, Dickson cites Thackeray's own
shortcomings as a defense of HF's.

870   Dilworth, E. N.   "Fielding and Coleridge: 'Poetic
       Faith.'"   N&Q, Jan. 1958, pp. 35-37.
       Contrasts the use of the phrase "poetic faith" in TJ
(VIII, 1) and Coleridge's Biographia Literaria (XIV) to con-
clude that in HF's pun is Coleridge's shibboleth; his wit is
Coleridge's sensation.

871   Dircks, Richard J.   "Cumberland, Richardson, and
       Fielding: Changing Patterns in the Eighteenth-Century
       Novel."   RS, 38 (1970), 291-299.
       Recalls that with its theme of a foundling coming into
an inheritance, Richard Cumberland's 1795 novel, Henry, is
modeled explicitly on HF's works.   Yet, Dircks shows,
Cumberland's overriding attitudes are keyed to the emerging
democratic order of his times and, as such, surpass HF's
in benevolence.   Dircks concludes somewhat oversimply that
Cumberland's positing of an innate sense of justice eclipses
HF's concept, which is based on a more or less rigid social
hierarchy.

872   Eaves, T. C. Duncan, and Ben D. Kimpel.   "The
       Reception of Clarissa; Richardson and Fielding, 1748-
       1750."   In their Samuel Richardson: A Biography.
       Oxford, England: Clarendon Press, 1971, pp. 285-321.
       Recounts Richardson's outburst of bitterness against
HF, especially his dislike for HF's improprieties.   Eaves
and Kimpel maintain that much of Richardson's antipathy was

due to his disappointment over the public reception of
Clarissa compared with that of TJ.

873   Esdaile, Mrs. "Fielding's Danish Translator: Simon
       Charles Stanley the Sculptor. " TLS, 3 April, 1937,
       p. 252.
       Notes that Stanley translated JA into Danish in 1749
and JW and "A Journey from This World to the Next" in
1759. It is probable that he knew HF through John Sander-
son, a London architect, himself a good friend of HF's in-
timate acquaintance, Hogarth.

874   Evans, James E. "The English Lineage of Diedrich
       Knickerbocker. " EAL, 10 (1975), 3-13.
       Specifies the influence of Swift, Sterne, and HF (in
that order) on Irving's use of the self-conscious narrator in
Knickerbocker's History of New York.

875   Ewald, Eugen. "Abbild und Wünschbild der Gessell-
       schaft bei Richardson und Fielding. " Diss. Köln, 1935.

876   Fernandez-Alverez, Jesus. "Un probable eco de Henry
       Fielding en La Fe de Armando Palacio Valdés. " FMod,
       33-34 (1969), 101-108.

877   Fleming, John P. "The Classical Retirement Theme
       in the Fiction of Defoe, Fielding, Johnson, and Gold-
       smith. " Diss. Bowling Green. DAI, 38 (1977), 2804A.

878   Frey, Bernhard. "Shaftesbury und Fielding. " Diss.
       Berne, 1952.

879   George, M. Dorothy. London Life in the Eighteenth
       Century (1930). Rpt. New York: Capricorn, 1965,
       pp. 5-7 and passim.
       Calls HF's magistracy a turning-point in London's so-
cial history. She notes his public spirit, his knowledge of
the underworld, and his desire to teach and reform.

880   Giddings, Robert. "Fielding, Smollett and Eighteenth-
       Century Criticism of the Novel. " In his Tradition of
       Smollett. London: Methuen, 1967, pp. 46-70.
       A useful discussion showing that HF and Smollett
agreed on the 18th-century critical standards of instruction,
delight, and truth. But he stresses that HF belongs to the
tradition of the comic romance, Smollett to that of the picaresque. For HF a novel was a concentrated symmetrical

study unified by its narrator's character, while for Smollett a novel is a large diffuse picture unified by its hero's character. Giddings contends that HF's innovation is the making of a moral point humorously, being deadly serious under a mask of comedy.

881   Glenn, Sidney E.   "Some French Influences on Henry Fielding. "   Diss. Illinois at Urbana-Champaign, 1932.

882   Goldgar, Bertrand.   "Fielding, Sir William Yonge, and the Grub Street Journal. "   N&Q, June 1972, pp. 226-227.
       Asserts that the Grub Street Journal's three-month attack on HF for dedicating The Modern Husband (1732) to Walpole in hope of partronage was not written, as previously was thought, by Sir William Yonge.   Yonge was a henchman of Walpole and would have had no reason either to attack a play dedicated to him or to associate with an Opposition journal.

883   Goldknopf, Irma.   "Crime and Prison-Experience in the Early English Novel: Defoe, Fielding, Smollett. "   Diss. Syracuse.   DA, 29 (1968), 1207A.

884   Goyne, Arley V. , Jr.   "Defoe and Fielding: A Study of the Development of English Novel Technique. "   Diss. Texas at Austin, 1954.

885   Grace, Matthew S.   "Fielding in the Eighteenth Century. "   Diss. Wisconsin.   DA, 25 (1965), 6624.

886   Graves, William T.   "National Characters in the Novels of Henry Fielding, Samuel Richardson, and Tobias Smollett. "   Diss. N. Y. U.   DAI, 31 (1971), 6549A.

887   Greene, Graham.   "Fielding and Sterne. "   In From Anne to Victoria.   Ed. Bonamy Dobrée.   New York: Scribner's, 1937, pp. 279-289.
       A light contrast of the two novelists.   Greene credits HF with introducing the poetic imagination into prose fiction both by bringing architectural order to the human experience and by investing that order with a high moral seriousness. Yet he concludes Sterne to be more readable and graceful.

888   Guthrie, William Bowman.   "The Comic Celebrant of Life. "   Diss. Vanderbilt.   DA, 29 (1969), 3098A.

889   Habel, Ursula.   "Die Nachwirkung des picaresken

Romans in England (von Nash bis Fielding und Smollett). " Diss. Breslau, 1930.

890   Halsband, Robert. "Fielding: The Hogarth of Fiction. " Saturday Review of Literature, 30 Sept. 1950, pp. 20-21.
Suggests that HF's main qualities--storytelling, characterizations, and ethical viewpoint--make him the Hogarth of prose fiction.

891   Hannaford, Alayne E. "'Conscience Like a Good Lawyer': Law in the Novels of Henry Fielding. " Diss. Indiana. DAI, 38 (1978), 4844A.

892   Harris, Elizabeth W. "Fiction and Artifice: Studies in Fielding, Wieland, Sterne, Diderot. " Diss. Yale. DA, 34 (1974), 7191A.

893   Harris, Kathleen. Beiträge zur Wirkung Fieldings in Deutschland (1742-92). Diss. Göttingen, 1960.

894   Hill, Rowland M. "Realistic Descriptive Setting in English Fiction from 1550 through Fielding. " Diss. Boston University, 1941.

895   Holloway, Jean M. "Law and Literature in the Age of Englightenment: Blackstone and Fielding. " Diss. Texas at Austin, 1950.

896   Honhart, Carol T. "Fielding, Smollett, Sterne, and the Development of the Eighteenth-Century Travel Book. " Diss. Duke. DA, 35 (1975), 5348A.

897   Horne, Charles F. The Technique of the Novel. New York: Harper, 1908. References passim.
Disparages the "immorality" and type characters of the novels. However, Horne admires HF's sound structure produced by a comedic plot with epic and episodic features.

898   Hubbard, Lester A. "Fielding's Ethics Viewed in Relation to Shaftesbury's 'Characteristics. '" Diss. California at Berkeley, 1934.

899   Itzkowitz, Martin E. "A Fielding Echo in She Stoops to Conquer. " N&Q, Jan. , 1973, p. 22.
Credits HF's JVL as the source of Marlowe's comment on good and bad inns in Goldsmith's comedy.

900   Jensen, Gerard E. "The Covent-Garden Journal Extra-
       ordinary. " MLN, 34 (1919), 57-59.
       Notes that this newly found 1752 burlesque of HF's
Covent-Garden Journal mocks his usage of Smollett, Amelia's
broken nose, and HF's second marriage. The author of the
pamphlet may have been Bonnell Thornton; however, no evidence exists that Smollett wrote it.

901   Johnson, E. D. H. "Vanity Fair and Amelia: Thack-
       eray in the Perspective of the Eighteenth Century. "
       MP, 59 (1961), 100-113.
       A workmanlike comparison of the two novels. Johnson
notes Thackeray's desire to imitate HF and stresses internal
evidence as well: the similarities in the characters and
situations of the two Amelias and the likenesses in character and function of others in the novels.

902   Kinkead-Weekes, Mark. Samuel Richardson: Dramatic
       Novelist. Ithaca, N. Y. : Cornell Univ. Press, 1973.
       See pp. 466-472.
       A useful general contrast of Richardson and HF. Be-
sides regarding Richardson as a dramatic novelist with a
main interest in character and HF as an epic novelist with
a main interest in design, Kinkead-Weekes contrasts their
views of morality. He juxtaposes Richardson's acute awareness of sin and evil with HF's cheerful muscular Christianity.
Accordingly, Kinkead-Weekes specifies faith to be dominant
in Richardson's vision, charity in HF's.

903   Kishler, Thomas C. "The Satiric Moral Fable: A
       Study of an Augustan Genre with Particular Reference
       to Fielding. " Diss. Wisconsin. DA, 20 (1959), 1352.

904   Lind, Levi Robert. "Lucian and Fielding. " The
       Classical Weekly, 20 Jan. 1936, pp. 84-86.
       Partially details the "unconscious influence" of Lucian
on HF, who was steeped in the Roman author's work. Lind
shows some parallels of character, situation, and technique
between various dialogues of Lucian and HF's "Journey from
This World to the Next. "

905   Lucker, Heinrich. "Die Verwendung der Mundart im
       englischen Roman des 18 Jarhunderts (Fielding, Smol-
       lett). " Diss. Darmstadt, 1915.

906   MacAndrew, Mary E. "The Debate Between Richardson
       and Fielding. " Diss. Columbia. DAI, 34 (1973), 280A.

907 McBurney, William H. "Mrs. Mary Davys: Fore-
     runner of Fielding." PMLA, 74 (1959), 348-355.
     Suggests that in three prose works of the 1720s, Mrs.
Davys prepares a readership for HF. Rejecting the role of
the fashionable learned lady, she introduces a non-stilted
style, realism and circumstantial detail, sprightliness and
humor as well as a number of Fielding-like characters and
situations (e. g., the country scene and its various personality
types). Her conscious theory of the novel--with its stress
on unity of action--also makes her a forerunner of HF.

908 McKee, John B. "Literary Irony and the Literary
     Audience: Studies in the Victimization of the Reader
     in Early English Fiction." Diss. Syracuse. DA, 33
     (1973), 5132A-33A.

909 McKillop, Alan D. Samuel Richardson: Printer and
     Novelist (1936). Rpt. Hamden, Conn.: Shoe String
     Press, 1960. See pp. 169-175 and passim.
     Documents Richardson's hostility toward HF. McKillop
describes Richardson's jealousy at the remarkable success
of TJ and his joy at the failure of Amelia.

910 Matthews, Grace. "Fielding in the Eighteenth Century."
     Diss. Wisconsin. DA, 25 (1964/65), 6624.

911 Mellen, Joan. "Morality in the Novel: A Study of
     Five English Novelists, Henry Fielding, Jane Austen,
     George Eliot, Joseph Conrad, and D. H. Lawrence."
     Diss. C. U. N. Y. DA, 29 (1968), 1543A.

912 Moore, Robert Etheridge. "Dr. Johnson on Fielding
     and Richardson." PMLA, 66 (1951), 162-181.
     Shows that HF and Johnson were at one on many funda-
mental positions: forthrightness, the novel as a lecture of
conduct, notions of morality and Nature. Yet Johnson pro-
fessed a high regard for Richardson at HF's expense. Moore
suggests that this paradox may have resulted from the flip-
pancy that masked HF's moral concern, from Johnson's deep
personal regard for Richardson, or from the reputed general
behavior of HF that Johnson disdained.

913 Nagourney, Peter J. "Law in the Novels of Henry
     Fielding." Diss. Chicago, 1971.

914 Nelson, Judith K. "Fielding and Molière." Diss.
     Rice. DAI, 32 (1971), 2064A.

915   Olybrius. "A Presentation Inscription by Fielding."
      N&Q, 27 April 1940, p. 298.
      Notices a copy of Horace inscribed by HF for Jane
Collyer in 1754.
      J. Paul de Castro (ibid., 11 May 1940, p. 337) prints
and analyzes a letter by Miss "Collier."

916   Orf, Rolf-Jürgen. Die Rezeption Henry Fieldings in
      Frankreich 1744-1812 und ihre Auswirkung. Baienfurt;
      1974. 212 pp.
      Review: N&Q, Aug. 1976, pp. 370-371.

917   Pappetti, Viola. "Amor sacro e amor profano in alcuni
      romanzi settcenteschi." EM, 24 (1973-74), 105-127.
      On Defoe, Fielding, and Goldsmith.

918   Parfitt, G. E. L'Influence français dans les oeuvres
      de Fielding et dans le théâtre anglais contemporain de
      ses comédies. Paris: Presses universitaires, 1928.

919   Parker, Alice. "Views of Crime and Punishment in
      Fielding and Smollett." Diss. Yale, 1939.

920   Price, Lawrence Marsden. "The Works of Fielding
      on the German Stage, 1762-1801." JEGP, 41 (1942),
      257-278.
      Highlights the intricate textual changes involved in
adapting HF's works to the German stage. Price states
that TJ, produced as drama and opera, was the most popular of HF's works. He concludes that the chief value of HF
adaptations was their reproduction of English customs, which
to the Germans often seemed crude and startling.

921   Pykare, Nina Coombs. "The Female Part of the
      Species: A Study of Women in Fielding." Diss. Kent
      State. DAI, 37 (1976), 991A.

922   Rader, Ralph Wilson. "Thackeray's Injustice to Field-
      ing." JEGP, 56 (1957), 203-212.
      Suggests that Thackeray so identified himself with HF
that his 1840 defense of him (the Times review) was a justi-
fication for his own behavior. Yet Thackeray's 1851 damn-
ing of HF (in the English Humorists) was an attempt to
palliate his guilty conscience for a dissolute life.

923   Raushenbush, Esther M. "Charles Macklin's Lost Play
      about Henry Fielding." MLN, 51 (1936), 505-514.

Reveals that a recently found manuscript of Macklin's play, The Covent-Garden Theatre, or Pasquin Turn'd Drawcansir, praises HF. Representing HF, the central character Pasquin emerges as the acute and benign critic who watches and comments as personifications of fashionable vices and follies incriminate themselves on stage. The play was performed only once: 8 April 1752.

924   Roberts, Edgar V.   "Mr. Seedo's London Career and His Work with Henry Fielding." PQ, 45 (1966), 179-190.
Provides biographical facts about the little-known Seedo (or Sydow or Sidow), a theater music director, composer, and organist in London from the mid 1720s until 1736. Roberts avers that Seedo's work for HF was extensive and included musical arrangements for versions of The Lottery, The Mock Doctor, and The Author's Farce. The artistic relationship lasted from 1731 to 1734, two years before the financially troubled Seedo returned home to Germany.

925   Roberts, W.   "Fielding in French." The National Review (London), 79 (1922), 721-728.
Claims that the life of HF's novels in France was longer than that of Richardson's, though the translations of HF were deplorable stylistically; indeed, they were often only adaptations. Still, his French readers comprised all classes. That his name had commercial value in France is shown in the ascribing of other novelists' works to him. He was credited, e. g., with authorship of Smollett's Roderick Random in translation.

926   Robinson, Roger.   "The Influence of Fielding on Barnaby Rudge." AUMLA, 40 (1973), 183-197.
Notices Dickens's borrowing of certain scenes, characters, and quotations from HF's novels.

927   Rolle, Dietrich.   Fielding und Sterne: Untersuchungen über die Funktion des Erzählers.   Neue Beiträge zur englischen Philologie, Band 2.   Münster: Verlag Aschendorff, 1963.   196 pp.
Reviews: JEGP, 64 (1965); NS, 13 (1964).

928   Ronte, Heinz.   Richardson und Fielding: Geschichte ihres Ruhms; literarsoziologischer Versuch.   Kölner anglistische Arbeiten, xxv.   Leipzig: Tauchnitz, 1935.   217 pp.

929   Rosenblood, Bryan N.   "Some Aspects of Henry Field-
      ing's Heroes. "   Diss. Pittsburgh.   DAI, 30 (1969),
      695A.

930   Ryan, Marjorie.   "The Tom Jones Hero in Plays and
      Novels, 1750-1800:   A Study of Fielding's Influence. "
      Diss. Minnesota.   DA, 19 (1958), 815.

931   Sackett, Samuel John.   "The Place of Literary Theory
      in Henry Fielding's Art. "   Diss. U. C. L. A. , 1956.

932   _____.   "'To Write Like an Angel. '"   WF, 18
      (1959), 250-251.
      Notes that HF's use of variations of the proverb, "to
write like an angel" (JA, I, 17 and Amelia, XII, 5), both
in reference to Latitudinarian divines, can be traced to I
Cor. 13:1.

933   Schmidt-Hidding, Wolfgang.   "Sieben Meister des
      literarischen Humors in England und Amerika. "   Diss.
      Heidelberg, 1959.

934   Schonzeler, Heinrich.   "Fieldings Verhaltnis zu Lesage
      und zu anderen Quellen. "   Diss. Weimar, 1915.

935   Sen, S. C.   "Richardson and Fielding: Moral Sense
      and Moral Vision. "   Bulletin of the Department of
      English, Univ. of Calcutta, 2 (1961), 38-40.

936   Sharp, Ruth M. M.   "Rational Vision and the Comic
      Resolution: A Study in the Novels of Richardson,
      Fielding and Jane Austen."   Diss. Wisconsin.   DAI,
      31 (1970), 369A.

937   Shea, Bernard D.   "Classical Learning in the Novels
      of Henry Fielding. "   Diss. Harvard, 1952.

938   Shepperson, Archibald Bolling.   "Types of the Burlesque
      Novel from Fielding to Thackeray. "   Diss. Virginia,
      1928.

939   Sherbo, Arthur.   "Fielding and Chaucer--and Smart. "
      N&Q, Oct. 1958, pp. 441-442.
      Suggests Christopher Smart's authorship of a Chaucerian
ballad in a 1752 number of HF's Covent-Garden Journal.

940   Sherwood, Irma, Z.   "The Influence of Digressive

Didacticism on the Structure of the Novels of Richardson and Fielding. " Diss. Yale. <u>DAI</u>, 30 (1970), 3436A.

941   Shoup, Louise. "The Use of the Social Gathering as a Structural Device in the Novels of Richardson, Fielding, Smollett and Sterne. " Diss. Stanford, 1950.

942   Sitter, John E.   "Cibber and Fielding's Quintessential Ode. " <u>N&Q</u>, Feb. 1978, p. 44.
Observes that Colley Cibber's quotation of HF's parody of a Cibberian ode in the <u>Historical Register</u> (I, 120-142) was meant to defuse HF's satire.

943   Skilton, David.   "Richardson and Fielding. "   In his <u>English Novel: Defoe to the Victorians.</u>   London: <u>David & Charles, 1977, pp. 19-31.</u>
Designates the chief innovations of Richardson and HF. Skilton credits Richardson with consummate characterization in (1) the integration of the moral, religious, social, and psychological aspects of an individual and (2) the use of interpersonal perceptions to produce complexity of character. He thinks HF's main innovations to be in (1) the introduction of classical form (epic and Roman city comedy) into prose fiction and (2) the use of irony as a technique to reveal inconsistencies in character and event.

944   Skinner, Mary Lynn.   "The Interpolated Story in Selected Novels of Fielding and Smollett. " Diss. Tennessee. <u>DA</u>, 29 (1969), 4020A.

945   Smith, LeRoy W. "Fielding and 'Mr. Bayle's' <u>Diction-ary.</u> " TSLL, 4 (1962), 16-20.
Suggests the possible influence of Pierre Bayle's <u>Critical and Historical Dictionary</u> (1697) on HF. If Bayle was not a direct source, he was at least a strong support for HF's views on the power of the passions and the presence of a capricious fortune in life. Moreover, the two authors shared attitudes of pessimism, tolerance, skepticism, and Christianity.

946   Solon, John J.   "Fielding in the Twentieth Century. " Diss. Wisconsin, 1955.

947   Stephenson, William A. , Jr. "Henry Fielding's Influence on Lord Byron. " Diss. Texas Tech. <u>DA</u>, 35 (1974), 478A.

948   Stern, Guy. "Fielding, Wieland, and Goethe: A Study in the Development of the Novel." Diss. Columbia. DA, 14 (1954), 1731.

949   _____. "A German Imitation of Fielding: Musäus Grandison der Zweite." CL, 10 (1958), 335-343.
Details HF's influence on Musäus' brilliant 1762 parody of Richardson's Sir Charles Grandison. Besides HF's method of mimesis, satiric bent, and characterization, Musäus used his subtle irony to introduce a note of sophistication into German fiction that reappears in Wieland, Goethe, and the "irony" of Germany's romantic poets.

950   Stewart, Maaja A. "The Artifice of Comedy: Fielding and Meredith." Diss. Michigan. DA, 27 (1967), 2163A.

951   _____. "Techniques of Intellectual Comedy in Meredith and Fielding." Genre, 8 (1975), 233-247.
Examines HF's technical influence on Meredith: the narrator who establishes a rational ideal and emotional distance and who generalizes characters, self-deceiving characters exposed by the narrative voice, and the parody of sentimental fiction to assert the novel's "reality."

952   Streeter, Harold W. The Eighteenth-Century English Novel in French Translation: A Bibliographical Study (1936). Rpt. New York: Benjamin Blom, 1970. See pp. 76-91.
Shows that though HF enjoyed a wide circulation in France, French critics differed in their views of him. Some praised his didacticism and moral earnestness while others attacked his vulgarity and discursiveness. Yet Streeter suggests that the French never really understood HF because of the poor translations and adaptations, the curious Anglo-Saxon manners depicted in his novels, and the love of sentiment against which he reacted.

953   Takács, Ferenc. Fielding Világa ["Fielding's World"]. Budapest: Európa, 1974. 213 pp.

954   Taylor, Douglas. Fielding's England. Living in England Series. London: Dobson, 1966.
A pleasant but unscholarly tour of early 18th-century England. Using HF's life and works as his organizational principle, Taylor offers interesting facts and anecdotes about living conditions then. Because it is ultimately a layman's

social history (short articles on such topics as Eton, prisons, ships, cricket, etc.), HF's work gets only passing notice. Profusely illustrated.

955   Todd, William B.   "Three Notes on Fielding." PBSA, 47 (1953), 70-75.
        (1) Lists misprints in two earlier editions of An Apology for the Life of Mr. T. C[ibber]. (1740), a burlesque bio-graphy usually ascribed to HF. (2) Likewise catalogues variants in two editions of A Dialogue between a Gentleman ... of London and an Honest Alderman of the Country Party (1747). (3) Claims that Amelia underwent only one edition in 1751 and 1752. The supposed second "edition" is really a ghost, indeed a second impression that involved only minor resetting. Amelia thus exists as a single impression of 5000 copies.

956   Touster, Eva Beach.   "The Literary Relationship of Thackeray and Fielding." JEGP, 46 (1947), 383-394.
        Demonstrates that in Thackeray's novels the HF in-fluence is strong: epic structure, picaresque touches with digressions, Quixotic humor, and intellectual realism with its satire on vanity and hypocrisy. But Thackeray stops short of depicting the "low." In this shirking of realism Thackeray was conditioned by the atmosphere of Victorian England, so his novels intentionally do not approximate HF's frank view of life.

957   Trzyna, Thomas N.   "Forgiveness: A Review of a Moral Conflict in Eighteenth-Century English Thought with Studies of Fielding, Goldsmith, Richardson, and Rowe." Diss. Washington. DAI, 38 (1977), 3524A.

958   Wendt, Allan Edward.   "Fielding and South's 'Luscious Morsel': A Last Word." N&Q, June 1957, pp. 256-257.
        Notes analogues of a passage on revenge in five of HF's works and identifies its source as an epigram in a sermon of Dr. Robert South: "Revenge is certainly the most luscious morsel that the devil can put into the sinner's mouth."
        Arthur Sherbo, ibid., Sept. 1957, pp. 378-379, notes that references to South recur in the Covent-Garden Journal and in JVL.

959   _____.   "Richardson and Fielding: A Study in the Eighteenth-Century Compromise." Diss. Indiana. DA, 17 (1957), 859.

960   Wicklein, Ernst. "Das 'Ernsthafte' in dem englischen komischen Roman des xviii Jarhunderts." Diss. Dresden, 1908.

961   Wilson, Robin Scott. "Henry Fielding and the Passionate Man." Diss. Illinois at Urbana-Champaign. <u>DA</u>, 20 (1960), 3285.

962   Wolfe, George H. "Lessons in Virtue: Fielding and the Ethical Imperative." Diss. North Carolina at Chapel Hill. <u>DAI</u>, 38 (1977), 814A.

AUTHOR INDEX

Allen, Walter 120
Allott, Miriam 534
Alter, Robert 121, 122, 415, 535, 536, 718
Amory, Hugh 57, 58, 59, 123, 400, 773, 774, 850
Anderson, Howard 537
Antal, F. 851
Arnold, Allen D. 538
Appleton, William W. 24, 305
Ashmore, Charles D. 124
Auty, Susan G. 125
Avery, Emmett L. 60, 306, 307, 308

Bailey, Vern D. 61
Baker, Ernest A. 126, 281
Baker, Myra M. 127
Baker, Sheridan W., Jr. 15, 39, 128, 129, 130, 309, 401, 416, 539, 540, 541, 719, 775
Balderston, Katherine C. 852
Banerji, H. K. 131, 310, 417, 542, 720, 776
Barnes, John L. 543
Bassein, Beth Ann C. 132
Bateson, F. W. 311
Battestin, Martin C. 2, 27, 30, 31, 62, 63, 133, 418, 418a, 419, 420, 421, 422, 423, 544, 545, 545a, 546, 547, 548, 777

Beach, Joseph Warren 134
Beasley, Jerry C. 135, 853
Beatty, Richmond Croom 136
Becker, Gustav 854
Bell, Inglis F. 4
Bell, Michael 549
Bennett, James O'Donnell 550
Bennett, Robert C. 855
Bensly, Edward 551, 552
Berger, Tjard W. 137
Bevan, C. H. K. 721
Billi, Marcella Mancioli 138
Biron, H. C. 64
Bissell, Frederic Olds, Jr. 139, 424, 553
Blake, Warren Barton 554
Blanchard, Frederic T. 140
Bliss, Michael 555
Bloch, Tuvia 556, 722, 723, 778
Boas, Frederic S. 312
Bolles, Edwin C. 856
Booth, Wayne 141, 557
Borinski, Ludwig 141a
Bort, Barry D. 558
Borthwick, Mary C. 857
Bosdorf, Eric 425
Bouce, P. -G. 477
Bowers, Fredson 27
Brack, O M 5, 36
Bradbury, Malcolm 142
Braudy, Leo 143, 426, 501, 559, 724
Bredvold, Louis I 144
Brewerton, Marti J. 6
Brogan, Howard O. 560

SUBJECT INDEX*

ADAPTATIONS OF HF'S WORKS
    into books   466, 655a, 930
    into films   482a, 546, 670a
    into plays   337, 458, 673, 676, 699, 920, 923, 930
    of JA   458, 466, 482a
    of TJ   337, 546, 655a, 670a, 673, 676, 677, 678, 699,
920, 930
    general   871, 920, 923, 925

ADVERSE OPINION ON HF
    146, 148, 182, 212, 219, 562, 565, 633, 659

THE CHAMPION
    131, 784, 796, 811, 812, 815, 833, 834, 835, 836, 838,
839, 840, 841, 843, 847

CHARACTER AND CHARACTERIZATION
    general   121 ("integration of c."), 127 (satiric c.), 130
(in plays and novels), 134 (psychology of c.), 181 (moral
psychology), 215 (c. and education), 217 (humors c.), 221
(irony and c.), 240 (motives), 270 (literary portraits), 286
(novels of c.), 296 (naming of c.), 304 (unrealistic c.) 886
(national c.), 897 (type c.), 929 (aspects of heroes)
    JA   419 (c. development), 427 (allusive methods of c.),
440 (slang names), 442 (supporting c.), 445 (clothing and c.),
446 (beasts and c.), 459 (burlesque and complex c.), 465
(uncertainty of c.), 468 (names in c.), 487 (literary portraits),
493 (Joseph as hero), 496 (the "good man"), 497 (high and
low c.)
    JW   512 (symbolic c.), 518 (failure of c.), 519 (c. as
clown), 527 (literary portraits)
    TJ   535 (design of c.), 539 (c. of Bridget), 540 (hero
as touchstone), 543 (charactonym), 544 (complex c. of pru-

---

*See under THEMES AND MOTIFS for highly specific topics.

dence), 560 (determinism and c.), 601 (c. and composition),
605, 630, 674, 685 (c. of Allworthy), 631, 632 (c. of
Partridge), 633 ("cardboard" c.), 647 (typological c.), 653
(c. and the seasons), 534, 608, 679, 685 (c. of Square),
650, 658, 667, 682, 688, 689, 696a, 698 (c. of Tom), 686
(literary portraits), 694 (c. of Blifil), 695 (c. and action),
697 (the "double"), 930 (the "TJ" hero)

    Amelia   718 ("progressive discovery" of c.), 722 (pas-
sions and c.), 727 ("conservation of c."), 756 (literary
portraits)

    journalism   779 (personae and c.)

COLLECTIONS OF ESSAYS ON HF
    201, 206, 211, 230, 239, 241, 255, 258, 267, 277, 278,
545a, 571

COMEDY AND HUMOR
    general   125 (benevolent c.), 142 (attitudinal c.), 154
(intellectual influences), 155 (wit and seriousness), 171 (h.
subversive of satire), 194 (HF as humorist), 196 (social
background of HF's h.), 200 (narrative c.), 216 ("thoughtful
laughter"), 226 (h. as aesthetic experience), 242 ("comic
alternative"), 247 ("c. of forms"), 282 (comic form), 284
(c. and good nature), 293 (comic and sentimental), 304 (festive and cultivated c.), 888 (comic celebration), 936 (comic
resolution), 950 (comic artifice), 951 (intellectual c.)

    plays   311 (comic drama), 322 ("c. of warning"), 324
(comic technique), 330 (farce technique), 389 (c. of manners), 390 (comedies)

    JA   460 (comic mythology), 471 (comic genre), 481
(merriment), 483 (comic method), 490 ("comic resolution"),
492 (amiable h.), 500 (festive c.)

    TJ   565 (urbane wit), 574 (c. and narrator), 587 (comic
irony), 589 (c., benevolism, and hope), 600 (comic celebration), 649 (voices of h.), 680 (sources of comic pleasure),
703 ("comic curve"), 714 (festive c.)

    Amelia   741 (comic action), 772 (festive c.)

THE COVENT-GARDEN JOURNAL
    131, 782, 809, 826, 900

"DIGRESSIONS" IN JA AND TJ
    general   198, 263, 940, 944
    JA   422, 429, 433, 438, 441, 449, 461, 462, 494, 495
    TJ   547, 595, 632, 642, 646, 681, 698

ETHICS, MORALITY, THOUGHT
    general   82, 124 (e.), 181 (moral psychology), 185 (HF

and philosophy), 188 (language and m.), 195 (social m.), 198, 199 (conflicting values), 203 (virtue and instinct), 212 (simplification of moral issues), 215 (educational theory), 217 (e. of humors characters), 249 (social concerns), 255 (m. and stylistic effects), 263 (beliefs and rhetoric), 266 ("layman's sermons"), 268 (moral-social outlook), 270 (literary portraits as ethical media), 274 (HF and Mandeville), 282 (progressive view of history), 283 (philosophy of history), 284 (comedy and m.), 287 (HF and Hume), 299 (moral purpose of epic), 301 (marriage and m.), 303 (HF as Christian censor), 858, 253 (attitudes toward the gentleman), 878, 898 (Shaftesbury and HF), 911 (m. in HF), 962 (ethical imperative), 289, 850, 859 (HF's library)

plays   322 (self-interest v. good nature), 336 (didacticism), 338 (good nature and virtue), 382 (language and moral meaning)

Shamela   404 (conservative social thought)

JA   422 (moral basis of HF's art), 475 (epic and m.), 485 (refutation of moral basis of HF's art), 498 (marriage and m.)

JW   506 (pessimism about human goodness), 510 (e.), 512 (ethical contrasts), 515 (Christianity and stoicism), 530 (moral indignation), 532 (moral allegory), 533 (marriage and m.)

TJ   534 (deist-orthodox controversy), 538 (social e.), 555 (philosophical theme), 560 (fiction and philosophy), 568, 654 (moral defense of HF), 589 (moral imperatives), 591 (non-humanism), 596a (spontaneous virtue), 602 (moral philosophy), 644 (benevolence), 654 (good nature), 656 (Christian allegory), 679 (satire on deism), 682 (Tom as Christ), 685 (benevolence and allegory), 708 (philosophical thought), 711 (marriage and m.), 717 (love and m.)

Amelia   718 (Christian hero), 712 (refutation of Mandevillian philosophy), 722, 757 (doctrine of the passions), 730 (view of mankind), 742 (spiritual change), 761 (Fortune and the passions), 767 (Amelia as ethical center)

journalism   817 (vacillation between orthodox and latitudinarian tendencies), 818 (ethical basis of satire), 847 (ethics in Champion), 849 (social thought in the pamphlets)

FOREIGN RECEPTION OF HF
    continental   663, 868
    Danish   881
    French   554, 583, 588, 683, 699, 916, 925
    German   857, 893, 920
    Mexican   629

INTELLECTUAL BACKGROUND
general 82 (religious milieu), 143 (historiography), 154
(intellectual influences on HF's comedy), 181, 236 (main i.
milieu), 185 (HF's philosophical contexts), 188 (Locke and
language), 198 (cultural contexts), 202 (HF's Weltanschauung),
205 (HF's philosophy), 215 (HF and Locke), 274 (HF and
Mandeville), 287 (HF and Hume), 289 (Renaissance critical
theory), 303 (Christian background), 802, 849, 895, 913
(legal background)
    JA 289 (Renaissance critical theory), 420 (general in-
tellectual background), 422 (latitudinarian thought)
    JW 510 (philosophical contexts), 532 (ethical contexts)
    TJ 289 (Renaissance critical theory), 560 (educational
thought), 589 (Christian background), 602 (philosophical background), 630 (HF and Barrow), 647 (romance tradition), 707
(historiographical trends)
    Amelia 745 (ideological trends)

IRONY
general 121 (i. in characterization), 128 ("i. of form"),
188 (language of irony), 221 (types and techniques), 232
(ironic power of narrator), 255 (i. as sarcasm), 261 (function
of i.), 382 (i. and moral meaning), 917 (literary i.)
    JA 441 (techniques of i.), 494 (ironic tension)
    JW 199 (ironic plot), 511 (crude i.), 516 (rhetorical i.),
528 (ironic structure), 530 (allegory of i.)
    TJ 587 (satiric and comic i.), 590 ("double i. "), 604
(i. and dramatic action), 609 (i. and moral-comic view),
621 (i. and prudence), 655 ("complex irony"), 657 (types of
i.), 666 (plot as i.)
    Amelia 718 ("reader-directed i. ")

LANGUAGE AND DIALOGUE
general 121 (uses of style), 129 (recurring clichés),
176 (familiar style), 188 (attitude toward l.), 193 ("world as
l. "), 257 (fictional d.), 267 (favorite phrases and mannerisms), 296 (names), 304 (versatile usage), 875 (legal l.),
189 (professional jargon)
    plays 82 (speedy d.), 377 (words as symbols)
    Shamela 406 (mannerisms)
    JA 422 (names of Adams and Joseph), 440 (name of
Tow-wouse), 469 (name of Didapper), 470 (rendering of
speech), 484 (dogs' names), 499 (uses of l.)
    JW 507 (political corruption of l.), 508 (l. and comic
play), 522 (use of cant)
    TJ 549 (l. as comic ritual), 574 (mock-heroic style),
626 (abstract diction), 634 (prose style types), 647 (stylistic

devices), 648 (rhetorical devices), 649 (HF's voices), 688
(virtuous speeches), 693 (conversational style)
    Amelia 258 (sarcasm), 736 (plain style), 770 (rhetoric)
journalism 778 (early usages)

LEGAL CAREER
    58 (uninfluential l. theory), 64 (review of HF's magis-
tracy), 65 (dates of appointments to bench), 67 ("lost" law
book), 69 (original penal theory), 74 (HF as publicist), 82
(contexts of HF's l. career), 87 (hard work as magistrate),
92 (survey of l. c.), 95 (health during Canning case), 98
(criminal and l. contexts), 99 (HF's theory on criminal
law), 100 (HF in court), 102 (dates of office), 103 (succession to office), 104 (murder and smuggling trials), 774
(l. manuscripts), 775, 792, 849 (l. pamphlets), 802 (l. beliefs), 859 (l. library), 879 (magistracy)

LETTERS
    57, 59, 81, 87, 93a, 104

LITERARY CRITICISM, POETICS, AND THEORY OF HF
    general 135, 159 (romance influence), 136, 251, 846
(HF as critic), 136, 302 (attitude toward critics), 139, 246
(t. of novel), 147, 271 (t. of fiction), 163, 932 (literary t.),
169 (picaresque influence), 171 (satiric and comic t.), 178,
289, 297 (epic influence), 233 (poetic t.), 240 ("anti-romanti-
cist"), 263 (rhetorical methods), 279 ([non] "epic impulse)
    plays 352 (HF as critic), 860 (attitude toward stage)
    JA 289 (t. of comic prose epic), 416 (romance t.), 424
(t. of novel), 428 (t. of number and pattern), 448, 482 (on
JA's Preface), 489 (p. of comic epics), 447 (continental
sources)
    JW 505, 517, 524 (mock form), 510 (traditional ingre-
dients), 514 (p. of "rogue ruined"), 530, 532 (allegorical
form)
    TJ 289, 687 (t. of comic prose epic), 536, 665, 704
(picaresque tradition), 540, 646, 647, 701 (romance tradition), 553 (t. of novel), 561 (numerological pattern), 617
(dicta on the novel), 622 (HF on composing the novel), 659,
708 (epic tradition)
    Amelia 719 (romance t.), 737, 750, 755 (epic models)

THE MISCELLANIES
    773, 776, 786, 793, 817, 818, 819, 842

NARRATOR AND NARRATIVE TECHNIQUE
    general 141 (self-conscious n.), 143 (dynamic n. t.),

153a (concern with storytelling process), 176 (familiar style
and narrative distance), 187 (author as puppet-master), 221
(HF's persona), 226 (intrusive n. as unifying device), 257
(authorial presence in dialogue), 267 (identity of HF and his
n.), 269 (intrusive n. as weakness), 285 (role of n.), 295
(origins of HF's n. t.)

    plays   329 (authorial dimension)

    JA   426 (n. t.), 441, 452 (HF's adaptation of authorial
intervention), 464 (n. as naive historian)

    JW   501 (historiographical t.)

    TJ   537 (n. t.), 555 (empathy for n.), 557 (intrusive n.),
563 (wordy n.), 574 (n. 's elevated language), 589 (obtrusive
presence of n.), 622 ("plot" of the prefaces), 628 (meditative
n. as central), 634 (n. 's prose styles), 642 (digressions as
parody of n.), 649 (HF's voices), 651 (persuasive power of
n.), 655 (n. 's sentimental and skeptical views), 691 (n. 's
epistemological presence), 705 (artifice of n. t.), 708
(authorial intrusions as sociable), 716 (first-person n.)

    Amelia   724, 734 (n. t.), 731 (dramatic mode), 733
(conflict of dramatic and authorial modes), 743 (narrative
structure), 747 (manipulated ending), 749 (use of exemplum),
752 (withdrawal of n.), 759 (psychic drama)

PAMPHLETS
    119, 418a, 775, 787, 788, 792, 795, 802, 805, 806,
807, 808, 820, 829, 831, 832, 844, 849, 863

PLOT
    JA   167 (dramatic structure), 441 (p. movements)
    TJ   539 (p. and plotting), 548 (symmetry of design, 570
(p. of fortunate fall), 572 (p. and reader), 589 (structure of
p.), 597 (failure of p.), 606 (diagram of p.), 558, 619, 658,
682 (allusive p. parallels), 622 ("p. " of the prefaces), 625
(main structures of mid-p.), 647 (archetypal p.), 666
(ironic p.), 703 (p. and tension), 708 (p. and social order)
    Amelia   740 (p. and prisons), 747 (deus ex machina),
754 (time scheme of p.)

POEMS
    43, 327, 773, 777, 799, 800, 817, 848, 942

POLITICS AND HF
    life   60 (attacks on government), 63, 104 (political
favors), 66 (HF and the Walpoles), 88 (changing attitudes
toward Walpole), 90 (HF and Jacobite threat), 92, 99, 119
(criminal legislation), 93 (HF and Dodington), 188 (p. and
language)

(s. on the professions), 200 (s. and comedy), 240 (HF as satirist), 851 (HF's and Hogarth's satiric targets), 855 ("satiric dance"), 863 (anti-Catholic s.), 903 (satiric moral fable)

plays 305 (s. in Historical Register), 309, 315, 356, 358, 359 (political s.), 341 (dramatic s.), 352, 384 (literary s.), 359 (s. and travesty), 363 (s. on pantomime), 367 (social s.), 368 (satiric touches), 382 (s. on audience)

Shamela 402 (Aesopic s.), 401, 402 (parodic aspects), 412 (review of literary, moral, social s.), 413 ("subtle s.")

JA 421 (s. on Hervey), 433 (s. on vanity and hypocrisy), 441 (satiric exposure), 437, 459 (burlesque of Pamela)

JW 502 (parody of criminal biography), 503 (sentimental burlesque), 507, 531 (political s.), 507, 508 (satiric language), 524 (mock-heroic), 525 (s. on Machiavelli), 526 (s. on Cibber), 529 (s. on "Great Man"), 531 (s. on Walpole)

TJ 291 (favorite satiric targets), 574 (mock-heroic diction), 587 (non-satiric instinct), 589 (satiric honesty), 604, 609 (s. and irony), 634 (parodic style)

journalism 805 (s. on physicians), 811 (focus of satiric attack), 818 (ethical basis of s.), 820 (s. on Royal Society), 822 (s. on royal family), 825 (s. and feeling), 826 (parody of Oldmixon)

SETTING
130, 192 (general s.), 894 (realistic descriptive s.)

SOCIAL BACKGROUND
general 68 (class system), 69, 82 (general s.b.), 98 (criminal b.), 196, 198 (s. influences), 204 (fashionable society), 244, 249, 260 (English scene), 268 (s. outlook), 272 (country squires), 279 (s. changes), 291 (political con-texts), 301 (marriage backgrounds), 953, 954 (HF's world)

plays 333 (law and marriage), 374 (1731 lottery)

JA 422 (religious contexts), 454 (s. contexts)

TJ 690 (HF's presentation of society), 696a (contexts), 702 (cultural milieu), 713 (s. atmosphere)

Amelia 745 ("new bourgeois ideal")

STRUCTURAL TECHNIQUES AND DESIGN
general 121 ("architectonic novel"), 138, 160, 167, 183, 250, 288 (narrative structure), 175 (poetic justice), 227, 289 (epic structure), 263 (rhetorical t.), 199 (structural tension), 247, 265 (symmetries), 270 (literary portraits), 187, 300 (providential design), 304 (artful contrivance), 941 (general structure)

plays 316, 324, 325, 330, 372, 758 (general t.), 329

hunt and pursuit   625, 703
incest   495, 539, 558, 658, 697
jargon   189, 339, 649, 867
law   123, 333, 339, 674, 760, 867, 891, 895, 913
lawyers and physicians   189, 497, 805
liberty   504, 817, 831
love   152, 210, 252, 429, 449, 621, 717, 917
marriage   273, 301, 333, 429, 449, 481, 624, 764
masquerade   273
nudity   267, 486, 490
pilgrimage and journey   198, 422, 477, 481
providence   232, 300, 422, 461, 545a, 548, 664, 761
prudence   495, 538, 544, 550, 570, 604, 609, 621,
    658
Rebellion of 1745   90, 198, 547, 569, 623a, 624,
    662, 806
rejection of solitude   709
religion   267, 300, 303, 422, 656, 682
rural retirement   213, 422, 439
search for parent   441, 476
seasons   653
self-interest   247, 322, 506, 510, 532, 712
sex   654, 667
social communities   157, 214, 709
squires   272
"thriving"   322
"true greatness"   350, 510, 512, 529, 817
vanity and hypocrisy   422, 438, 483, 817
wisdom   544, 658
women   225, 259, 301, 338, 404, 654, 921

THACKERAY AND HF
    140, 869, 901, 922, 956